J. W. (James Williams) Tyrrell

Across The Subarctics of Canada

A Journey Of 3.200 Miles

J. W. (James Williams) Tyrrell

Across The Subarctics of Canada
A Journey Of 3.200 Miles

ISBN/EAN: 9783741117985

Manufactured in Europe, USA, Canada, Australia, Japa

Cover: Foto ©Andreas Hilbeck / pixelio.de

Manufactured and distributed by brebook publishing software (www.brebook.com)

J. W. (James Williams) Tyrrell

Across The Subarctics of Canada

J. W. TYRRELL.
(In Eskimo costume.)

ACROSS THE SUB-ARCTICS OF CANADA, A JOURNEY OF 3,200 MILES BY CANOE AND SNOW-SHOE THROUGH THE BARREN LANDS

BY J. W. TYRRELL, C.E., D.L.S.

INCLUDING A LIST OF PLANTS COLLECTED ON THE EXPEDITION, A VOCABULARY OF ESKIMO WORDS, A ROUTE MAP AND FULL CLASSIFIED INDEX. WITH ILLUSTRATIONS FROM PHOTOGRAPHS TAKEN ON THE JOURNEY, AND FROM DRAWINGS BY ARTHUR HEMING

LONDON: T. FISHER UNWIN
PATERNOSTER SQUARE

CONTENTS.

CHAPTER		PAGE
I. Toronto to Athabasca Landing		7
II. Down the Athabasca		19
III. Running the Rapids		36
IV. Chippewyan to Black Lake		49
V. Into the Unknown Wilderness		70
VI. The Home of the Reindeer		80
VII. A Great Frozen Lake		90
VIII. On the Lower Telzoa		102
IX. Meeting with Natives		114
X. The Eskimos		127
XI. Customs of the Eskimos		147
XII. Down to the Sea		172
XIII. Adventures by Land and Sea		181
XIV. Polar Bears		189
XV. Life or Death?		199
XVI. Fort Churchill		210
XVII. On Snowshoes and Dog-Sleds		219
XVIII. Crossing the Nelson		229
XIX. Through the Forest and Home Again		240

APPENDIX

I. Plants Collected on the Expedition		251
II. Eskimo Vocabulary of Words and Phrases		273

ILLUSTRATIONS.

	PAGE
J. W. Tyrrell	*Frontispiece*
J. Burr Tyrrell	8
Our Canoemen	11
Hudson's Bay Company's Traders	13
A Hudson's Bay Company's Interpreter	15
A Pioneer of the North	16
Indians of the Canadian North-West	18
Trooper, N.-W. Mounted Police, in Winter Uniform	26
Landing of Scows above Grand Rapid	29
Grand Rapid, Athabasca River	31
English-Chippewyan Half-Breed	32
Neck Developed by the Tump-Line	35
Shooting the Mountain Rapid, Athabasca River	40
Store, Fort McMurray	41
Chippewyan Camp	42
Starving Cree Camp, Fort McMurray	44
A Dandy of the North. A Voyageur	46
An English-Cree Trapper	48
Fort Chippewyan	50
Steamer "Grahame"	52
Landing on North Shore, Lake Athabasca	56
A Typical Northland Father	59
Indian Log House	64
Cataract, Stone River	65
A Difficult Portage	67
Indian Rafts Loaded with Venison	69
A. R. C. Selwyn, C.M.G., F.R.S.	74
Scotch-Cree Half-Breed	79

ILLUSTRATIONS.

	PAGE
Telzoa River	82
Rapids, Telzoa River	83
Herd of Reindeer	85
Ice on the Shore of Markham Lake	91
Tobaunt Lake	94
French-Cree Half-Breed	101
Rapids on the Lower Telzoa	103
Musk Oxen	104
Eskimo "Topick," Telzoa River	106
Eskimo Hunters	121
Group of Eskimos	122
Icelandic Settler	125
An Eskimo, Eskimo Woman	126
Half-Breed Hunter with Wooden Snow-Goggles	134
Section Through Igloe	136
Eskimo Kyack	141
Eskimo Oomiack	142
Dog-Whip, Walrus Tusks and Bows and Arrows	146
Harpoons, Lances and Spears	154
Eskimo Games and Toys	163
Half-Breed Boy	180
Blackfoot Boy	188
Encounter with Polar Bears	196
The Last of Our Provisions	199
French-Salteaux Girl	209
Rev. Joseph Lofthouse and Family	212
Ruins of Fort Prince of Wales	216
Ice-Block Grounded at Low Tide	218
N.-W. M. P. "Off Duty"	228
Half-Breed Dog-Driver	229
Hudson's Bay Company's Store, York Factory	238
Red-Deer Cow-Boy	239
Dog-Train and Carryall	240
Cree Hunter's Prize	250

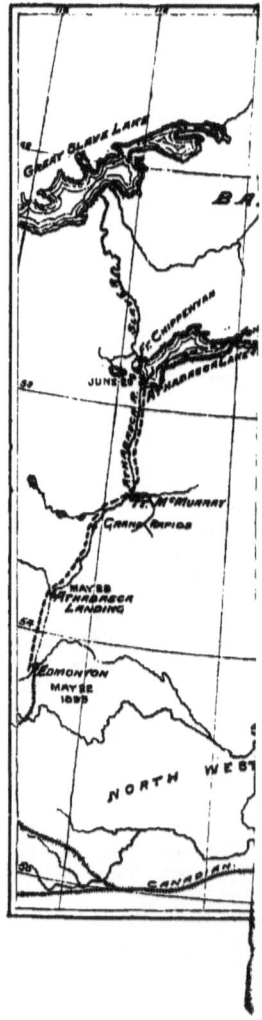

vi   *ILLUSTRATIONS.*

	PAGE.
Telzoa River	82
Rapids, Telzoa River	83
Herd of Reindeer	85
Ice on the Shore of Markham Lake	91
Tobaunt Lake	94
French-Cree Half-Breed	101
Rapids on the Lower Telzoa	103
Musk Oxen	104
Eskimo "Topick," Telzoa River	105
Eskimo Hunters	121
Group of Eskimos	122
Icelandic Settler	125
An Eskimo. Eskimo Woman	126
Half-Breed Hunter with Wooden Snow-Goggles	134
Section Through Igloe	136
Eskimo Kyack	141
Eskimo Oomiack	142
Dog-Whip, Walrus Tusks and Bows and Arrows	146
Harpoons, Lances and Spears	154
Eskimo Games and Toys	163
Half-Breed Boy	180
Blackfoot Boy	188
Encounter with Polar Bears	196
The Last of Our Provisions	199
French-Saltkaux Girl	209
Rev. Joseph Lofthouse and Family	212
Ruins of Fort Prince of Wales	216
Ice-Block Grounded at Low Tide	218
N.-W. M. P. "Off Duty"	228
Half-Breed Dog-Driver	229
Hudson's Bay Company's Store, York Factory	238
Red-Deer Cow-Boy	239
Dog-Train and Carryall	240
Cree Hunter's Prize	250

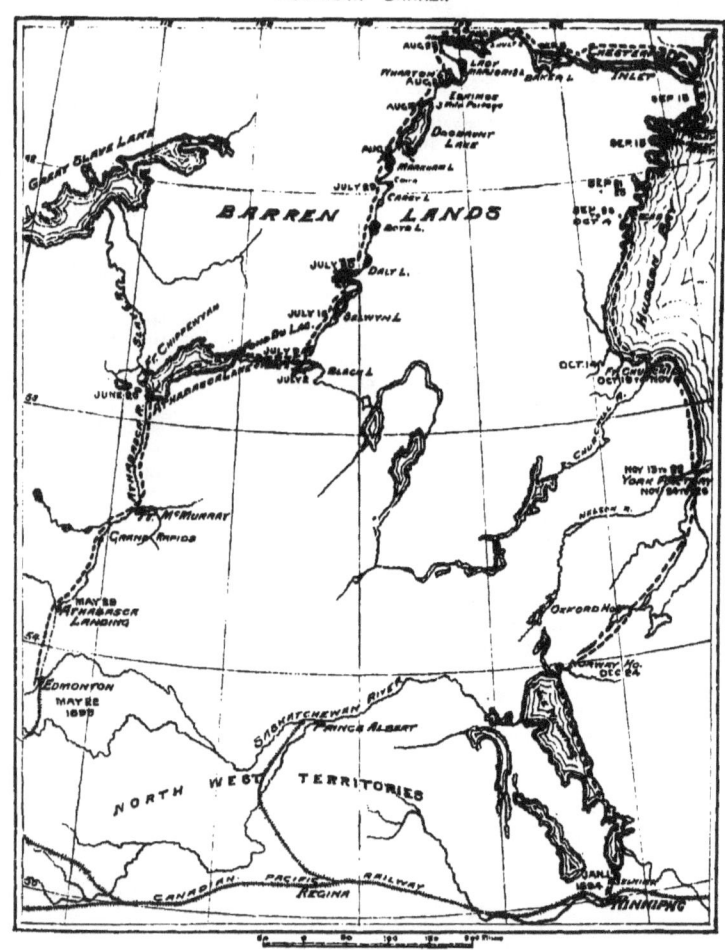

ACROSS THE SUB-ARCTICS OF CANADA.

CHAPTER I.

TORONTO TO ATHABASCA LANDING.

On the morning of the 10th of May, 1893, in response to a telegram from Ottawa, I took train at Hamilton for Toronto, to meet my brother, J. Burr Tyrrell, of the Canadian Geological Survey, and make final arrangements for a trip to the North.

He had been authorized by the Director of that most important department of the Canadian Government to conduct, in company with myself, an exploration survey through the great mysterious region of *terra incognita* commonly known as the Barren Lands, more than two hundred thousand square miles in extent, lying north of the 59th parallel of latitude, between Great Slave Lake and Hudson Bay. Of almost this entire territory less was known than of the remotest districts of "Darkest Africa," and, with but few exceptions, its vast and dreary plains had never been trodden by the foot of man, save that of the dusky savage.

During the summer of 1892 my brother had obtained some information concerning it from the Chippewyan Indians in the vicinity of Athabasca and Black Lakes, but even these native tribes were found to have only the vaguest ideas of the character of the country that lay beyond a few days' journey inland.

In addition to this meagre information, he had procured sketch maps of several canoe routes leading northward toward the Barren Lands. The most easterly of these routes commenced at a point on the north shore of Black Lake, and the description obtained of it was as follows: "Beginning at Black Lake, you make a long portage northward to a little lake, then across five or six more small ones and a corresponding number of portages, and a large body of water called Wolverine Lake will be reached. Pass through this, and ascend a river flowing into it from the northward, until Active Man Lake is reached. This lake will take two days to cross, and at its northern extremity the Height of Land will be reached. Over this make a portage until another large lake of about equal size is entered. From the north end of this second large lake, a great river flows to the northward through a treeless country unknown to the Indians, but inhabited by savage Eskimos. Where the river empties into the sea we cannot tell, but it flows a great way to the northward."

From the description given, it appeared that this river must flow through the centre of the unexplored territory, and thence find its way either into the waters of Hudson Bay or into the Arctic Ocean. It was by this route we resolved to carry on the exploration, and, if possible, make our way through the Barren Lands.

One of the first and most important preparations for the journey was the procuring of suitable boats, inasmuch as portability, strength and carrying capacity

J. BURR TYRRELL.
(Leaving Fort Churchill.)

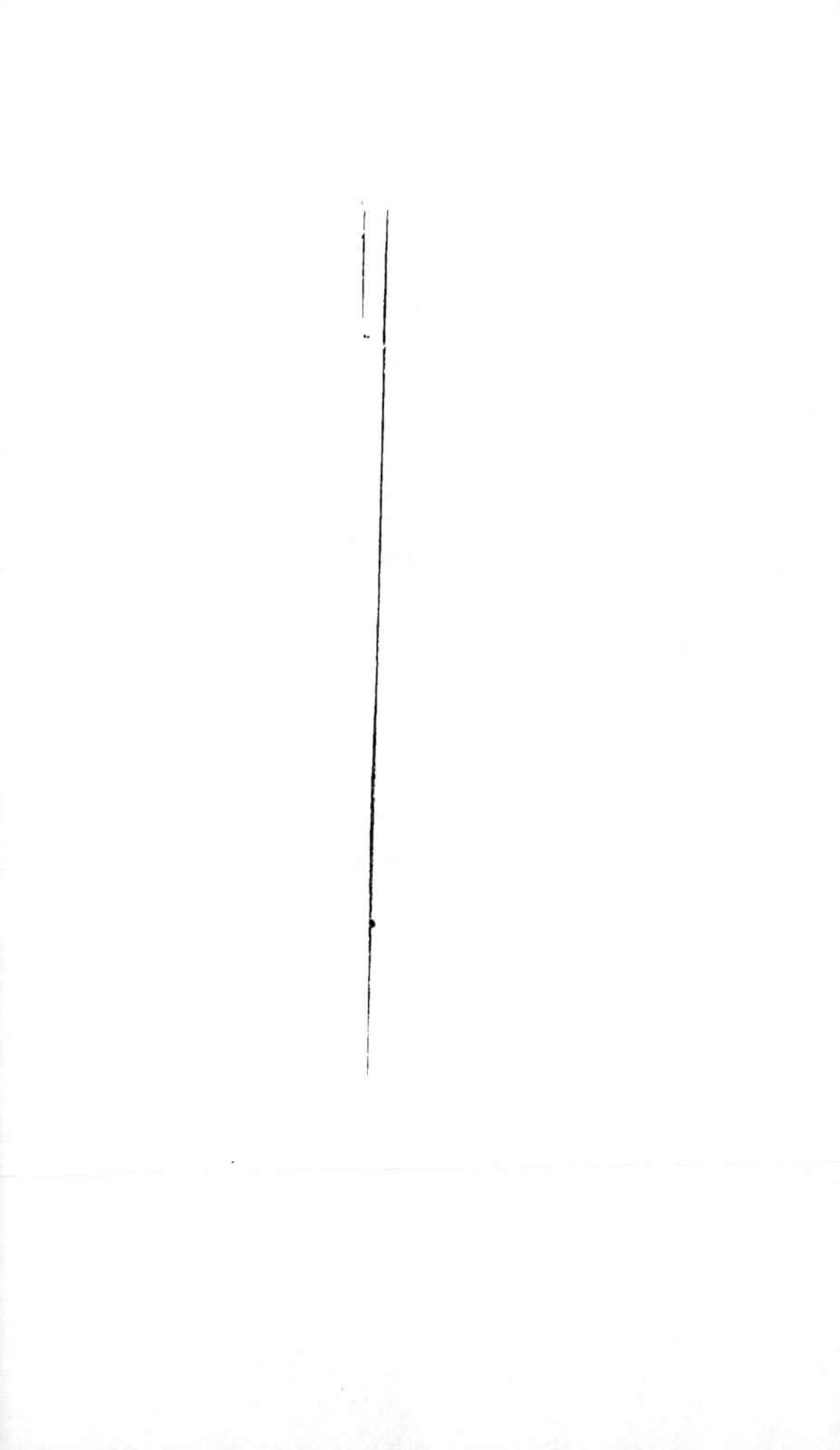

were all essential qualities. These were obtained from
the Peterboro' Canoe Company, who furnished us with
two beautiful varnished cedar canoes, eighteen feet in
length, and capable of carrying two thousand pounds
each, while weighing only one hundred and twenty
pounds. Arrangements had also been made to have a
nineteen foot basswood canoe, used during the previous
summer, and two men in readiness at Fort McMurray on
the Athabasca River.

Four other canoemen were chosen to complete the
party, three of them being Iroquois experts from
Caughnawaga, Quebec. These three were brothers, named
Pierre, Louis and Michel French. Pierre was a veteran
canoeman, being as much at home in a boiling rapid as
on the calmest water. For some years he had acted as
ferryman at Caughnawaga, and only recently had made
a reputation for himself by running the Lachine Rapids
on Christmas day, out of sheer bravado. His brother
Louis had won some distinction also through having
accompanied Lord Wolseley as a voyageur on his
Egyptian campaigns; while Michel, the youngest and
smallest of the three, was known to be a good steady
fellow, boasting of the same distinction as his brother
Louis.

The other man, a half-breed named John Flett, was
engaged at Prince Albert, in the North-West. He was
highly recommended, not so much as a canoeman, but as
being an expert portager of great experience in northern travel, and also an Eskimo linguist.

The two men, James Corrigal and François Maurice,
who through the kindness of Mr. Moberly, the officer
of the Hudson's Bay Company at Isle-à-la-Crosse, were

engaged to meet us with a third canoe at Fort McMurray, were also western half-breeds, trained in the use of the pack-straps as well as the paddle, and were a pair of fine strong fellows. Thus it was arranged to combine in our party the best skill both of canoemen and portagers.

Our reasons for not employing the Indians from Lake Athabasca were, that these natives had on nearly all previous expeditions proved to be unreliable. Such men as we had engaged, unlike these Indians, were free from any dread of the Eskimos, and as we advanced soon became entirely dependent on us as their guides. Besides, they were more accustomed to vigorous exertion at the paddle and on the portage than the local Indians, who are rather noted for their proficiency in taking life easy.

Next in importance to procuring good boats and canoemen was the acquisition of a complete set of portable mathematical instruments, but after some difficulty these, too, were obtained. The following is a list of them: One sextant with folding mercurial horizon, one solar compass, two pocket compasses, two prismatic compasses, one fluid compass, two boat logs, two clinometers, one aneroid barometer, a pair of maximum and minimum thermometers, one pocket chronometer, three good watches, a pair of field-glasses, an aluminum binocular, and a small camera. These, though numerous, were not bulky, but they comprised a part of our outfit over which much care had to be exercised throughout the journey. A bill of necessary supplies was also carefully made out, and the order for them forwarded to the Hudson's Bay Company's store at Edmonton, with

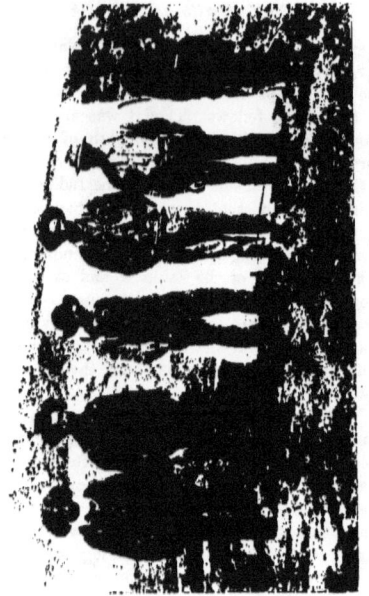

OUR CANOEMEN.

François Maurice. Pierre French. John Piett. Jim Corrigal. Michel French. Louis French.

instructions to have them freighted down the Athabasca River to Fort Chippewyan, on Lake Athabasca, as early as possible.

The above and a hundred and one other preparations having been completed, my brother and I bade farewell to our homes, and on the 16th of May boarded the North Bay evening express at Toronto. The journey was not begun without the stirring of tender emotions, for to me it meant separation, how long I knew not, from my young wife and baby boy five months old, and to my brother it meant separation from one too sacred in his eyes to mention here.

Once aboard the train we made ourselves as comfortable as possible for a five days' ride. I do not propose to weary my readers with a detailed account of the long run across continent by rail, as it is not reckoned a part of our real journey; in passing I will merely make the briefest reference to a few of the incidents by the way.

It was not until after many delays between North Bay and Fort William on the Canadian Pacific Railway, owing chiefly to the disastrous floods of that year, which inundated the track for long distances, washed it out at several points and broke one of the railway bridges, that we arrived at Winnipeg, the capital of the Province of Manitoba. Upon reaching the city it was found that our canoes, which had been shipped to Edmonton some time previously, had not yet passed through. After considerable telegraphing they were located, and it was found that they would arrive on the following day. In consequence of this and other business to be transacted with the Commissioner of the Hudson's Bay Company, we were obliged to remain here for a day. During our brief stay we were warmly greeted by many friends, and were most kindly entertained at Government House by the late Lieutenant-Governor, Sir John Schultz, and Lady Schultz, to whom we were indebted for the contribution to our equipment of several articles of comfort.

The next day we bade our Winnipeg friends good-bye and took the C. P. R. train for the West. The route lay

HUDSON'S BAY COMPANY'S TRADERS.

through vast areas of the most magnificent agricultural country, as a rule level and unbroken, save by the innumerable and ancient but still deep trails of the buffalo. Little timber was observed, excepting in isolated patches and along the river valleys, and for the most part the land was ready for the plough. Passing through many new but thriving towns and settlements by the way, we arrived early on the morning of the 22nd at the busy town of Calgary, pleasantly situated in the beautiful valley of the South Branch of the Saskatchewan River, and just within view of the snow-clad peaks of the Rocky Mountains. From Calgary our way lay toward the north, *via* the Edmonton Branch of the C. P. R., and after a stay of only a few hours we were again hurrying onward. On the evening of the same day, in a teeming rain, we reached Edmonton, the northern terminus of the railway.

Edmonton is a town situated on both banks of the North Branch of the Saskatchewan, and at this time was in a "booming" condition, particularly upon the southern bank. Many large business houses were being erected, and property was selling at stiff prices. Edmonton is chiefly noted for its lignite mines, which are worked to a considerable extent, and produce coal of very fair quality. The seams are practically of unlimited extent, and are easily accessible in many places along the river banks. Gold is also washed from the sands in paying quantities, while the town is surrounded by a fair agricultural and grazing country. Petroleum, too, has been discovered in the vicinity, and indications are that in the near future Edmonton will be a flourishing city.

The older part of the town is situated on the north side of the river, and communication is maintained by means of an old-fashioned ferry, operated by cables and windlass. As the Hudson's Bay Company's stores and offices from which our supplies were to be forwarded are situated on the north side, we crossed over on the ferry, and engaged rooms at the Jasper House. Upon enquiry we were gratified to find that the supplies and men, excepting the two who were to meet us later, had all arrived in safety. Our provisions, which were to be freighted down as far as Lake Athabasca by the Hudson's Bay Company, had not yet gone, but were already being baled up for shipment. The completion of this work, which was done under the supervision of my brother and myself, together with the making up of accounts and transaction of other business, occupied several days. But by the morning of the 27th of May our entire outfit, loaded upon waggons, set off on the northward trail leading to Athabasca Landing, a small trading-post situated one hundred miles distant on the banks of the great Athabasca River.

Two days later, being Monday morning, my brother and I, accompanied by a driver only, started out in a light vehicle in rear of the outfit. The weather was showery, and the trail in many places very soft. Occasionally deep mud-holes were encountered, bearing evidence of the recent struggles of the teams of our advance party, but as we were travelling "light," we had little difficulty in making good progress. Later in the day the weather cleared, permitting us to enjoy a view of the beautiful country through which we were passing. As to the soil, it was chiefly a rich black loam, well covered, even at this early season, between the clumps of poplar scrub, by rich prairie grass. A few settlers were already in the field, and had just built or were building

A H. B. C. INTERPRETER.

16   ACROSS THE SUB-ARCTICS OF CANADA.

log cabins for themselves on one side or other of the trail. A little farther on our way the country became more hilly, the soil more sandy, and covered by the

A PIONEER OF THE NORTH.
(Drawn from life by Arthur Heming.)

most beautiful park-like forests of jack-pine. Many of the trees were as much as fifteen inches in diameter, but the average size was about eight.

After passing through some miles of these woods we again emerged into more open country, wooded alternately in places by poplar, spruce and jack-pine. About nine o'clock that evening, when half-way to the Landing, we reached the Height of Land between the two great valleys of the Saskatchewan and Athabasca rivers. Here, upon a grassy spot, we pitched our first camp. As the night was clear no tents were put up, but, after partaking of some refreshment, each man rolled up in his blanket and lay down to sleep beneath the starry sky. We rested well, although our slumbers were somewhat broken by the fiendish yells of prairie wolves from the surrounding scrub, and the scarcely less diabolical screams of loons sporting on a pond close by. An effort was made to have the latter nuisance removed, but any one who has ever tried to shoot loons at night will better understand than I can describe the immensity of the undertaking.

About nine o'clock on the evening of the 30th of May we arrived at Athabasca Landing, only a few hours after the loads of supplies, which we were glad to find had all come through safely.

INDIANS OF THE CANADIAN NORTH-WEST.

(Drawn from life by Arthur Heming.)

CHAPTER II.

DOWN THE ATHABASCA.

THE town of Athabasca Landing consists in all of six log buildings, picturesque ╵ t in the deep and beautiful valley of one of the greatest rivers of America. Though not of imposing size, it is nevertheless an important station of the Hudson's Bay Company, being the point from which all supplies for the many northern trading-posts along the Athabasca and Mackenzie rivers are shipped, and the point at which the furs from these places are received. In order to provide for this shipping business, the Company has a large warehouse and wharf.

It is a fact I think not very well known, that from this place up stream for about one hundred miles and down for fifteen hundred miles to the Arctic Ocean, this great waterway, excepting at two rapids, is regularly navigated by large river steamers, owned by the Hudson's Bay Company and employed in carrying supplies for their posts and the furs which are secured in trade. Because of these two impassable rapids the river is divided into three sections, necessitating the use of three steamers, one for each section. Goods are transported from one boat to the other over the greater part of the rapids by means of scows, but for a short distance, at the Grand Rapid, by means of a tramway built for the purpose.

As we had previously ascertained, the steamer *Athabasca* was due to leave the Landing on her down-stream trip on or about the 1st of June, so, taking advantage of the opportunity, we shipped the bulk of our stuff to Fort Chippewyan, situated about three hundred and fifty miles down the river on Lake Athabasca. Everything excepting the canoes and provisions sufficient to take us to Chippewyan was loaded upon the steamer. Letters were written and sent back to Edmonton by the drivers, and on the evening of the last day of May we launched our handsome "Peterboroughs" in the great stream, and commenced our long canoe voyage.

The arrangement of the party was as follows: My brother occupied a central position in one canoe, and I a corresponding place in the other. As steersman he chose the eldest of the Iroquois, Pierre, with Michel as bowman. The remaining Iroquois, Louis, took the steering paddle of my canoe, and John, the western man, occupied the bow. Thus were our little crafts manned, each person, including my brother and myself, being provided with a broad maple paddle. Our loads being light, we were in good speeding condition. Just after launching we met some native Indians in their bark canoes, and by way of amusement and exhibition of speed paddled completely around them in the current, much to their amazement. Then with farewell salute, and the stroke of our paddles timed to the song of the canoemen, we glided swiftly down the stream.

As the start had been made late in the afternoon, not many miles were passed before it became necessary to look for a camping place. The banks of the river, formed of boulder clay, were very high, and good landings were scarce. In places the mud on the shore was soft and deep, but about seven o'clock a landing was effected and camp pitched for the night. At this time only two small tents were used, an "A" tent for the canoemen and a wall tent, affording a little more head room, for ourselves. The banks being well wooded with white and black poplar, spruce and birch, plenty of fuel was available. A fire was soon kindled and our evening meal prepared, in the cooking of which John was given the first opportunity of distinguishing himself. He was assisted by little Michel, who proved to be a very good hand. Having some bread and biscuits in stock, baking was not yet a necessity.

The weather now being fair and cool, and the great pest of camp life, the mosquito, not having yet arrived, our experience at this time was most enjoyable. It was the season of spring, and the sweet perfume of the Balm of Gilead, so abundant in the valley of the Athabasca, permeated the air. The leaves on many of the trees were just opening, so that everywhere the woods presented a remarkable freshness and brilliancy of foliage. These were our environments at the commencement of the canoe voyage, and at our first camp on the banks of the Athabasca. How different were they to be at the other end of the journey!

On the morning of the 1st of June camp was called early, and we continued on our way. As we glided down stream a succession of grand views passed, panorama-like, before us. The banks were high, towering in some places three, four or five hundred feet above the river;

here abrupt and precipitous, consisting of cut banks of stratified clay; in other places more receding, but by a gradual slope rising, beneath dense foliage, to an equal elevation.

At this season of the year the water being high and the current swift, we made good time, covering a distance of sixty miles for the first full day's travel. About noon on the 2nd, having reached a narrow part of the river, very remarkable massive walls of ice were found upon either bank, some distance above the water's edge. These walls were of irregular thickness, and from eight to ten feet in height; but the most striking feature about them was that they presented smooth vertical faces to the river, although built of blocks of every shape and shade from clear crystal to opaque mud. They extended thus more or less continuously for miles down the river, and had the appearance of great masonry dykes. The explanation of their existence is doubtless as follows: Earlier in the season the narrowness of the channel had caused the river ice to jam and greatly raised the water level. After a time, when the water had reached a certain height and much ice had been crowded up on the shores, the jam had given way and caused the water to rapidly lower to a considerable extent, leaving the ice grounded above a certain line. Thus the material for the wall was deposited, and the work of constructing and finishing the smooth vertical face was doubtless performed by the subsequent grinding of the passing jam, which continued to flow in the deeper channel. After the passing of the first freshet, and the formation of these great ice walls, the water had gradually lowered to the level at which we found it.

Late in the afternoon the first rapid of the trip was sighted, but the water being high we had no difficulty in running it. In the evening camp was made on a beautiful sandy beach. During supper-time we had a visit from an old Cree Indian, who came paddling up the river in a little bark canoe. Of course he landed at our camp, for it is a principle strictly observed by every Indian to lose no opportunity of receiving hospitalities, and in accordance with his ideas of propriety, refreshments were given him. He received them as those of his race usually receive all favors, as no more than his right, and without a smile or the least visible expression of pleasure, seated himself by the fire to enjoy them.

On the following morning the great walls of ice, which we had been passing for miles, began to disappear as the channel of the river became wider. At about 9.30 we reached a place known as the Rapid of the Jolly Fool. It is said to have received its name from the fact that at one time an awkward canoeman lost his life by allowing his canoe to be smashed upon the most conspicuous rock in the rapid. We wasted no time examining it, as it was reported to be an easy one, but keeping near the left bank, headed our little crafts into the rushing waters. We had descended only a short distance, and were turning a bend in the stream, when, a little ahead of us, my brother noticed moving objects on the shore. One of the men said they were wolves, while others maintained they were bears, but my brother getting his rifle in readiness, cut the discussion short by demanding silence. As we swept swiftly down with the current, the objects were seen to be a moose deer and her calf. Having no fresh meat on hand, these new-found acquaintances were hailed as "well met." Not until our canoes had approached within about one hundred and fifty yards did the old moose, standing in the shallow water near the river bank, appear to notice us. Then, apparently apprehending danger, but without alarm, she turned toward the shore, and, followed by her calf, walked up the bank towards the woods. As she did so my brother fired from his canoe, wounding her in the hind-quarters. I then fired, but struck the clay bank above the animal's head, and in attempting to fire again the shell stuck in my rifle, making it impossible for me to relond. Just as the moose was disappearing into the woods my brother fired again, and inflicted a body wound; but in spite of all away went the deer.

As our canoes were thrust ashore I succeeded in extracting the shell from my rifle, and leaving some of the men in charge of the canoes, my brother and I gave chase. The trail of blood was discovered on the leaves, but it led into such a jungle of fallen timber and thicket that it was no easy matter to follow. Scouts were sent out on either side, while with our rifles we followed the trail, running when we were permitted, jumping logs that came in the way, and clambering over or through windfalls that the moose had cleared at a bound. Presently through the leafy thicket we had a glimpse of our prey. Bang went both rifles and away bounded the moose with two more slugs in her body.

We were now pretty badly winded, but being anxious to complete the work we had undertaken, the chase was kept up. We knew from the wounds already inflicted that the capture was only a matter of physical endurance on our part, and we were prepared to do our best. More than once the trail was lost in the windfalls and jungle, but at length, getting another side view, I shot her through the heart, bringing the noble beast with a thud to the ground. Nothing had been seen of the calf since the beginning of the hunt, but going back to the shore to get assistance, I found that the men had captured and made it a prisoner beside the canoes. Taking charge of the captive myself, I sent the men into the woods to skin the deer and "pack" the meat out to shore. The little calf, which I held by the ear, was very young, and not at all wild. Indeed, though I let go my hold, the little creature did not care to go away, but kept on calling for its mother in such a pitiful way that it made me heartily sorry for having bereft it. After the space of an hour or so my brother and the men returned, well loaded with fresh meat and a fine moose-hide. The meat was placed in sacks and stowed away in the canoes, but the hide being heavy and of little value to us, was placed on a big stone in the sun to dry and await the ownership of the first Indian who should pass that way.

As it was now nearly noon, it was decided to take dinner before re-embarking, and while the cooks were devoting their attention to bannocks and moose-steaks my brother and I were debating as to what we should do with the calf. We had not the heart to deliberately shoot it, but were unable to take it with us alive, as we would like to have done. Through a suggestion of one of the men a happy alternative was decided on. Other moose were doubtless in the vicinity, so that the calling of the calf would likely attract some of them, and in the event of this taking place it was said that the little moose would attach itself to another female. With the hope that such kind fortune would befall it, my brother, after having taken its photograph, led it away by the ear into the shelter of the woods, and there left the little creature to its fate.

' During the afternoon of the same day, the head of the Grand Rapid of the Athabasca, situated just 165 miles below the Landing, was reached. Here we met a detachment of the Mounted Police, in charge of Inspector Howard; and as it was late in the day, and Saturday evening, it was decided to pitch camp. The police camp was the only other one in the neighborhood, so the first question which suggested itself was: What possible duty could policemen find to perform in such a wild, uninhabited place? The answer, however, was simple. The place, though without any settled habitation, is the scene of the transhipment of considerable freight on its way to the various trading-posts and mission stations of the great Mackenzie River District. The river steamer *Athabasca*, belonging to the Hudson's Bay Company, was now daily looked for with its load from the Landing. Mission scows, loaded with freight for Fort Chippewyan and other points, were expected, and free-traders' outfits were liable to arrive at any time. It was for the purpose of inspecting these cargoes and preventing liquor from being carried down and sold for furs to the Indians, that Inspector Howard and his detachment were stationed here.

From the Grand Rapid, down stream for about eighty miles to Fort McMurray, the river is not navigable for steamers, and so all goods have to be transported over this distance by scows built for the purpose. The head of the Grand Rapid is thus the northern steamboat

TROOPER, N.-W. MOUNTED POLICE, IN WINTER UNIFORM.

terminus for the southern section of the river. The whole distance of eighty miles is not a continuous rapid, but eleven or twelve more or less impracticable sections occur in it, so that no great length of navigable water is found at any place. As its name suggests, the Grand Rapid is the main rapid of the river, and has a fall of seventy or eighty feet. This fall occurs mostly within a distance of half a mile, though the total length of the rapid is about four times that. The upper part is divided by a long narrow island into two channels, and it is through these comparatively narrow spaces that the cataract rushes so wildly. Above and below the island, the river may with great care be navigated by the loaded scows, but the water upon either side is so rough that goods cannot be passed down or up in safety. The method of transportation adopted is as follows: About a mile above the island, at the head of the rapid, the steamer *Athabasca* ties up to the shore. There she is met by a number of flat-bottomed boats or scows capable of carrying about ten tons each, and to these the boat's cargo is transferred. When loaded the scows are piloted one by one to the head of the island in the middle of the river, where a rough wharf is built, and to it all goods are again transferred, whence they are carried to the lower end of the island by means of a tramway. The unloaded scows, securely held with ropes by a force of men on the shore, and guided with poles by a crew on board, are then carefully lowered down stream to the foot of the island, where they again receive their loads. Accidents frequently happen in passing down the unloaded scows, for the channel (the eastern one always being chosen) is very rough and rocky. From the foot of the island in the Grand Rapid the scows are then floated down the river, with more or less difficulty, according to the height of water, through the long succession of rapids to Fort McMurray, where they are met by the second steamer, the *Grahame*, which receives their freight and carries it down the river to Fort Chippewyan on Lake Athabasca, and thence onward to Fort Smith, on Great Slave River, where a second transhipment has to be made over about sixteen miles of rapids. From the lower end of these rapids the steamer *Wrigley*, under the command of Captain Mills, takes charge of the cargo and delivers it at the various trading-posts along the banks of the Mackenzie River, for a distance of about twelve hundred miles, to the Arctic Ocean.

But to return to our camp at the head of the Grand Rapid. Inspector Howard and his men proved to be interesting companions. I soon discovered, to my surprise, that the Inspector was a cousin of my wife's, and that I had met him in former years in Toronto. Meeting with even so slight an acquaintance in such a place was indeed a pleasure; and in justice to the occasion a banquet, shall I call it, was given us, at which moose-steak and bear-chops cut a conspicuous figure. In conversation with the Inspector some information was obtained regarding the character of the rapids now before us, and all such was carefully noted, since none of our party had ever run the Athabasca. We had with us the reports of William Ogilvie, D.L.S., and Mr. McConnell, who had descended the river and published much valuable information regarding it, but even they could not altogether supply the place of a guide. We were putting

LANDING OF SCOWS ABOVE GRAND RAPID.

great confidence in the skill of our Iroquois men at navigating rapids, and now in the succeeding eighty miles of the trip there would be ample opportunity of testing it.

On the morning following our arrival at the Grand Rapid, being the 4th of June, a number of mission scows, loaded with goods for Chippewyan and other mission stations, arrived. As they appeared, following each other in quick succession around a bend in the river, each boat manned by its wild-looking crew of half-naked Indians, all under the command of Schott, the big well-known river pilot, who is credited by Mr. Ogilvie with being the fastest dancer he has ever seen, they drew in towards the east bank, and one after the other made fast to the shore. The boats were at once boarded by Inspector Howard and his men, and a careful search made for any illegal consignments of "firewater." Liquor in limited quantities is allowed to be taken into the country when accompanied by an official permit from the Lieut.-Governor of the Territories, but without this it is at once confiscated when found. Out of deference to those for whom these cargoes were consigned, I had better not say whether a discovery was made on this occasion or not. When confiscations are made, however, the find is, of course, always destroyed. The news of the arrival of the scows was welcomed by us, not because of anything they brought with them, but because we expected to obtain directions from Schott regarding the running of the many rapids in the river ahead, and the transport of the bulk of our canoe loads to Fort McMurray, below the rapids. After some consideration, rather less than most Indians require to

take, these matters were arranged with Schott, and all but our instruments, tents, blankets and three or four days' provisions were handed over to him.

On the evening of the 4th, the steamer *Athabasca* also put in an appearance, and made fast to the shore a little above the scows. Grand Rapid was no longer an uninhabited wilderness, but had now become transformed into a scene of strange wild life. Large dark, savage-looking figures, many of them bare to the waist, and adorned with head-dresses of fox-tails or feathers, were everywhere to be seen. Some of them, notably those of the Chippewyan tribe, were the blackest and most savage-looking Indians I had ever seen. As it was already nearly night when the last of them arrived by the steamer, the work of transhipping was left for the morning. In the dark woods the light of camp-fires began soon to appear, and around them the whole night long the Indians danced and gambled, at the same time keeping up their execrable drum music.

ENGLISH-CHIPPEWYAN HALF-BREED.

At daylight the next morning the overhauling of cargoes was commenced. One by one the scows were loosened and piloted down the middle of the rapid to the wharf at the head of the island. Here they were unloaded, and after being lightened, were lowered down

DOWN THE ATHABASCA.

through the boiling waters by means of lines from the shore and the assistance of poles on board, to again receive their loads at the foot of the island. Two or three scows were also similarly engaged in transporting the cargo of the steamer, of which our supplies formed part, and, much to our annoyance, there was considerable delay on account of having to repair the tramway across the island. We were informed that the *Grahame* could not now reach Chippewyan before the 20th of June, which would be ten days later than we had expected to be able to leave that place. However, we could only accept the inevitable, and try to make the best use of the time.

While Schott and his crews were thus engaged with their transport, our own men were not idle. They had been told that the rapid would have to be portaged, as no canoeman would venture to run it; but having walked down the shore and themselves examined the river, the Iroquois asked and obtained permission to run it by taking one canoe down at a time. Schott and his Indians thought them mad to try such a venture, but seeming to have every confidence in their own abilities, we determined to see what they could do. John gladly chose the work of portaging along the rough boulder shore and over precipitous rocks in preference to taking a paddle, but the three Iroquois took their places, Louis in the bow, Michel in the middle, and old Pierre in the stern. As the three daring fellows pushed off from the shore into the surging stream, those of us who gazed upon them did so with grave forebodings. They had started, and now there was nothing to do but go through or be smashed upon the rocks. Their speed soon attained that of an express train, while all about them the boiling waters were dashed into foam by the great rocks in the channel. Presently it appeared as if they were doomed to be dashed upon a long ugly breaker nearly in mid-stream; but no! with two or three lightning strokes of their paddles the collision was averted. But in a moment they were in worse danger, for right ahead were two great rocks, over and around which the tumbling waters wildly rushed. Would they try the right side or the left? Only an instant was afforded for thought, but in that instant Pierre saw his only chance and took it—heading his canoe straight for the shoot between the rocks. Should they swerve a foot to one side or the other the result would be fatal, but with unerring judgment and unflinching nerve they shot straight through the notch, and disappeared in the trough below. Rising buoyantly from the billows of foam and flying spray, they swept on with the rushing waters until, in a little eddy half-way down the rapid, they pulled in to the shore in safety. They were all well soaked by the spray and foam, but without concern or excitement returned for the second canoe. In taking this down a valise of stationery and photographic supplies, inadvertently allowed to remain in the canoe, got a rather serious wetting, but as soon as possible its contents were spread out upon the smooth clean rocks to dry. Past the remainder of the rapid a portage was made and camp pitched at the foot. While our Iroquois were thus occupied, Schott and his men had been hard at work running down their scows and had been unfortunate enough to get one of them stranded on a big flat rock in the middle of the rapid. Had it not been for the timely assistance of our party and the generalship of old Pierre, he would probably never have gotten it off. As it was, the accomplishment of the task occupied our united energies for several hours.

NECK DEVELOPED BY THE TUMP-LINE.

CHAPTER III.

RUNNING THE RAPIDS.

BEFORE leaving the Grand Rapid several good photographs of it were obtained, and then on the morning of the 7th of June, bidding adieu to Inspector Howard, and leaving our supplies in the freighters' hands, we started down the river for Fort McMurray. The first object of special interest passed was a natural gas flow, occurring on the left bank about fifteen miles below the Rapid. At this place a considerable volume of gas is continually discharging, and may be seen bubbling up through the water over a considerable area, as well as escaping from rifts in the bank. The gas burns with a hot pale blue flame, and is said to be used at times by boatmen for cooking purposes. Eight or ten miles farther down stream came the Brûle Rapids, the first of the long series, and though they might easily have been run, we did not try it, as my brother wished to remain on shore for some time to collect fossils. Meanwhile our stuff was portaged, and without difficulty the empty canoes run down to the foot of the rapids, where camp was made. Just at this place commence the wonderful tar sand-beds of the Athabasca, extending over an enormous area. These certainly present a very striking appearance. During warm weather, in many places, the faces

of the river banks, from three to five hundred feet in
height, presents the appearance of running tar, and here
and there tar wells are found, having been formed by
the accumulation of the viscid tar in natural receptacles
of the rock. Thus collected it has been commonly made
use of by workmen in the calking of the scows on the
river.*

Sixteen miles farther down, the Boiler Rapid, so called
from the fact that in 1882 a boiler intended for the
steamer *Wrigley* was lost in it, was successfully run on
the following day, and early in the afternoon the third
rapid was reached In attempting to run it on the left
side, we found, after descending perhaps half-way, that
there were too many rocks in the channel ahead, and
therefore an effort was made to cross to the right side,
which looked to be clearer. My brother's canoe, steered
by old Pierre, avoided all rocks and was taken successfully across, but mine was not so fortunate. In
attempting to follow, we struck a large rock in mid-
channel, but happily the collision occurred in such a way
that my canoe was not seriously damaged. It was
merely whirled end for end in the current and almost
filled with water, though not quite sufficiently to sink
us. Leaving the two Indians to pull for the shore, I
seized a tin kettle and lost no time in dashing out some
of the water. After a sharp struggle we managed to
land. Of course all we had in the canoe—instruments,
blankets, provisions and clothing—was soaked, and it was
therefore necessary to unload and turn everything out.

* For further particulars regarding this most interesting locality,
see the report of Mr. McConnell, published in 1893 by the Geological
Survey of Canada.

My brother, seeing that something had happened, went ashore also, and with his men returned to assist us. The weather was fine, and our goods soon became sufficiently dry to allow us to re-embark.

An examination having been made of the rapid below, a short run was made down and then across to the opposite side, where we landed, and, because of the extreme shallowness of the channel and the many rocks that showed ominously above the surface, the canoes were lowered for the remaining half mile with the lines. The whole length of this rapid is perhaps a mile and a half, and it is sometimes designated as two, the Drowned and Middle Rapids. Following these in quick succession, at intervals of from two to ten miles, we passed through the Long Rapids, which occasioned no difficulty; then the Crooked Rapids, well named from the fact that they occur at a very sharp U shaped bend in the river, around which the current sweeps with great velocity. Just below this the Stony Rapid was passed, and then in turn the Little and Big Cascades, both of which are formed by ledges of limestone rock, about three feet high, extending in more or less unbroken lines completely across the river.

At the Big Cascade a portage of a few yards had to be made, and below this, smooth water was found for a distance of eight or nine miles, until the head of the Mountain Rapid was reached. Judging from the name that this would be a large one, we decided to go ashore to reconnoitre. For a considerable distance the rapid was inspected, but no unusual difficulty appearing, we resolved to go ahead. About a mile farther on, a bend occurred in the rapid, and so high and steep

RUNNING THE RAPIDS.

were the banks but only with great difficulty could we see the river beyond. As far as the bend, though the current was swift, there appeared to be but few rocks near the left bank, and plenty of water. We therefore decided to go ashore at that point, if necessary, and examine the stream beyond.

As we proceeded the stream became fearfully swift and the waves increasingly heavy. At the speed we were making the bend was soon reached, but just beyond it another bluff point came in view. We would have gone ashore to make a further inspection, but this was impossible, as the banks were of perpendicular or even overhanging walls of limestone. So alarmingly swift was the current now becoming that we eagerly looked for some place on the bank where a landing might be made, but none could be seen. Retreat was equally impossible against the enormous strength of the river: all we could do was to keep straight in the current. My brother's canoe, steered by old Pierre, being a little in advance of my own, gave me a good opportunity of seeing the fearful race we were running. Suspicions of danger were already aroused, and the outcome was not long deferred. As we were rounding the bluff, old Pierre suddenly stood up from his seat in the stern, and in another instant we likewise were gazing at what looked like the end of the river. Right before us there extended a perpendicular fall. We had no time for reflection, but keeping straight with the current, and throwing ourselves back in the canoes in order to lighten the bows we braced ourselves for the plunge, and in a moment were lost to sight in the foaming waters below. But only for an instant. Our light cedars, though partly filled by the foam and spray, rose buoyantly on the waves, and again we breathed freely. It was a lucky thing for us that the canoes were not loaded, for had they been they never would have floated after that plunge, but would have disappeared like lead in the billows. We afterwards found we had taken the rapid in the very worst spot, and that near the right side of the river we might have made the descent free of danger. Without a guide, however, such mistakes will sometimes occur in spite of every precaution.

Poor John, my bowman, was badly unstrung as a result of this adventure, and declared that he did not want to shoot any more waterfalls: and for that matter, others of us were of much the same mind. One more small rapid, the Moberly, completed the series, and then for a few miles we enjoyed calm water until, toward evening, we reached Fort McMurray.

This settlement, containing in all five small log buildings—a warehouse, a store, the traders' dwelling and two Indian houses—is situated on a cleared tongue of land formed by the junction of the Clear Water River with the Athabasca, and is about two hundred and fifty miles below the Landing. The site of the post is at an elevation of forty or fifty feet above the water, but in the immediate background, and on both banks of the river, the ground rises abruptly, and is covered by a thick growth of poplar, spruce and birch trees. At the time of our arrival two parties of Indians, one Cree and the other Chippewyan, occupying in all a dozen or more lodges, were encamped at the place, and were to be seen in groups here and there idly putting in the time, while everywhere their mangy canines skulked and prowled

SHOOTING THE MOUNTAIN RAPID, ATHABASCA RIVER.

about, seeking what they might devour—old moccasins, pack straps, etc., apparently being their favorite dainties.

Naturally, our first inquiry upon arriving at the Fort was whether or not our two men and canoe from Isle-à-la-Crosse had arrived; but the appearance of an upturned "Peterborough" on the shore soon answered the question, and a few minutes later two stout half-breeds made their appearance, and informed us they were

STORE, FORT McMURRAY.

the men who had been sent by Mr. Moberly to meet us My brother had expected the two men who had accompanied him on his trip of the previous year, but they having been unable to come, these two, Jim Corrigal and François Maurice, had been engaged in their stead. Jim was a man of middle age, tall and of muscular frame; while his companion was probably not more than twenty years of age, and in appearance rather short and of heavy build. Jim spoke English fairly well, though Cree was his tongue; but François, while speaking only very broken English, could converse in French, Cree and Chippewyan, his knowledge of the last making him subsequently very useful as an interpreter.

Our party, consisting of eight men, with three canoes, was now complete, and thus assembled, the cleanest

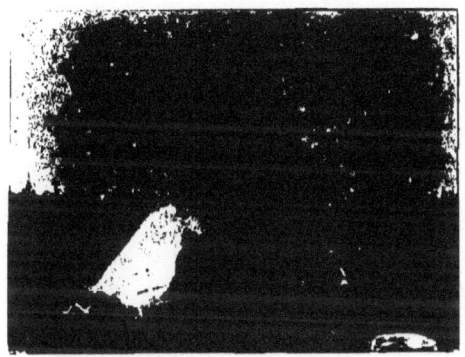

CHIPPEWYAN CAMP.

available ground remote from Indian lodges was chosen, and camp pitched to await the arrival of the four hundred pounds of supplies left with Schott at Grand Rapid. We soon found we were not the only ones waiting, and that anxiously, for the arrival of the scows from the south. The entire population then at Fort McMurray was in a state of famine. Supplies at the post, having been insufficient for the demand, had become exhausted, and the Indians who had come in to barter their furs were thus far unable to obtain food in exchange, and were obliged, with their families, to subsist upon the few rabbits that might be caught in the woods. We were also out of supplies, but now the scows were hourly expected. Expectations, however, afforded poor satisfaction to hungry stomachs, and no less than five days passed before these materialized. In the meantime, though we were not entirely without food ourselves, some of the natives suffered much distress. At one Cree camp visited I witnessed a most pitiable sight. There was the whole family of seven or eight persons seated on the ground about their smoking camp-fire, but without one morsel of food, while children, three or four years old, were trying to satisfy their cravings at the mother's breast. We had no food to give them, but gladdened their hearts by handing around some pieces of tobacco, of which all Indians, if not all savages, are passionately fond.

In addition to the unpleasantness created by lack of provisions, our stay at Fort McMurray was attended with extremely wet weather, which made it necessary to remain in camp most of the time, and to wade through no end of mud whenever we ventured out.

On the evening of the 14th the long-looked-for scows with the supplies arrived. It will readily be imagined we were not long in getting out the provisions and making ready a supper more in keeping with our appetites than the meagre meals with which we had for several days been forced to content ourselves. The cause of delay, as Schott informed us, was the grounding of

STARVING CREE CAMP, FORT McMURRAY.

some of the boats in one of the rapids, in consequence of which the cargoes had to be removed by his men, and carried on their shoulders to the shore, the boats then freed, lowered past the obstruction, and reloaded. Such work necessarily entails considerable delay, and is of a slavish character, as all hands have to work in the ice-cold water for hours together.

Receiving again our four hundred pounds of supplies from Schott, we lost no more time at Fort McMurray, but at seven o'clock next morning the little expedition, consisting now of eight men and three canoes, pushed out into the river, and with a parting salute sped away with the current, which being swift, and our canoemen fresh, enabled us in a short time to place many miles between us and the Fort. At five o'clock in the evening, having then descended the river a distance of about sixty miles we were delighted to meet the steamer *Grahame* on her up-stream trip from Fort Chippewyan to McMurray to receive the goods brought down the rapids by the scows. The steamer, being in charge of Dr. McKay, the Hudson's Bay Company's officer from Chippewyan, who had been informed of our expedition, was at once brought to a stand in the river, and we were kindly invited on board. When I commenced to clamber up the steamer's deck, whose hand should be offered to assist me but that of an old friend and fellow-shipmate for two years in Hudson Straits, Mr. J. W. Mills. The acquaintance of Dr. McKay and of the Bishop of Athabasca, who happened to be on board, was also made, and with right genial companions an hour quickly and very pleasantly passed. Mr. Mills, who was attired in the uniform of a steamboat captain, had lately been appointed to the command of the steamer *Wrigley*, plying on the lower section of the river below Fort Smith, to which place he was to be taken by the *Grahame* on her return trip from Fort McMurray. Before parting company, the Doctor promised to meet us again at Chippewyan on the 19th inst., and after this

A DANDY OF THE NORTH.   A VOYAGEUR.

short meeting, and many parting good wishes, as well as blessings from the Bishop, we resumed our separate ways.

Notwithstanding the hour's delay, and the fact that rain fell all day, we made the very good run of seventy-two miles. As we swept along with the winding river, the most beautiful and varied scenes were continually presented. The banks, though not so high as above Fort McMurray, were bold and thickly draped with spruce and poplar woods. Taking advantage of the discovery of some straight spruce saplings, we landed as night approached, and a number of our men were sent to select a few for the purpose of making good tent-poles, to take the place of the rough ones we had been using. Besides spruce and other varieties of timber, balsam trees, the last seen on the northward journey, were found at this camp.

On the morning of the 16th, though the weather continued showery and a strong head wind had set in, we were early on our way, for we were anxious to reach Chippewyan a day or two before the return of the *Grahame*, that we might rate our chronometer and make all necessary preparations for a good-bye to the outermost borders of civilization. In descending the Athabasca we were making no survey of the course, nor any continuous examination of the geological features of the district, but were chiefly concerned in getting down to Chippewyan, where we were to receive our full loads of supplies, and from which place our work was really to begin. Despite the unpleasantness of the weather, therefore, our canoes were kept in the stream and all hands at the paddles, and by nightfall another stretch of about sixty miles was covered. We had now reached the low flat country at the delta of the river, where its waters break into many channels, but still a strong current was running, and this we were glad to find continued until within a distance of six or eight miles from the lake. Some parts of the river were much obstructed by driftwood grounded upon shoals; the banks, too, were low and marshy, and landing-places difficult to find. Several flocks of wild geese were seen, but none secured.

During the morning of the 17th some gun-shots were heard not far distant across the grassy marsh, and turning our canoes in that direction we soon met several bark canoes manned by Chippewyan Indian hunters. François, being the only man in our party who could understand or talk with them, was much in demand, and he was instructed to ask them the shortest way through the delta towards Chippewyan. Indian like, he entered into conversation with the strangers for ten minutes or so, doubtless chiefly about their wives and daughters, and then with a wave of the hand said, "We go dis way." So that way we went, and by three o'clock in the afternoon found ourselves in the open waters of Lake Athabasca. Two hours later we had crossed the end of the Lake and drawn up our canoes on the rocky shore in front of Fort Chippewyan. It was Saturday evening, and the distance travelled thus far since launching the canoes, was, according to Mr. Ogilvie, 430 miles. As we were already aware, Dr. McKay, the Hudson's Bay Company's agent, was not at the Fort, but we were received by the assistant trader, Pierre Mercredie, a half-breed, and shown to a camping-ground in front of the Fort, or otherwise on Main Street of the town. During the evening we had the pleasure of meeting Mrs. McKay and her children, and also Mr. Russell, an American naturalist, who was sojourning at this place on his way down the Mackenzie River.

AN ENGLISH-CREE TRAPPER.

CHAPTER IV.

CHIPPEWYAN TO BLACK LAKE.

FORT CHIPPEWYAN is an old and important trading-post of the Hudson's Bay Company. Before many of our Canadian and American cities came into existence, Chippewyan was a noted fur-trading centre. From here—or rather from a former site of the post, a few miles distant—Alexander Mackenzie (afterwards Sir Alexander) started, in 1789, on his famous journey down the great river which now bears his name. About the beginning of the present century the post was moved to the position it now occupies on the rocky northern shore of the west end of the Lake.

The Fort consists of a long row of eighteen or twenty detached log buildings, chiefly servants' houses, connected by a high strong wooden fence or wall, so as to present an unbroken front to the water, behind which, in a sort of court, are situated the Factor's dwelling and two or three other good-sized log buildings. At the west end of the row stands an Episcopal Mission church and the Mission house, which at the time of our visit was occupied by Bishop Young, the see of whose diocese was formerly here, but since removed to Fort Vermilion, some 270 miles distant on the Peace River. Within easy sight, a short distance farther west, across a little

FORT CHIPPEWYAN.

CHIPPEWYAN TO BLACK LAKE.

bay, the Roman Catholic Mission church, and various buildings connected therewith, are situated. This mission is a large and flourishing one, and is the see of the Roman Catholic Diocese of Athabasca. All the buildings of Chippewyan are neatly whitewashed, so that, particularly from the front, it presents a most striking appearance. At the back of the Fort, between the rocky hills, plenty of small timber for house-building and firewood is found, and over at the Catholic Mission a little farm is cultivated, and many luxuries in the way of root vegetables obtained from it.

The staple food, however, for both man and dogs (which latter are important members of the community) is fish, several varieties of which are caught in abundance in the lake close at hand. One or two whitefish, according to size, is the usual daily allowance for a dog.

In the north the dog takes the place which the horse occupies in the south, and it is a very interesting sight to see the canine population of the town, perhaps thirty or forty in all, receiving their daily meal. They are called together by the ringing of a large bell, erected for the purpose at all Hudson's Bay Company posts. At the first stroke all dogs within reach of the sound spring to their feet and scamper off to the feeding place, where they find a man in charge of their rations. Forming round in a circle, each dog waits for the portion thrown to him, which he at once trots away with to enjoy in some quiet retreat. Occasional snarls and fights take place, but it is astonishing to see how orderly Chippewyan dogs are able to conduct themselves at a common mess.

The day after our arrival at the Fort being Sunday, we

FORT CHIPPEWYAN.

had our last opportunity for several months of attending Divine service, and were privileged to listen to an excellent sermon preached by His Lordship Bishop Young. Some of our men, being Roman Catholics, were able to avail themselves of the opportunity of attending mass as well, and of receiving a parting blessing from the priest.

STEAMER "GRAHAME."

The next day being the 10th, the date on which Dr. McKay had promised to rejoin us at the Fort, his return with the *Grahame* was eagerly looked for. We had made all the preparations for departure that could be made until he and our supplies should arrive. During the afternoon a strong breeze sprang up from the east, raising a heavy sea, and it was not until sunset that the belated steamer tied up to the wharf. She had had a rough passage, so rough that the Doctor declared it was the last time he would ever be a passenger on her in such water, a not unwise resolution, for the steamer, top-heavy and drawing only about three feet of water, was not unlikely to roll over in rough weather.

With the return of the Doctor, Captain Mills and the Captain of the *Grahame*, we now formed a merry party, and spent a pleasant evening at the Doctor's house. Captain Mills and I talked over old-time adventures in Hudson Straits, and recalled many incidents from our mutual experiences in the north in bygone days. But as the Doctor had determined to leave again with the steamer on the following day for the Great Slave Lake river posts, there was no time to be lost in social pleasures. In compliance with my brother's request, sent by letter some months previously, Dr. McKay had engaged the best available Indian guide to accompany us from this place through Lake Athabasca and as far beyond as he knew the country. With the success of this arrangement we were greatly pleased, as it was desirable that as little time as possible should be lost in seeking trails and river routes. The guide's name was Moberly—a Christian name, though borne by a full-blooded Chippewyan Indian, who, before we were through with him, proved himself to be anything but a Christian. He was acquainted with our route for about one hundred miles to the northward from Black Lake, and even in this distance his services, we thought, would likely save us several days.

The next morning the Fort was a scene of hurry and bustle. Goods were landed from the steamer, cordwood taken on board, and much other business attended to.

I took charge of our own supplies, and checked each piece as it was brought ashore. Our chest of tea was the only article that had suffered from the effects of frequent transhipment. It had been broken open and a few pounds lost, but the balance—about sixty pounds—had been gathered up and put in a flour bag. Before noon everything was safely landed on the shore, and it formed a miscellaneous pile of no small extent. Following is a list of the articles: "Bacon, axes, flour, matches, oatmeal, alcohol, tin kettles, evaporated apples, apricots, salt, sugar, frying-pans, dutch oven, rice, pepper, mustard, files, jam, tobacco, hard tack, candles, geological hammers, baking powder, pain killer, knives, forks, canned beef—fresh and corned—tin dishes, tarpaulins and waterproof sacks. Besides the above, there were our tents, bags of dunnage, mathematical instruments, rifles and a box of ammunition. The total weight of all this outfit amounted at the time to about four thousand pounds.

A sail-boat which my brother had used in 1892, and which was in good condition, rode at anchor before the Fort, and for a time it was thought we would have to make use of this as far as the east end of the lake to carry all our stuff. Moberly, the guide, particularly urged the necessity of taking the big boat, for his home was at the east end of the lake, and he had a lot of stuff for which he wished to arrange a transport, but as we were not on a freighting tour for Moberly, and as we found by trial that everything could be carried nicely in the canoes, we decided to take them only. At this the guide became sulky, and thought he would not go. His wife and two daughters, who were to accompany him as far as their home, tried to persuade him, but Indian-like he would not promise to do one thing or the other. At last we told him to go where he chose, as we were in no way dependent on him, but knew our own way well enough.

As arranged, the *Grahame* steamed away during the afternoon, for the Great Slave River, with Dr. McKay, Captain Mills and Bishop Young on board, but our own start was deferred until the next morning, and in the meantime home letters were written, for a packet was to go south from here about the 16th of July.

On the morning of the 21st of June, the whole outfit being snugly stowed in the three canoes, our party set out on the eastward course. Old Moberly, the guide, was also on hand with his family and big bark canoe. The morning was beautifully fair and calm; all nature seemed to be smiling. But soon the smile became a frown. The east wind, as if aroused by our paddles, began to stir himself, and before long made things unpleasant enough, coming not alone but with clouds of mist and rain. Though we could make but slow progress, we persisted in travelling until 9.30 p.m., when, having made about twenty-four knots, we pitched camp in a little sandy bay, worthy to be remembered because of the swarms of mosquitos which greeted us on landing. We had been reminded of the existence of these creatures at Chippewyan and at former camps, but here it was a question of the survival of the fittest. Mosquito nets, already fixed to our hats, had to be drawn down and tightly closed, and mosquito oil or grease smeared over the hands.

The whole north shore of the lake, being bold and

LANDING ON NORTH SHORE, LAKE ATHABASCA.

rocky, and consisting chiefly of Laurentian gneiss, is of little geological interest except at a few points, which will be spoken of as they are reached. The south shore, which was examined by my brother in 1892, was found to be of entirely different character, low and flat, and its rocks cretaceous sandstones. The chief varieties of timber observed as we passed along were spruce, white poplar and birch, and with these, though of small size, the country was fairly well covered.

Our second day on the lake was even less successful than the first, for though we made a start in the morning, we were soon obliged to put to shore by reason of the roughness of the water and a strong head-wind. At noon we succeeded in getting our latitude, which was 59° 6′ 32″ N.

About six o'clock that evening, shortly after our second launch, we met a party of Indians in their bark canoes, sailing with hoisted blankets before the wind. There were quite a number of them, and as they bore down towards us they presented a picturesque and animated scene. Moberly was some distance in the rear, but François was on hand to interpret, and as we met a halt was made. The first and most natural question asked by the Indians was, "Where are you going?" "To h—," was François' prompt but rather startling reply. In order that we might have an opportunity of securing information about the country (not that to which François had alluded, however), it was decided that we should all go ashore and have some tea; so our course was shaped for the nearest beach, a mile or so away. Upon landing we found that some of these Indians were men of whom Dr. McKay had spoken as being shrewd, intelligent fellows. From one old hunter in particular, named Sharlo, we obtained interesting sketch-maps of canoe routes leading northward from Lake Athabasca. Of course tea and tobacco had been served out before such information was sought, for no man of any experience would think of approaching an Indian for the purpose of obtaining a favor without first having conferred one. Our object accomplished, canoes were again launched, and the struggle with the east wind was renewed. Though we travelled until 10.30 at night we made only 16.4 knots during the day, as indicated by the boat's log; and then in the mouth of the Fishing River we found a sheltered nook in the thick woods for a camping-ground.

The next day, the high wind continuing and rain falling freely, the lake was too rough for us to venture out. A collection of all the many varieties of plants occurring in the vicinity was carefully made. Nets were set out, and some fine fish taken; trolls were also used with fair success, and with my revolver, much to the amusement of the party, I shot and killed some distance under water a fine large pike. A few geese were seen also, but none could be secured.

On the following morning, though it was still raining, the wind had fallen, and we were able to go ahead. Because of the wet we had great difficulty in using our surveying instruments and in making notes. During the forenoon while ashore at Cypress Point, a long sand-beach timbered with jack-pine woods, and extending a mile or more out into the lake, we observed a sail not far ahead. A sail-boat in these waters was an unusual sight, but on this occasion we were able to guess its meaning. It was Mr. Reed with his party returning from Fort Fond du Lac (now a small winter post only) to Chippewyan with the last winter's trade. We had been told we would likely meet him on the lake, and here he came before the breeze in his big York boat. As he approached and sighted us he made in to where we were, and ran his boat on the sand beach.

Besides Mr. Reed, the young trader, there were with him two French priests returning from their season's labor among the Indians. One of them, now an old man, had spent the greater part of his life in mission work in this district, and was about laying down his commission, to be succeeded by his younger companion. As it was nearly noon, our men were instructed, though it was raining heavily, to kindle a fire and prepare lunch for the party. Beneath some thick fir-trees a shelter was found, and the tea being made and lunch laid out on

A TYPICAL NORTHLAND FATHER.

the ground, we all seated ourselves about, and spent a delightful half-hour together. But to us every hour was precious, and without further delay we wished each other God-speed, and continued our courses. By nightfall the log-reading showed our day's travel to be thirty-two knots, equivalent to about thirty-seven miles. So far we had been fortunate in finding comfortable camping grounds. With a guide who knew the shore we should be expected to do so, but with a guide such as ours, who was commonly several miles behind, his connection with the party made little difference, excepting in the consumption of "grub."

Three more days passed, and despite the unfavorable weather, seventy miles of shore-line were surveyed. Then a discovery of some interest was made. Just east of the Beaver Hills we found a veritable mountain of iron ore, and that of the most valuable kind, hæmatite. Coal to smelt it is not found in the vicinity, though there is plenty of wood in the forest. The shore of this part of the lake was very much obscured by islands, upon the slopes of which the remains of the last winter's snow banks could still be seen.

We made an early start on the morning of the 18th, breaking camp at five o'clock, but before we had made any distance a fog settled over the lake so dense that we could not see ten yards from the canoes. For some time we groped along in the darkness, every little while finding our way obstructed by the rocky wall of some island or point of land, and finally, meeting with a seemingly endless shore, we were obliged to wait for the weather to clear. All hands landed and climbed the precipitous bank, with a view to discovering something about the locality, but all was obscurity. Toward noon the fog lifted, and we were able to make out our position, which was on the mainland and north of Old Man Island. On this point we observed a solitary grave, and near by the remains of an old log house. As to who had been the occupant of this solitary hut, or whose remains rested in the lonely grave, we knew not, but their appearance on this uninhabited shore made a realistic picture of desolation and sadness.

On the morning of the 29th of June, high west winds and heavy rain were again the order of the day, but venturing out, we made a fast run before the wind and reached the Fort in a heavy sea. Fond-du-Lac is a fort only in name, and consists in all of two or three small log shanties and a little log mission church, situated on a bare, exposed sandy shore, without any shelter from the fierce winter storms which hold high carnival in this country six or seven months of the year. Having already met the white residents of Fond-du-Lac on the lake, most of their houses, few though they were, were locked up or deserted. Two or three Indians and their families were living at the place, and with one of them letters were left with a hope that they might be taken safely to Chippewyan, and thence forwarded by the Hudson's Bay Company's autumn packet to Edmonton. This was undoubtedly the last chance, though only a chance, of sending any news to our friends until we should return to civilization.

From Fond-du-Lac eastward the lake is quite narrow, having much the appearance of a broad river. It is only five miles in width, but extends a distance of fifty miles. On the south shore could be seen a large group of Indian lodges, and at this camp was the home of our guide. It was here that his family were to be left, so we all went across to the Indians' encampment. Moberly now appeared to be very indifferent as to whether or not he should go any farther with us. Indeed he seemed more inclined to remain with his friends, for to accompany us meant more exertion for him than he was fond of. Various reasons were given why he must remain at this place; but after much parleying, and the offer of liberal inducements, he promised to secure a companion canoeman, and follow our track in the morning. With this understanding we parted, and proceeded along the south shore until evening, when, finding an inviting camping-ground in the open jack-pine wood, we went ashore, while the cooks soon prepared supper, with us the principal meal of the day.

So far our fare had been exceedingly good, for it had been the policy to dispose of luxuries as soon as possible, in order to reduce the weight of the loads on the portages. Our limited stock of canned fruits was, therefore, used with a free hand at first.

June closed with a bright, clear and unusually calm day, which was also marked by the absence of mosquitos and black flies. Under these unusual circumstances, at noon-hour, an event transpired which was seldom repeated during the remaining part of our journey, viz., the taking of a bath.

Just as lunch was ready we were again joined by Moberly and his companion, an old Indian named Bovia. We were glad, if not a little surprised, to see them, for we had a suspicion that the guide had no serious intention of keeping his promise. During the afternoon, however, as before, his canoe lagged far behind, not so much because of his inability to keep up with us, as because of his serene indifference and laziness. The paddles used by him and his comrade were like spoons as compared with our broad blades, and the position of old Bovia, as he pulled with one elbow resting on the gunwale of his canoe, was most amusing. By this way of travelling it was very evident that the guides were going to be a drag rather than a help to us, so it was resolved that before proceeding farther a definite understanding must be arrived at.

Beside the evening camp-fire, accordingly, the matter was broached to the Indians. They were told plainly that if they were to continue with us they would be required to go in advance and show us the way as far as they knew the route and further, that they would be expected to assist in portaging our stuff whenever that might become necessary. In consideration of this, as already agreed upon, they were to receive their board and eighty skins ($40.00) per month, upon their return to Chippewyan. This arrangement was accepted as being satisfactory to them, and it was hoped that it might result satisfactorily to ourselves.

During the morning of the 1st of July, with a little Union Jack flying at the bow of my canoe, we arrived at the east end of the lake, and concluded a traverse, since leaving Chippewyan, of 210 miles. Here at the extremity of the lake we found several Indian families living, not as is usual, in their "tepees" or skin-covered lodges, but in substantial log huts. One of these, we learned, was the property of our brave Moberly, and in front of it he and old Bovia deliberately went ashore, drew up their canoe, and seated themselves upon the ground beside some friends.

Their action at once struck us as suspicious, but presently they made an open demand for a division of our bacon, flour, tea and tobacco. Some pieces of tobacco and a small quantity of tea had already been given, but any further distribution of the supplies was declined. At this Moberly became very angry, and said he would go with us no farther, and not another foot would he go. From the first his quibbling, unreliable manner, characteristic of the tribe to which he belonged, had been most unsatisfactory, and now having received board for himself and his family in journeying homeward, besides a month's pay in advance, he had resolved to desert us. There was no use in trying to force him

INDIAN LOG HOUSE.

to continue with us against his inclinations, nor could we gain anything by punishing him for his deception, though punishment he richly deserved. He was given one last opportunity of deciding to go with us, but still refusing, we parted company with him without wasting strong language, which he could not have understood.

With our three canoes only we thereupon commenced the ascent of what had been named the Stone River, the outlet of Black Lake. We had gone only a short distance when we were met by a canoe and four Indians coming down with the current. They appeared to be delighted to see us, and turning back accompanied us to the first rapid, where a short portage had to be made. The natives willingly assisted us, and for their labor were liberally rewarded with tea, tobacco and a few lumps of sugar. With this they volunteered to return

CATARACT, STONE RIVER.

on the following day and assist us in crossing some longer portages, the first of which we would meet before nightfall. Of this offer we were quite glad, and promised good pay for the work as inducement for them to keep the engagement, but in the meantime they went down to the log houses where we had left our guides, and we continued our course up the river.

The next day, Sunday, we spent in camp at the foot of a wild and beautiful cataract. The weather was warm, and the black flies and mosquitos swarmed in the woods and about camp so thickly that we could nowhere escape from their ceaseless hum and dreaded bite. In this neighborhood they did not appear to have the customary respect for the smudge. Dense smoke was made about camp, but the flies only appeared to revel in it.

At camp the men were variously employed. A fishing net had been put out in an eddy at the foot of the rapids the previous night, and when taken up in the morning some of the finest fish I have ever seen were found in it. Two salmon trout measured three feet one inch and three feet two inches in length respectively, and the white fish, of which there were a large number, ranged in weight from six to ten pounds. I may add, in deference to a suspicion which statements of this nature sometimes give rise to, that these facts can be amply verified. Towards evening we looked for the return of the four natives who had promised us their assistance, but they came not.

Following this day of rest came one of most laborious, exhausting work. Our camp was not only at the foot of a beautiful fall, but in consequence was at the lower end of a rough, rocky portage, found to be three miles in length, and the canoes were all heavily loaded, containing some four thousand pounds of cargo to be transported. One of our men, Corrigal, was unfortunately laid up for the time with an ugly gash in the knee, so we had only five packers: but being fresh and in high spirits they went at their work with a rush, notwithstanding a rocky hill of two hundred feet which had to be climbed, and a deep muskeg which obliged them to wade. Long before night, however, their

A DIFFICULT PORTAGE.

spirits had dropped many degrees, and it became evident that the task was telling heavily on the men. Before evening their feet were fearfully blistered, and all complained of pains in one place or another. They had each carried six loads to the upper end of the portage, which represented a walk of thirty-three miles, eighteen of which were travelled with one-hundred pound loads upon their backs, over rocky hills and through swamps knee-deep with mire. This was disheartening work at the outset, but it was good training for what was to follow.

The next morning the weather was hot and the flies were out in swarms, as on the day before. The men were all foot-sore and stiff, but without a grumble resumed their work. They were obliged to make two more trips before everything was across, and by that time it was nearly noon; still, without a pause for rest, they loaded the canoes, pushed out into the lake—a small expansion of the river—and headed for the opposite shore, where we soon discovered the mouth. When yet far out on the lake we could see the river's foaming water, and as we drew nearer could plainly hear the unmistakable roar of a cataract. Some distance to the right, on a sand-beach, we went ashore, and found ourselves at the foot of a second long portage.

Because of the condition of our men camp was now ordered to be pitched, so as to give them some chance to recruit. My brother and I walked across the portage, and found it to be three and one-half miles in length. It was, however, much less difficult than the former one, being more level and less rocky. Its upper end terminated on the shore of Black Lake, where we hoped to find Indians who would help us across. But in this we were disappointed, and, instead of Indians, found only old forsaken "tepee" poles and blackened fireplaces. We tried to rest for a while upon the shore of Black Lake, but the flies swarmed about us with such frightful fury that we were compelled to beat a retreat, and seek rest where alone it could be found, beneath our mosquito awnings at camp.

By the way, there is an Indian tradition which says that it was on these very portages that the Great Spirit first made these black flies, and our experience, we thought, would tend to bear out that belief.

On the afternoon of the 7th we started out in a northeasterly direction, following the shore of Black Lake (explored by my brother in 1892) for a distance of about sixteen miles, until we reached the hunting trail, of which

INDIAN RAFTS LOADED WITH VENISON.

he had been informed by the Indians, leading away to the northward. This place until now had been our objective point, and the way to it was known; but beyond this point we knew nothing of the road, or of the country through which it would lead us, excepting for the first few days' travel, to which the Indians' description, quoted at the beginning of this narrative, would apply. From this point northward, for a distance of one hundred miles, or thereabouts, we had expected to be guided by that old humbug Moberly, but he having deserted us we were now dependent on our own resources.

CHAPTER V.

INTO THE UNKNOWN WILDERNESS.

On Saturday morning, the 8th of July, without guide or map, we commenced our journey into the great untravelled wilderness. The trail commenced with a portage two miles in length, leading through thickets, swamps, and over rocky hills, but by this time the men were accustomed to their work, and went about it in a steadier and more methodical manner. My brother's time was chiefly devoted to the general direction of the party, and an examination of the geology of the country.* My own time was largely taken up in making the survey and topographical notes of the route, and in collecting the flora of the country; but when our duties permitted and occasion required we both took a turn at the pack-straps, as we did on this portage.

In order to make an easier trail than the existing circuitous one, which led over sharp angular stones and precipitous rocks, we were obliged to cut our way through a thicket for a distance of half a mile. Having done this, the work of portaging through the forest was begun. During the remainder of the day, and indeed until ten o'clock at night, we continued our labor.

---

* For a full description of geological features, etc., see J. B. Tyrrell's Report for 1893-94, Geological Survey.

Corrigal, who had been crippled, was now at work again, and proved to be a capital hand. All hands worked well, but it was amusing to note the craftiness of the Iroquois, who invariably tried to secure such articles to carry as biscuits, tents or dunnage bags. With immense loads of comparatively little weight they would then stagger off like old Atlas himself.

When the last loads for the week were laid down at camp, we were a thoroughly tired party. For the past six days we had been laboring on long portages, and during that time had carried the entire outfit for a distance of about eight miles, over the roughest kind of country, representing a total transport of fifty-six miles, or a walk of 104 miles for each man. Sunday was spent, therefore, by all in enjoying complete rest. The weather continued fine and warm, as it had been all week.

During the succeeding day and a half six little lakes and as many short portages, leading in a northerly direction, were crossed, and then at noon on the 11th inst. Wolverine Lake was discovered and its position in latitude determined. This lake, only about three miles in width by six in length, is by no means a large body of water, but because of its many deep shore indentations and consequent coast-line of forty or fifty miles, it was thought by us to be large enough before we discovered our road out of it, which we knew to be by the ascent of a large river from the north. The shores of the lake were heavily and beautifully wooded with spruce and birch timber, and its surface was studded with islands. At nightfall, after exploring the uttermost recesses of several deep bays, without discovering any trace of the river, we pitched camp, and obtained shelter from a cold drizzling rain.

The next morning being cool, and flies scarce, a plunge bath was the first item on the programme. After disposing of our usual breakfast of bacon and bannocks, the search for the route was resumed. After much careful search, occupying nearly the whole day, the mouth of the river was found, close to where we had first entered the lake. It was much obscured by islands, and owing to the depth of the channel had an almost imperceptible current; but beyond all doubt it was the road described by the Indians, and though rain was again falling, no time was lost in commencing the ascent.

About seven miles up stream we were obliged to seek camp, but a suitable one was not to be found, as the shores were low and flooded with water. A place none too dry was finally selected, and in a drenched condition we scrambled or waded ashore.

As I was enjoying a mug of tea, my brother came into our tent and reported having heard a cariboo calf in the swamp close by. Though it was already nearly dark, I picked up my rifle and started out in the direction from which he had heard the noise, in quest of venison. The dense spruce swamp was literally alive with mosquitos, which at every step rose up from the wet grass in swarms, and beat into my face. A runway was soon found, and I hurried noiselessly along through the gloom of the forest, hoping soon to hear something of the calf. Many other runways were crossed, and after travelling some distance without any signs of success, I was about to return, for fear of being overtaken by darkness, when a little distance ahead I heard the cracking of a stick. It was, no doubt, caused by the foot of the fawn. Quickly but silently I proceeded. Again and again the noise was heard, and each time nearer than the last. My advance was continued cautiously, until very soon, in a thicket of scrub, only a few yards ahead, I noticed the moving of some branches. Still no deer could I see, but in creeping up closer, at a distance of not over twenty yards, I suddenly came within full view of an immense black bear, seated on his haunches and occupied in rubbing the mosquitos off his nose. Although taken by surprise at the proportions of the supposed calf, I dropped on one knee, and, levelling my rifle, fired at the back of bruin's head, whereat he also exhibited considerable surprise by leaping into the air, making several delirious revolutions, and bolting away into the gloom of the swamp. Though in all probability badly wounded, it was too dark to follow him. The gloom had already spoiled my aim, so without further pursuit I groped my way back to camp.

During the following day the ascent of Wolverine River was continued, and three short portages, the longest one being half a mile, were made. As we proceeded northward the banks of the river became more rocky. In many places bald hilltops were visible, rising two or three hundred feet above the level of the river. Such timber as there was consisted of spruce, birch and jackpine.

On the 14th, Birch Lake, a small body of water about nine miles long by two wide, was discovered and surveyed, and near its northern extremity a large rapid stream was found emptying into it its foaming waters. Judging the course of this stream to be our route, a

74   ACROSS THE SUB-ARCTICS OF CANADA.

portage of half a mile was made past it. This brought us to the southern extremity of another larger lake, which we assumed to be the Indians' so-called "Big Lake," and which in honor of the then Director of the Geological Survey we have named Selwyn Lake. Being

A. R. C. SELWYN, C.M.G., F.R.S.,
Director Geological Survey, 1869-1895.

too wide to admit of both shores being sketched from our line of survey, this lake was traversed on the east side only.

In the evening camp was pitched on an island a little distance off shore. On this island a lonely grave was discovered, at the head of which stood a plain wooden cross. It was, doubtless, the grave of some Christian Indian who had been taught by the priests at Fond-du-Lac, and who, when out on a hunting expedition, had been stricken down by the great reaper, and by his companions had been laid here to rest.

This island camp recalls an incident connected with John, our baker. For some time past, notwithstanding the appetites of the men, his bread had not been giving satisfaction. Some of the party were afraid to eat it on account of the possibilities of canoeing accidents, which would be almost certain to result fatally, for with John's bread in one's stomach there could be little hope of remaining afloat. At first John had confined his baking to the making of grease bannocks, which, after being formed in a pan, were removed and cooked before the fire on a stick; and so long as he baked in his accustomed way he was fairly successful, but as soon as he undertook the use of baking powder, and the production of bread from a reflector (a camp oven) he grievously failed. Being anxious to uphold the dignity of his profession at this camp, he sat up all night endeavoring to improve on his methods, but with little success. Two days later he again undertook the prosecution of his calling, and after cleaning his hands, brought out his dutch-oven, bake-pans, sack of flour, baking powder, etc. My brother, noticing these preparations, strolled over to a convenient log and there seated himself to watch John's *modus operandi*. The sack was opened and the top of it rolled down until it formed a ring over the flour, in which a hollow was then made with the hands.

Into this basin a quart or more of water was poured, and *into the water the prescribed quantity of baking powder was stirred and allowed to effervesce*. We now understood the secret of John's failures, and gave him instructions on the use of baking powder. After this we enjoyed better bread.

A week had now passed since leaving the end of the long portage out of Black Lake, and during that time we had made only about eighty miles. This was a slow rate of travel, and if possible would have to be improved on. One day had been lost in discovering the outlet from Wolverine Lake, another spent in ascending the river, and considerable time had been occupied on the several portages.

Sunday, the 16th of July, was spent quietly and profitably at camp after the six days of hard travel, and, strange to say, the flies which had filled the air and made our lives a burden the previous evening had now almost entirely disappeared. The day was bright and warm, affording a good opportunity for lake bathing. This pleasure was highly prized. After one has been subjected to the continual lacerations and stings of flies and mosquitos, and the liberal application of tar-oil for a week or two, a bath is not only a luxury, but a necessity.

On Monday morning the exploration of Selwyn Lake was continued. The shore-line was still found to be irregular and indented by deep bays. Some of these were passed by, but those toward the north end of the lake were carefully examined to their extremities, in our search for the portage, of which we had been informed, leading over the Height of Land.

Towards evening our party was surprised by the appearance of a canoe some distance away, and not far from it, on a little island, an Indian camp. Shaping our course for the camp, a salute was fired, and was promptly answered by the Indians. Reaching the camp we were not a little astonished to find that some of the Indians were the very same men who had agreed to assist us over the portages out of Athabasca and Black Lakes. They had, no doubt, after meeting old Moberly, been prompted to leave us to shift for ourselves, and had returned in such a way as to avoid meeting us again. From them we now inquired for the Height of Land portage, and were pleased to learn that it was near at hand. Having obtained as much information from these fellows as v. could, and arranged once more for three or four of them to assist us over in the morning, we pitched our own camp on a neighboring island.

During the evening most of the Indians paddled across to where we were, and from some of them sketch-maps and useful information were obtained; but their attention was chiefly devoted to filling the men with stories of the fearful dangers and certain disasters which we would encounter should we attempt to descend the Telzoa River. They said we would meet with great impassable canyons, and that the country through which it flowed was inhabited by savage tribes of Eskimos, who would undoubtedly eat us. These and similar stories produced a deep impression on the minds of some of our men, and might have given rise to serious trouble or even the disorganizing of the whole party. Jim went to my brother, and with a sad face unbosomed his trouble. He said that if he were a single man he would not feel so badly, but having a family dependent on him he could not run into such destruction as he now learned awaited us. Most of the men, excepting, perhaps, François, who cared for nothing, were equally affected, and it was with some difficulty we managed to reassure them. We told them that these Indians were a set of miserable liars, and were only trying to prevent us from going into their hunting grounds; that I had lived with the Eskimos for nearly two years, and had found them to be far better people than these Indians who were trying to deceive them. We referred them to Moberly, the untrustworthy and false, as a sample of their tribe, and at length persuaded them into disbelieving the stories.

On the morning of the 18th, accompanied by five native Indians, we arrived at our portage near the northern extremity of the lake, and about fifty miles from the rapids where we had entered it. The portage led, as we had been informed by the Indians, over the Height of Land to the northward. It was found to be a mile and a quarter long. Its northern end terminated on the shore of another large lake, the level of which was ascertained to be about fifty feet lower than Selwyn Lake. Separating the two lakes, rocky hills rose to elevations of two or three hundred feet (fourteen or fifteen hundred feet above sea level), and between them wound the trail, which was comparatively level and easy. With the help of the natives, our stuff, already considerably reduced, was soon portaged, and the canoes again launched and loaded. Before these operations

INTO THE UNKNOWN WILDERNESS. 79

were completed, realizing the fact that we had now reached a summit of the continent, it seemed to me a most suitable place to leave the emblem of our country. Selecting, therefore, a tall, straight tamarack, and providing myself with bunting and hatchet, I climbed to the top of the tree and there nailed securely the flag of Canada. As I descended, I lopped off the branches and thus made of the tree an excellent flag-pole.

SCOTCH-CREE HALF-BREED.

CHAPTER VI.

THE HOME OF THE REINDEER.

From Lake Athabasca to the Height of Land our course had constantly been up stream, but from this point to the sea the way must ever be with the current. Having launched our little fleet in the lake on the north side of the watershed, the new stage of the journey was begun with a strong, fair breeze.

The lake is a large one, and has been named Daly Lake—after the Hon. T. M. Daly, then Minister of the Interior for Canada. Towards the centre of it was discovered a peninsula, which is connected with the west shore only by a very narrow neck of land, across which a portage was made. For a day and a half we were delayed here by a gale, the most severe we had so far encountered. So wild was the lake during this storm that water-spouts were whirled up from its billows and carried along in great vertical columns for considerable distances.

Certain remarkable physical features in the shape of great sand "Kames," or high ridges, were also observed at this locality. They were composed of clear sand and gravel, were sixty or seventy feet in height, trended in a north-easterly and south-westerly direction, were quite narrow on top, and so level and uniform that they might well be taken to be the remains of the embankments of ancient railways. Geologists, however, have another theory accounting for their origin, namely, that they were formed by fissures or splits in the ancient glaciers.

On the sheltered southerly slopes of these ridges many new varieties of plants were found, and some others which had been collected farther south were here seen for the la   me on the journey. Notable among the latter was t!   en, of which several stunted, gnarled specimens were observed. When the storm had abated sufficiently the traverse of the lake shore was resumed, when other notable features appeared.

A large part of the country was now composed of frozen mossy bogs, sloping gently down towards the lake. In the higher portions of the bogs the moss was still growing, but elsewhere it was dead, and excepting a few inches, was imbedded in solid glaciers. In many instances these frozen bogs or glaciers were found to be breaking off into the lake, and in such places they presented brown mossy vertical faces, from ten to twenty feet above the water. In examining these vertical sections they were observed, as on top, to consist of frozen moss to within about a foot of the surface. The first of the moss glaciers, if I may call them such, were observed near the Height of Land, but towards the north end of Daly Lake they composed a large part of the country, and timber occurred only in scattered, isolated patches.

According to our Indian information we should now be near the outlet of the lake. During the morning of the 22nd, after a good deal of searching in many deep

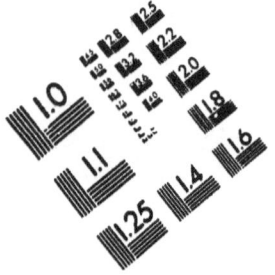

**IMAGE EVALUATION
TEST TARGET (MT-3)**

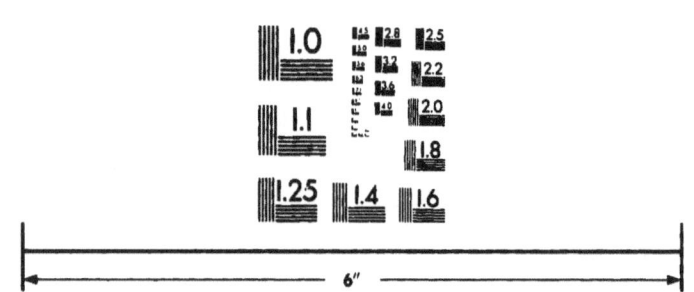

Photographic
Sciences
Corporation

23 WEST MAIN STREET
WEBSTER, N.Y. 14580
(716) 872-4503

bays, the entrance to the Telzoa (broad shallow river) was discovered. It was indeed a great, broad and rapid river, broken up into many shallow channels, whose waters seemed to have been, as it were, spilled over the edge of the lake in the lowest places. This was the river we had set out to explore, and with nothing more than conjectures as to where it would lead us, we pushed

TELZOA RIVER.

our canoes into the stream, and sped away to the northward. Landings were made when necessary to carry on the survey and examination of the country, but at other times the canoes were kept in the stream, and the men at the paddles. Many rapids were run, but our veteran steersman Pierre, with his skill, judgment and unflinching nerve, was usually able to map out his course and steer it successfully, sometimes between rocks and through channels little wider than his canoe.

Upon one occasion, which I well recollect, Pierre led the way for the centre of a wild, rocky rapid. We soon saw that he was making for a heavy shoot between two great boulders, where the channel was barely wide enough to allow us to pass. I determined to follow, but our third canoe sought a channel nearer shore. Pierre, by keeping straight in the centre of the current, was shot through the notch like a rocket, but my steersman, less skilful, allowed our canoe to be caught by an eddy. Like a flash it was whirled end for end, and happily for us struck the shoot stern first instead of sideways and was carried through safely—no thanks to the steersman. The third canoe fared worst of the three, for it was dashed upon a great flat rock and broken in the bottom. Its occupants, by jumping out upon the rock, managed to hold it until assistance could be given them. The load of the disabled canoe was safely landed by one of the others, and the damage soon repaired.

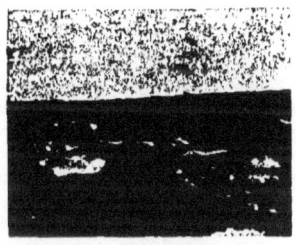

RAPIDS, TELZOA RIVER.

We were now fairly beyond the limit of woods, which for some time past had been gradually becoming thinner more scattered, and of more stunted growth. On this account it is impossible to lay down any definite line as the limit of the forest. Outlying patches of spruce and tamarack might still be found here and there in the most favored localities, but as a whole the country was now a vast, rolling, treeless wilderness.

On the evening of the 28th of July we reached the north end of an expansion of the river, named Barlow Lake. Our supply of meat was already running low. Being quite unable to carry provisions with us for the whole trip, we had, in starting, taken only a limited quantity of this kind of food, trusting to our ability to replenish the supply from time to time by the way. Up to this time, however, we had seen nothing in the shape of game since leaving Lake Athabasca, excepting the one black bear, and he made good his escape. Plenty of old deer-tracks were to be seen, but not a single deer, and in consequence we were beginning to feel some anxiety. If game should not be found within a week or ten days, we would have to return, or proceed with the probability before us of starvation.

We had only begun to think seriously on this question when on the evening above-mentioned, just as we had gone ashore to camp, a moving object was noticed on a little island out in the lake. By means of our field-glasses we could tell it was a deer, and I need hardly say that no time was lost in manning a canoe and pulling for the island. As we approached the deer watched us closely; and soon satisfied of danger, bounded into the air, galloped to the farther side of the island, plunged into the water, and struck out for the nearest shore. The rate at which the frightened animal tore its way

HEAD OF REINDEER.

through the water was really marvellous, and for a time it looked as if we would not be able to overtake it with our light canoe and four paddles. Every muscle was strained, both of deer and men, so that the hunt resolved itself into a veritable race for life. Unfortunately for the poor animal, though, the course was too long, and before it could reach the shore we had overhauled and shot it. That night we enjoyed our first meal of venison.

The next day, after descending the river a distance of five or six miles, and getting into a body of water named Carey Lake, through which we were steering a central course, one of the party called attention to something moving on the distant shore to our right. It turned out to be not one but a band of deer. Our canoes were headed to leeward of the band, that they might not scent us as we approached the shore. Drawing nearer we found there was not only one band, but that there were many great bands, literally covering the country over wide areas. The valleys and hillsides for miles appeared to be moving masses of reindeer. To estimate their numbers would be impossible. They could only be reckoned in acres or square miles.

After a short consultation a place for landing, near a small grove of tamarack—one of the last we saw—was chosen. Rifles were examined, and an ample supply of cartridges provided. Shot-guns and revolvers were furnished to four of the men, and thus prepared we landed and drew up the canoes. So far the deer had apparently not seen us, but to prevent a general stampede, it was arranged that I should go around to the rear of a large detachment of the herd, near by, while my brother should approach them from the shore. Accordingly I was given fifteen minutes to run around, a mile or so, behind some rising ground. Meanwhile the rest of the party scattered themselves about in different places, and at the given time my brother, having approached within easy range, opened the fray by bringing down a noble buck. At this first shot the whole band—a solid mass of several thousands of deer—was thrown into confusion, and they rushed to and fro, not knowing which way to flee. Simultaneously with my brother's shot, I opened fire on them from the rear, and our armed men charged from the sides, while the other two were obliged to take refuge upon a great boulder to avoid being trampled to death. The band was speedily scattered, but not before a woful slaughter had been made, and an abundant supply of fine fresh meat secured, for which we were sincerely thankful. It was fortunate that there was wood at hand to make a fire with and dry the meat. Having slain as many animals as we required, the men were set to work to prepare dried meat for the rest of the trip.

This stroke of good fortune gave us much encouragement, as we thought we had now nothing to fear from lack of provisions. Several days were spent in drying the eighteen or twenty carcases, which were preserved, and while this work was progressing my brother and I had ample time to roam over the hills and view and photograph the bands of deer which were still everywhere about us. After the slaughter of the first day we carried no rifles with us, but armed only with a camera walked to and fro through the herd, causing little more alarm than one would by walking through a herd of cattle in a field. The experience was delightful, one

THE HOME OF THE REINDEER.

never to be forgotten. The reindeer, which is the same as the Barren Ground caribou, is an animal of exceptional interest. To those whose imaginations dwell on visions of St. Nicholas and his coursers it is the ideal steed; while to the hardy native of the frigid zone it is a faithful and efficient servant, and is undoubtedly the most useful and valuable of the fifty or more known varieties of deer.

In different localities, and at different seasons of the year, reindeer vary in appearance; they range in weight from one hundred to four hundred pounds. During the months of June and July they present their poorest appearance, being then lean and scrawny, and their half-shed coats ragged and frowsy. By the month of August they have discarded their tattered last-winter garments, and have assumed sleek glossy brown summer coats, which give them a smaller but much more comely appearance. From this time, both because of increasing flesh and length of hair, they become gradually larger and more handsome, until, by the month of November, when they don their winter suits of white and grey, they are transformed in appearance into the noblest animals of the chase.

Then it is that the enormous antlers of the male deer have attained their full, hard growth, and he is thus armed for the many battles habitually fought during the months of November and December for the possession of favored members of the fair sex. During the month of January these antlers of the male deer, having served their purpose as weapons of warfare, are annually cast. Within a few weeks of the falling of the old horns, soft new ones begin to form beneath the skin, and gradually they increase in size until they reach maturity the following autumn. During growth the antlers remain comparatively soft, and are covered with skin and fine short hair, known as the "velvet." At maturity a circular burr is formed at the base of the horn. This has the effect of cutting off the blood-vessels, and causing the velvet to dry and shrivel and ultimately peel off. The peeling of the velvet is also hastened by the deer rubbing its antlers upon rocks and trees. With each successive year the antlers are supplemented by one additional prong, so that the number of prongs or tines is a positive indication of the age of the deer. I have counted as many as twenty-two prongs on one horn, or twice that number on the pair. Unlike every other variety of deer, the caribou is antlered in both sexes, the only difference being that in the case of the females the horns are rather smaller, and are more slender and delicate in their formation than those of the males.

The hoofs of the reindeer are very large in proportion to other parts of the body, and, being cloven, they spread greatly in walking. This characteristic peculiarly fits them for travelling upon the crusted snow, through which other deer would break and flounder in a hopeless manner.

Concerning the habits of the reindeer, they are both gregarious and migratory. During the summer season their resort is the open plain or the sea-coast, where, to some extent, they escape from their tormentors, the mosquitos and black flies, and find abundance of food in the tender grasses, the ground birch, or the willow buds. In the autumn they turn their steps toward the woodlands or more sheltered districts, where they spend the long, severe winter, subsisting on tree-buds, moss or lichens.

The breeding season occurs in the early spring, before winter quarters are vacated; and the number of fawns borne by a doe at one time ranges from one to three.

From an economic or commercial point of view, the reindeer is highly prized. By the Laplanders and other people it is domesticated, and takes the place of the horse, the dog, the cow or the goat of other countries. As a traveller it is swift and enduring, being capable of hauling from two to three hundred pounds upon a sled, as much as one hundred miles per day; and as compared with the dog, it possesses the great advantage of being able to obtain its food by the way.

As a source of venison it cannot be excelled, especially in the autumn season, when it is in prime condition. During September and October the males are rolling fat; and as food their flesh is then equal to the finest beef. Of all meats I have ever tasted, certainly reindeer tongues take the first place for daintiness and delicacy of flavor.

From the skins of the reindeer the natives of the Arctic regions make almost every article of winter clothing. For this purpose it is most admirably suited, both because of its great warmth and its remarkable lightness. Through different methods of tanning and dressing it is made adaptable to a great variety of other uses. Sewing thread, lashing twine and other strong lines are also made from sinew obtained from along the spine of this animal.

What the buffalo was to the North American Indian in days gone by, the reindeer is now to the Eskimos and other natives of the north country.

CHAPTER VII.

A GREAT FROZEN LAKE.

BEFORE leaving "Reindeer Camp" a cairn of rocks was built on the top of an immense boulder, conspicuously situated on the summit of a point reaching out into the waters of Carey Lake. A record of our journey to date was placed in it, and the "flag that for a thousand years has braved the battle and the breeze," left floating overhead.

On the 2nd of August the journey was resumed, and during the day a remarkable grove was found on the north shore of the lake, in latitute 62° 15' north. As a whole the country was now a treeless, rocky wilderness, but here by a little brook grew a clump of white spruce trees, perhaps thirty in all, of which the largest measured eight feet in circumference at two feet above ground. Such a trunk would be considered unusually large in a forest a thousand miles to the south, but here it and its fellows stood far out in the Barren Grounds with their gnarly, storm-beaten tops, like veritable Druids of old.

In this grove many varieties of plants were found—among others wood violets, which were here seen for the last time on the trip. Not the least enjoyable feature of this little oasis was that it afforded us an opportunity of having a good noon-day fire, which of late had been a rare luxury.

Pushing out our canoes, we continued the traverse of the coast to the westward in search of the Telzoa, but it could not be found that day.

On the morning of the following day, at the northwestern extremity of the lake, our course was again discovered. It commenced with a wild rapid of about

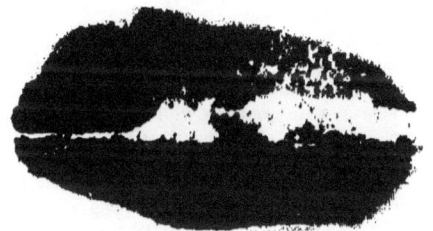

ICE ON THE SHORE OF MARKHAM LAKE.

thirty feet fall, and this we found to be followed within a distance of twenty miles by seven others, all of which together aggregated a fall of about 120 feet, which took us to the level of Markham Lake, named in honor of Admiral A. H. Markham, R.N.

While traversing this lake a decided change in the climate was observed. For the first time since the early part of the season snow-banks were seen on the hillsides, and the weather, which had been as a rule wet

and cold since leaving the woods, became decidedly
colder. Toward the north end of the lake we passed
great piles of rafted ice on the shore. Such conditions
during the month of August were highly suggestive of
the character of climate which must exist here in the
winter season.

Near the outlet of Markham Lake was found an exceptionally interesting little island. For weeks we had
seen nothing but Laurentian or Huronian hills, but here
was a solitary out-lier of white Cambrio-Silurian limestone. The size of the island was perhaps not more
than ten acres, but its whole composition was quite
different from anything in the district, and growing on
it were found many entirely new varieties of plants.
Several hours were spent here with fruitful results, and
then as the shadows of evening were stealing from the
rocky hills far across the lonely plains, we discovered,
at the north end of the lake, our river, upon the bare
high rocky bank of which we pitched camp.

It is worthy of note that at this point some very old
moss-grown "tepee" poles and fragments of birch bark
were found, indicating clearly that in days gone by the
spot had been visited by Indians, though it was now
known to them only in legends. We had seen no recent
traces of Indians since entering the Telzoa, but at some
time they had descended thus far, and had camped on the
same bald hill which we now occupied. There was more
than sentiment to us in the fact, for from the old rotten
poles, few and small though they were, we built a fire
that gave us not a little comfort and cheer.

On the 5th of August, after partaking of a hurried
breakfast of venison—of which, by the way, our supplies

now almost entirely consisted—the canoes were again launched in the swift stream, in which during the day rapid after rapid was run, until six were successfully passed and a descent of over a hundred feet had been made.

At about six o'clock in the evening, having made twenty miles, a fortunate incident occurred. As we were approaching a seventh rapid we suddenly found ourselves enveloped in a dense chilling mist, which so obstructed the view that we were unable to proceed. As we went ashore at the head of the rapid we discovered, much to our delight, a little patch of stunted black spruce trees. They were twisted and gnarled, and not more than four or five feet in height, but as fuel they were the source of much comfort, and beside them we decided to camp. It was Saturday night. During the day's run we had been soaked by the spray of the rapids, and were therefore in good condition to again enjoy the warm, cheerful blaze of a fire, around which we all huddled and sat far into the night, drying our clothing, rehearsing adventures of the day and discussing the prospects of the future.

The morrow being Sunday we had a further opportunity of enjoying the camp-fire, cooked provisions, and dry clothing, all which are rare luxuries in the Barren Lands. Our fishing nets, which had been set in the river the night before, were taken up loaded with magnificent whitefish and trout, the former ranging from six to ten pounds in weight, and the latter up to twenty-five pounds.

During the afternoon, as my brother was tramping in the interior he reached the summit of an adjacent hill, where a most dreary and chilling scene opened to his vision. To the east and northward not many miles away, and extending as far as the eye could reach, there appeared a vast white plain shrouded in drifting clouds of mist. It was evidently a great lake, still covered in the month of August with a field of ice, and was probably the Doobaunt or Tobaunt Lake, known in a legen-

TOBAUNT LAKE.

dary way to the Athabasca Indians, and sighted over one hundred years ago by Samuel Hearne when on his journey to the Copper Mine River. Its re-discovery was now a matter of the deepest interest to us. Was it to form an insurmountable obstacle in our path was the question at once suggested, and judging from appearances, most of the men were of opinion that it would.

On Monday morning, the 7th of August, all undismayed, we broke camp early, and bidding good-bye to the last vestige of growing timber to be seen, continued down the river toward the frozen lake. Four more rapids were passed, and about 10 a.m., retarded by a strong east wind, we went ashore on a little island in the broad mouth of the river. Here we built another cairn of rocks, upon which was painted, with red enamel, the latitude of the spot and the date and name of the expedition.

In the afternoon, the wind having moderated, we started out for the mainland to the north. We followed it for some miles to the eastward, and then struck across to a long point, which appeared to be the outermost point of the river shore. Up to this time we had seen nothing of the ice-field, but here it was, tight in against the shore and defying farther advance by canoe. Towards the edge of the pack the ice was much broken and honey-combed, but it was far too heavy to be tackled by canoes or even stout boats. It was decided, therefore, to turn into what we supposed was a bay just passed, and from the shore get a view of the pack. We had no sooner altered our course than a deer was sighted close by, shot, and taken on board for fresh meat. It was found that the point was that of a long island, and that the supposed bay was a channel through which we might pass unobstructed by ice.

By this time, however, the wind was again blowing strongly, and a cold heavy rain setting in drove us to camp. During the night the wind increased to a gale, accompanied by torrents of rain, which flooded the tents and saturated our clothing and blankets. Not a vestige of fuel was to be found in the country, but

with a spirit lamp we made hot tea and appeased
our sharp appetites with some remnants of boiled
venison. For three days the storm continued. On the
fourth it turned to snow and the temperature went
down to freezing—rather inhospitable weather for the
10th of August.

Next morning, the gale having sufficiently subsided,
camp was called about four o'clock, and we continued
on our way through the channel we had entered, and
along the west shore of the lake in open water until 8
a.m., when we again found ourselves hemmed in by
heavy floating ice, which in several places was measured
and found to be seven feet in thickness. To advance
here in the canoes was impossible, so a favorable spot
for landing was selected, at the base of the point where
the ice was hard ashore.

Just as we were landing, a small band of deer was
seen feeding on a grassy plain not far away, and as our
supply of fresh venison was nearly gone, we made plans
for a hunt. It was arranged that my brother and I
should take up our positions in concealment on a low
neck of land between the shore and a small lake, and
that the men should so place themselves as to drive the
band within range of us. We managed to reach our
vantage ground unobserved, but one of the canoemen
in attempting to carry out his instructions awkwardly
exposed himself and alarmed the deer, causing them to
speedily scatter. Some of them, however, bounded past
within range of our rifles, and three were brought down,
which were sufficient to replenish the larder.

Not far from the landing place was a high hill, so providing ourselves with field-glasses we set out for its summit. As we proceeded across the country we found the ground frozen and all the little ponds covered by new ice. Such a condition of things was not the most enlivening, and it was a point of discussion with us whether the season of this land was spring or autumn. Upon reaching the hill-top we were well repaid for our labor. Away to the south and the east, as far as we could see, the ice-field extended, but to the north there lay much open water, and near the base of the hill there was a comparatively narrow neck of land across which we might portage our outfit and get to the open water. This we decided to do.

Having accomplished this task we were once more free, but before nightfall were again blocked by the pack. In a deep bay by the mouth of a small river we went into camp, feeling somewhat disheartened by our ill fortunes. Neither wood nor moss could here be found with which to make a fire, but with alcohol some hot tea was made, and from it as much comfort was extracted as possible, for there was little elsewhere to be found. Meeting with so much ice at this season of the year made the prospects of farther advance northward anything but encouraging, but we were resolved, if it were possible, to push on and see the end of the great river we had thus far descended.

The morning of the 12th broke cold and dreary. New ice everywhere covered the ponds, but camp was astir early, and it was with much pleasure we discovered that the ice-pack, which had forbidden our advance the night before, had now moved off the shore and left in its stead a channel of open water. Into this we gladly made our way, and once more the paddles were plied lustily. During the day we encountered much ice, solid fields of which extended out from the land, but we were able to get along without much obstruction. Several white wolves were seen on the shore as we passed, and at some places, where landings were made, numerous little ermines were observed darting about among the rocks. The formation of the coast was found to consist largely of a remarkable looking ferruginous conglomerate, and despite the extremely barren and dreary aspect of the country, a large variety of beautiful little flowers were collected.

At nightfall, after a long day's struggle with the opposing elements, as we were hauling the canoes ashore towards the shelter of some rocky cliffs, we were suddenly set upon by a pack of huge grey wolves. A great gaunt, hungry-looking brute with dilated eyeballs led the attack. He was the largest wolf in the pack and a daring brute, but for once, at least, he met with a surprise, as he was promptly bored from end to end with a slug from my brother's rifle. The leader of the pack having been thus treated, the others fled, but revenged themselves by howling at us all night long from the surrounding hills.

With the pack several little wolves had been noticed, and when the old ones beat their retreat an effort was made to capture some of them, but unsuccessfully, for just as young partridges suddenly and mysteriously disappear in the leafy woods when danger threatens, so did these young wolves disappear among the rocks, and though we searched carefully and must have been within a few yards of them, we could not get sight of one.

I have said the wolves here encountered were grey.

This seemed a little peculiar, since any that we had seen for some time had been of the white Arctic variety, which do not travel together in packs, like those of the timber country.

At this locality, which was close to the north-west extremity of Tolmunt Lake, the country was more than ordinarily broken, and was distinctively marked by the existence of several great hills of sand. The highest of these sand mountains I became ambitious to climb, in order to obtain a view of the surrounding country and have a look for the outlet of the lake. In the open country one can often, in an hour or two, obtain more information in this way from a prominent elevation than would otherwise be possible in two or three days' travel. So it was on this occasion, when in company with two canoemen I obtained a variety of information.

From the summit one could get a grand view of the whole surrounding country, and thus an opportunity was afforded of gaining much interesting topographical information. In the performance of this work my binoculars were of invaluable assistance, enabling me to trace the natural features of the country for a considerable distance.

While thus scanning the broad dreary plains from my vantage point, scattered bands of deer could be seen here and there, also two or three wolves and a wolverine. This latter animal, also known as the glutton, being not very far distant, afforded us some amusement. We had no rifles with us, but I had my revolver, and seeing that François was keen for a chase, I offered him the use of it.

Opportunities for excitement were seldom neglected

by our dare-devil young Westerner, and on this occasion, quickly availing himself of my offer, he started down the steep hill at a break-neck pace, followed by John, in a bee-line for the wolverine.

No sagacious Indian cunning, of which we so often read, was brought to play in the hunt. It was merely a question of which could run the faster and keep it up the longer. The wolverine is not a swift animal, nature having provided him with only short limbs, but on this occasion he used such as he had to the very best possible advantage, and with a rolling gait made his way off across the rough stony plains at a record-breaking pace. His pursuers were, however, soon observed to be gaining on him, and as the distance between the runners gradually lessened, the race became exciting, even to me, looking on from the hill-top.

Once or twice in their wild chase the men had bad tumbles, but recovering themselves, continued to gain on the wolverine until they had almost overhauled him. Then "bang" went the revolver, and the glutton, unhurt, dodging around some rocks, was almost run upon by François, who in his excitement fired again, and at the same time took a header. It appeared as if he had shot himself instead of the wolverine, but he had done neither: he had only experienced another bad tumble on the rough, rocky ground. Gathering himself up again, François followed in hot pursuit, making a most determined chase, but just as he was about to do the tragic act, Mr. Wolverine disappeared among the broken rocks, and could not any more be found.

Thus ended the hunt, and the men, greatly disgusted, wearily recrossed the plain and climbed the hill.

Finding great quantities of moss in the neighborhood, several large piles of it were collected, tied up into bundles and taken back with us to camp for fuel. Two varieties of this moss fuel were commonly found growing upon the stony hill-tops, the one, reindeer moss (*lichen rangiferinus*), being almost white, and the other, black and wiry looking, and the better fuel of the two. Either variety, of course, had to be dry in order to burn, and that was a condition in which we seldom found it, as incessant wet weather had been experienced since entering the Barren Grounds.

When dry moss was found, therefore, it was our custom to keep the kettles boiling all or most of the night, in order to cook enough meat to supply camp for several days.

FRENCH-CREE HALF-BREED.

CHAPTER VIII.

ON THE LOWER TELZOA.

UNTIL the evening of the 15th of August, we paddled on through varied scenes of ice and open water, following the barren shore-line in search of the outlet of Tobaunt Lake.

In addition to game already mentioned, two young broods of wild geese, not yet able to fly, were seen. It is commonly said that the breeding place of the wild goose has never been discovered, but here, at any rate, was the breeding place of these.

On the morning of the 16th we were early aroused by the voice of a howling gale and the pelting rain, which was freely beating through our flapping tents. Of these, our meagre shelters, some of the guys were broken, and the tent occupied by my brother and myself was only prevented from being blown away by the unpleasant performance of scrambling out in the darkness, exposing ourselves to the piercing wind and driving rain, and securing it with new ropes and piles of stones. Upon this occasion, also, blankets and clothing not yet dry since the last wetting were again saturated. Everything in the way of instruments, photographic supplies, note books, etc., were piled together at one side of the tent and well covered by a rubber sheet, and at the other side we made ourselves as comfortable as possible, which was in truth pretty miserable.

This storm continued with fury for two days, and during this time, wet and shivering in the tents, we found our only spark of comfort in the brewing and

RAPIDS ON THE LOWER TELZOA.

imbibing of hot chocolate prepared over the spirit lamp. On the afternoon of the second day, the rain ceased and the wind fell sufficiently to enable us to faintly hear to the north the roar of heavy rapids. Stimulated by the sound, we struck camp at seven o'clock in the evening and started out for what we hoped might prove to be the Telzoa flowing out of the lake, and after a long and late pull we were gratified to find our hopes realized. On account of the lateness of the hour we had no opportunity that night of examining the river, further than to observe that it was unobstructed by ice, which observation afforded us great satisfaction.

On the morning of the 18th we launched in the clear, strong stream of the Lower Telzoa, and very soon found ourselves at the head of the rapids we had heard. At the second rapid the first unmistakable signs of the recent habitations of Eskimos were discovered. They consisted of rings of camp stones, an old bow, several broken arrows, a whip-stock and numerous broken or partly formed willow ribs of a "kyack" or canoe.

About six miles or so down from Tobaunt Lake we arrived at the head of a wild rapid, where the broad river rushes down through a narrow, rocky gorge, not more than fifty yards in width, and about two and a half miles in length. Over this entire distance the river forms one continuous boiling, tumbling stream of foaming water, which at every rock in its course is dashed high in air into myriad particles of spray. At the foot of the rapid the river again widens out beyond its usual width into a little lake, which was still more than half covered by the last winter's ice.

Past the entire length of this rapid a portage of everything had, of course, to be made. Camp was pitched at the foot, and near it were found bones of musk oxen. Later, on the opposite side of the rapid, two of these animals were seen.

On the morning of the 19th we started across the little ice-bound lake in a northerly direction, and within

a distance of about four miles discovered to the left the mouth of another small river flowing in from the westward, and, much to our delight, upon its sandy beaches found dead willow drift-wood in such quantities that we were able to load the canoes with it. Signs of Eskimos were also observed here. Three miles farther north, just west of a remarkable white sand-hill or moraine, three hundred feet in height, the Telzoa, now a broad swift stream, was again entered.

Towards evening we ı ‗ ed upon the right bank, some distance ahead of us, the solitary lodge of an Eskimo. In front of the doorway stood a man gazing toward us, and behind and around him excited women and children were gathered. These were all quickly placed inside the "topick" or lodge, and the doorway laced up securely. But he, remaining outside, continued to watch us intently. Our canoes were no doubt taken to be those of the "Ik-kil-lin" (the Indians) from the south—their hereditary enemies—so they expected no good thing from us.

Our own men, recalling to mind the stories of the "savage Eskimos who would undoubtedly eat them," were scarcely less fearful than the solitary native, who, as we drew nearer, was observed through our glasses to be nervous and trembling. As soon as we had approached to within calling distance, I stood up in my canoe and shouted, "*Chimo! chimo! cudloona uvugut peeuweunga tacko Enuit*" (Halloo! halloo! we are white men, glad to see the Eskimos). Before my words were finished the doorway of the topick was torn open, and with great rejoicing and excited gestures all the inmates scrambled out to meet us at the shore as we landed.

The Eskimo himself was a tall, well-built, stalwart man, with a shrewd, intelligent face, and wore the pleasant characteristic grin of his race. With him were his two wives and six children, and all joined in extending to us a hearty welcome.

Their lodge was a large well-formed, clean-looking one, made of deer-skin parchment, and supported by

ESKIMO "TOPICK," TELZOA RIVER

stout spruce poles, which must have been brought from some distant place. Into this dwelling we were cordially invited and most hospitably received. Seats of deer-skin were offered by the hostesses and venison was placed before us, while we in return handed around presents of beads, tobacco, matches, and such things. About us were to be seen evidences of communication with traders, such as a large tin kettle, two old guns and a pair of moleskin trousers. Upon inquiry I was told they had received them in trade from other "Enuits" (Eskimos). We satisfied ourselves that this family were accustomed to meet with the Eskimos from Hudson Bay who trade at Fort Churchill or Marble Island, and for that reason the Telzoa must in all probability flow into the bay. We were, moreover, soon convinced of this by getting the Eskimo to draw us a sketch of the river's course.

From the natives we also secured several articles, such as horn spoons, personal ornaments, and two or three deer-skin coats, to do us service, if necessary, later in the season. In exchange for these we were asked for powder, bullets and gun-caps, all of which they were badly in need of. About camp there appeared to be an abundance of venison for the present support of the family, but the hunt for musk oxen was what had brought this venturesome hunter far up the river in advance of his tribe.

As Eskimo interpreter I had little difficulty in conversing with the natives, though I found that many of my words as used by the Eskimos on the east coast of Hudson Bay and the north shore of the Straits were not understood. It was not so surprising that many of their words were not understood by me. In the main, however, I found the language to be the same as that spoken by the Eskimos of various other districts formerly visited.

Among those of us who for the time shared the hospitality of this native family was our worthy cook, John, who also laid claim to the distinction of being an

Eskimo linguist. It was noticeable, however, at this time that John was unusually silent and backward, more so indeed than anyone in the party. After leaving the lodge I asked him if he had understood what the natives were saying, and was not a little amused when he replied, " Y-e-s, but,—b-u-t, t-h-e,—the trouble was I couldn't get them to talk." After a pleasant but brief visit of less than one hour, during which time we received some valuable information about our route, as well as much assurance and encouragement, with many hearty "tabowetings" (good-byes), we parted. As we did so Louis, my steersman, with an expression of pleasant disappointment on his face, exclaimed, "They are not savage, but real decent people."

The current being strong, our friends at the topick were soon far behind. They had told us that from there to the sea (Hudson Bay) was about a twenty days' journey, and though we thought we could likely make it in half that time, we were impressed and spurred on by the knowledge of the fact that we were now far into the interior of the country, and at the least eight hundred miles by our road from the nearest Hudson's Bay Company's post, Fort Churchill. This day and the next after visiting the Eskimos we had beautifully bright weather, but the enjoyment of it was marred by our encountering swarms of black flies.

As we glided down the river several white wolves were seen upon the shore, gnawing at the carcass of a deer, and at a distance of about ten miles below the topick we entered another lake.

While traversing the shores of this body of water, which is about twenty miles in length, and which has been christened Wharton Lake, a number of magnificent specimens of reindeer in prime condition were seen, and several of them shot at ranges of from two to four hundred yards. By this time—the 22nd of August—the skins as well as the carcases of the deer were at their best, and the centres of several of the hides were saved and dried for use as sleeping mats, while all of the fine fat meat secured was applied to the replenishing of our severely taxed larder.

After describing nearly the entire circumference of this lake, the outlet, much obscured by a labyrinth of islands, was discovered on the east side, close to a conspicuous hill of white quartzite, 230 feet in height.

At the foot of this hill an Eskimo cache, consisting of a "kometic" (sled), snow-shovels, musk-ox horns, etc., was discovered, and here on the night of the 22nd camp was pitched. As no moss or other description of fuel could be found in the vicinity, some of the men considered they had "struck a bonanza" in finding the "kometic," and carried it to camp, intending to utilize it for boiling the kettle. A slat or two had already been knocked off when, happily, I arrived on the scene just in time to prevent its destruction and preserve our good name with the natives.

To the Eskimo who owned the sled it was an invaluble possession, and for us to have destroyed it for one "mess of pottage" would have been a flagrant shame. It was therefore repaired, and carried back to where it had been found; and for a peace-offering a plug of tobacco was left upon it.*

From our camp at White Mountain, on the morning of the 23rd, we again entered the river, which for ten or twelve miles carried us off to the eastward; then turning sharply to the northward and flowing swiftly between high, steep banks of sand, it widened out into what has been named Lady Marjorine Lake, a body of water about ten miles long by three or four wide. Through this we passed and at its north-western extremity regained the river.

It began with a rough, rocky rapid, in running which my canoe struck a smooth rock, was smashed in the bottom, and nearly filled with water; but though in a sinking condition we managed to get it ashore. Though the contents were soaked, everything was landed without serious damage. After a delay of two hours we were again in the stream, and being borne away to the westward—the direction opposite to that we were now anxious to follow.

The river was here a noble stream, deep and swift, with a well-defined channel and high banks of rock or sand. Near the north bank there extended for some miles a high range of dark but snow-capped trappean hills, of about five hundred feet in height.

On the night of the 24th we camped at the base of two conspicuous conical peaks of trap, named by us the Twin Mountains.

---

* My brother in revisiting the Barren Lands during the summer of 1894 was hailed by the natives many miles south of the scene of this incident as the "Kudloonah Peayouk" (good white man) who had regard for the goods of an Eskimo, and left on his "kometic" a piece of tobacco.

During the whole of the 25th our course continued to be westerly and north-westerly, and because of this we began to feel anxious. We had now passed the latitude of Baker Lake, where, according to information obtained from the Eskimos, we were expecting the river to take us. Instead of drawing nearer to it, we were heading away toward the Back or Great Fish River, which discharges its waters into the Arctic Ocean, and was, on our present course, distant only two days' journey.

Towards evening, however, a marked change was observed in the character of the river. The banks grew lower and consisted of soft, coarse-grained sandstone. The water became shallow and the channel broadened out into a little lake, containing numerous shoals and low islands of sand. Just beyond this, much to our surprise and pleasure, we suddenly came upon abundance of drift-wood—not little sticks of willow or ground birch, but the trunks of trees six or eight inches in diameter, as heavy as two men could carry. No growing trees were to be seen in the district, nor had we seen any during the previous three or four hundred miles of our journey. At first, therefore, the occurrence of the wood seemed unaccountable, but the theory soon suggested itself that we must be close to the confluence of some other stream flowing through a wooded country. No other could account for its existence in this remote region, and accordingly this theory was borne out by the discovery, within a short distance, of a river as large as the Telzoa, flowing in from the westward and with it mingling its dark-colored waters.

The abundance and condition of the drift-wood, which was not badly battered, would indicate that upon the west branch few rapids and no lakes exist between the confluence and the woodland district, which is perhaps in the vicinity of Great Slave or Clinton Golden Lake. Lakes occurring on the course of a river act as catch-basins to prevent the further passage of drift-wood. According to information obtained from the Eskimo, some distance up this river there were great numbers of his people engaged in the building of kyacks. We would have been pleased to visit them, but deeming it unwise at this late season to go out of our way, we pulled on with the stream, which was now double its former strength and flowing again to the northward.

Many geese were seen about the low grassy shores and islands, upon one of which latter camp was pitched on the evening of the 25th, and a great blazing, roaring fire of drift-wood kindled.

It was hoped that henceforward for some time this supply of fuel might continue, for of late we had been entirely without fire for warming purposes. The miserable smudges made of moss or ground birch mixed with deer tallow or sprinkled with alcohol were useful for the purpose of cooking our venison, but for nothing else.

From camp on the morning of the 26th, for a distance of four or five miles, the river still flowed toward the Arctic, but in latitude 64° 41′ north it swerved around to the east, and then the south-east, and bore us down to the western extremity of a magnificent body of water, which has been named Aberdeen Lake, in honor of their Excellencies Lord and Lady Aberdeen. It was a lovely calm evening when the track of our canoes first rippled the waters of this lake, and as we landed at a bluff point on the north shore and from it gazed to the eastward over the solitary but beautiful scene, a feeling of awe crept over us. We were undoubtedly the first white men who had ever viewed it, and in the knowledge of the fact there was inspiration.

For two days following we enjoyed fine weather—something unusual in the Barren Land districts—and this enabled us to carry on the exploration of the large lake with very little delay. We found the total length to be about fifty miles. Portions of the shore toward the west end were low and sandy, and at one point of landing the remains of an old Eskimo camp, and beside it parts of a human skeleton, were found.

Towards the east end other remarkable traces of Eskimos were seen in the shape of stone pillars, well and uniformly built, but for what purpose I confess I cannot tell. If they had been located at conspicuous points, or upon hill-tops, I would say they were intended for landmarks. Several were found on the shore of the bay forming the eastern extremity of the lake, and others in more or less obscure places. I am inclined to think the object in building these stone pillars has been in some way connected with the hunting of musk oxen or deer, but they were evidently not intended merely for shelters or hiding places.

CHAPTER IX.

MEETING WITH NATIVES.

BORNE down by the river we had launched on the bosom of Aberdeen Lake without effort, but not so easy a matter was it to find our way out. With the hope of saving unnecessary search, it was resolved to climb to the top of a hill not far back from shore, and view the country with our field-glasses.

From the summit, which was found by the aneroid to be four hundred feet above the lake, we obtained a magnificent view of the surrounding country, and from the base of the hill could clearly trace the course of the river, winding away to the northward. While my brother and I were thus engaged in viewing and sketching the country, hammering the rocks, tracing the lines of ancient sea-beaches, etc., which were here clearly defined at no less than seven different elevations, varying from 60 to 290 feet above the surface of the lake, the men were usefully employed in collecting black moss, which in this neighborhood was found in abundance.

Since entering the lake nothing more had been seen of the drift-wood, but on our return from the hill in the evening we found camp already pitched, and near it a big kettle of venison simmering over a fire of moss. More than this, some flour, a little of which still remained, had been baked into grease cakes by John, and with these, the venison and hot tea, we enjoyed one . the heartiest meals of our lives.

On the morning of the 29th, enshrouded by a dense fog, we entered the river, and though for a time we could see neither bank, we knew our course from my sketch made on the hill-top. Later in the day the weather, clearing, enabled us at noon, as we entered the west end of Schultz Lake (so called in honor of the late Lieutenant-Governor of Manitoba), to ascertain our latitude, which was 64° 43′ north. Along the north shore of this lake extended a high range of rocky, snow-clad hills, from four to five hundred feet in height. The south shore was also bold and rocky, but of considerably less elevation.

The next day the old story of looking for the "hole" out of the lake was repeated. At noon, while lunch was being prepared, my brother climbed a hill on the south shore, and from its summit discovered the outlet, four or five miles distant on the opposite side.

As soon as possible after my brother's descent we started straight across on our course for the river. Light wolfy clouds were already scudding across the sky, and after them dark masses began to roll up from the horizon and soon overshadowed us. We were evidently in for a blow, and in order to avoid being overtaken on the open lake, every man exerted himself to the utmost. No sooner had we reached shore than the storm burst upon us, but once in the river channel we were able to obtain shelter from the force of the gale if not from the pelting rain.

We had now reached the second of two points of

highest latitude attained on our journey, namely 64° 48′ north. This as a high latitude does not, of course, amount to anything, but the attainment of a high latitude was not an object of our expedition, though scores of times the question has been asked of me, "How far north did you get?"

At this entrance to the river a large area of highly glaciated granitic rocks was observed, and the channel was well formed and deep. Both banks were high and rocky, and the current swift. Notwithstanding the weather our canoes were kept in the stream, though it was with difficulty I was able to carry on the survey and keep my notes.

About seven miles down stream a very rocky rapid was discovered. On examination we found it could be run for a considerable distance, and that for the remaining distance only a short portage would have to be made.

The contents of the canoes being all safely landed below the rapids, they themselves were run down by the Iroquois through the foaming waters. Had it not been for our good steersman Pierre many and many a rapid through which our little crafts were guided in safety would have caused us much laborious portaging. If a rapid could be run at all in safety, Pierre had the skill and nerve to do it. During the scores of times that he piloted our little fleet through foaming waters, I believe I am correct in saying that his canoe never once touched a rock; but that is more than can be said of those who followed him.

After reloading the canoes we sped down with the current at a rate of about eight miles an hour, with the wind beating the cold rain and the spray from the crest of the waves in our faces, our only consolation was that we were making miles on the journey. The shores continued to be bare steep walls of rock; not a shrub was anywhere to be seen. About twelve miles below Schultz Lake we decided to camp. Tents were pitched, and within them our soaked and shivering party sought comfort. Little, however, was to be found, for the wind, which continued to increase in violence, drove the rain through our shelters, saturating the blankets and making us generally miserable. The morning brought no improvement, for the storm still continued.

It was impossible to make a fire, supposing moss or other fuel could have been found, for they would have been saturated with water. A little alcohol still remaining, tea was boiled with it, and dried venison completed our menu. As those who have used it well know, this description of meat is not the most palatable. It is good strong, portable food, but may be better compared to sole leather than any article of diet.

By the morning of the first of September the rain had ceased and the clouds partially cleared away. The gale, however, still continued to blow so fiercely as to frequently whip clouds of spray off the surface of the river, so that we were quite unable to travel in canoes.

On the following morning, the wind having fallen sufficiently, the canoes were again pushed into the current, and we glided down stream, in a south-easterly direction, at the rate of seven miles an hour. The channel was deep and about three hundred yards in width, while the banks, continuing to be bold and high,

were formed of dark Huronian schists and clay. The
schists were chiefly micaceous and hornblendic, such as
those occurring about the Lake of the Woods, and were
found dipping at high angles.

Four or five miles to the east was a conspicuous
range of snow-covered hills, probably six hundred feet
in height, while between them and the river appeared a
broad plateau, or a high level lake—which of the two we
could not determine from the river bank. Time would
not permit of our making side investigations when it
was possible to be travelling, so on we sped, pulling at
the paddles as well as being hurried along by the
current. Thus for a time we made good progress, and
as the long miles were quickly passed the spirits of our
little party were cheered.

Late in the forenoon, as we were rounding a bend in
the river, an Eskimo in his kyack was sighted ahead,
and much to our amusement he was soon much farther
ahead. The poor fellow, seeing our fleet of canoes, and
being himself alone, evidently thought his safest move
was to get out of the way, and this he did, leaving us
farther behind at every stroke, though we were doing
our best to catch him.

I shouted to him in his native tongue, but it was of
no use; he did not slacken his pace until, some distance
down the river, he reached an Eskimo encampment
of several topicks. Here he landed, hauled up his
kyack, and informed the other natives of our approach.
All eyes keenly watched us. As we drew nearer they
soon observed by our canoes and personal appearance
that we were not Indians, as they had supposed, but
were "Kudloonahs" (white men), the friends of the Eski-

mos. I shouted to them, "*Chimo! Kudloonah uvagut peeuweeunga tacko Enuit.*" To this they responded with cheers and wild gesticulations, and as we landed we were received with hand-shaking and great rejoicing. None showed the least sign of hostility. Indeed the ladies exhibited an embarrassing amount of cordiality, so much so that it was thought wise to make our visit as brief as possible. Having "greeted all the brethren," I proceeded to obtain what information I could from them regarding our road to the sea, and was much pleased to learn that we were close to the mouth of the river. I also obtained a sketch map of our course thence to the "sea" or Hudson Bay. There was now no doubt as to the route. We were to reach the Bay through Chesterfield Inlet, which was now not far distant, and at this certain knowledge we felt much encouraged. Besides this information, several skins were obtained from the natives, some skin clothing and a few trinkets. One very old man of the camp asked to be given a passage down the river a few miles to another native village. Placing him in our third or freighting canoe, and accompanied by an escort of three kyacks, we departed, amid a generous exchange of salutes.

We were pleased to learn from the natives that there were no more rapids or obstructions to be encountered. As we proceeded, however, we found the current both strong and swift, and quite rough in some places, but the Eskimos in their kyacks shot ahead from time to time and showed us the best charnels. Sometimes they fell behind, evidently for the sake of having the opportunity of showing how quickly they could repass. Just as we had been able to paddle around the

Indians in their bark canoes, so were these little fellows able to paddle around us. Soon after leaving the Eskimo camp we went ashore. The river bank here was abrupt and high, in the neighborhood of one hundred feet, and on the side of this steep bank several new species of plants were collected. Marine shells and marl were also found thirty feet above the river, while on the top of the bank some Eskimo graves were discovered. Out of consideration for our native escorts, the graves, already broken by bears or wolves, were not molested. When lunch was announced, and we, seating ourselves, proceeded to work with the customary plates, knives and forks, the Eskimos were very much amused, and stood watching our operations with great interest. Some refreshments were offered them, but to our surprise they declined, informing us that they had plenty of meat. For their own lunch they each took a lump of raw venison and a drink of water from the river, a very simple but no doubt wholesome meal.

Before re-embarking I secured several good photographs of the Eskimos. At first they were not prepared to be "shot" by the camera, but after explaining what I wished to do, they were pleased and amused to have their pictures taken, and changed their positions when I asked them to do so. By the time we had descended eight or ten miles farther down the river, our native escorts commenced cheering, hallooing and acting in a most hilarious manner. At first we wondered what had possessed them, but the cause of their strange actions was soon disclosed as we switched around a bend in the river and found ourselves close upon a large Eskimo

ESKIMO HUNTERS.

village. As we pulled ashore this time there was no need of introducing ourselves. Our coming and our character had already been lustily proclaimed from half a mile or so up the river until the time of landing, so that we were received with great demonstrations.

Upon going ashore one of the first objects which attracted my attention was a small topick, or lodge,

GROUP OF ESKIMOS.

constructed of beautiful musk-ox robes. I felt inclined to doubt my own eyes, for it seemed such a strange waste of luxury. I proceeded to this princely dwelling, and finding the owners—three young brothers—entered into negotiations with them for its purchase. The value asked in exchange for the robes being very moderate, they were secured and made into a snug little bale. Next my attention was drawn to a pile of skins lying on the rocks. As I approached these skins, several Eskimos sat upon them, telling me as they did so that the owner of them was away hunting, and therefore I could not buy them. I assented, but asked to be allowed to look at them. Even this, however, was stoutly refused, as the owner was not present. I could not help admiring these fellows for their fidelity to one of their number. Some time was then spent in collecting information about the country, and in purchasing nicknacks of one kind and another, and while doing so the owner of the skins returned. He at once proceeded to open up his furs, which, with the exception of one wolf skin, were all musk-ox robes, but of inferior quality. The four best skins were picked out and reserved, and the frowsy remnant then offered to us. The poor skins, I told him, were not the ones we wanted, but for a time he positively refused to sell the good ones. After a little discussion, however, the crafty hunter came to the conclusion that he wanted a small kettle and some gun-caps (for he had an old gun), and so offered me one of the skins for these articles. We happened to have a kettle in which we had carried our butter, but which had now become only an article of extra baggage, so after some " serious consideration," I concluded to let him have the kettle and some caps for the skin.

It was then my turn to make him an offer. I produced a telescope, a jack-knife, and an old shirt, and offered them for the three remaining robes. The temptation proved too great; the skins were handed over, and the telescope, knife and shirt accepted with great delight and many thanks. Although it was now time to camp, and many pressing invitations were extended to us to spend the night at the village, it was thought wisest for the moral well-being of our party not to do so. Besides this, the surface of the country in the neighborhood of the village was exceedingly rough, being formed entirely of boulders. The Eskimo topicks were pitched upon the rocky shore, and it was thought we might find smoother ground. Before leaving the village one old Eskimo surprised us very much by making a remark in English. I said to him, "Oh! you understand English," whereat he made the amusing reply, "No, me no understand English." I tried then to find out from the old man where he had learned to speak our language, but the only reply I could get from him was that he had always been able to speak it. It may be that he had accompanied Sir George Back, Sir John Richardson, or Dr. Ray, on one of their Franklin search expeditions, or perhaps he had come from Hudson Bay, where he had been associated with some of the American whalers who frequent its waters.

Followed by many hearty cheers and "tabowetees" (farewells), we parted from our new but warm-hearted friends. As before, we were accompanied by an escort of kyacks, but after a time they fell behind and returned to the village.

As we had been informed by the natives, so we soon found, we were at last at the mouth of the great Telzoa, and gradually as we passed out into the broad shallow delta and gazed over the deep blue limitless waters beyond, the gratifying fact forced itself upon us that we had accomplished what we had started out to do, viz., to explore a route through the heart of the Barren Lands,

MEETING WITH NATIVES.

where certainly no other white men, if indeed Indians or Eskimos, had ever passed. We were still, of course, a long way from being out of the Barren Land country, but once on the waters of Baker Lake, as we now were, the remainder of the road was to some extent known to us.

Before proceeding further with my narrative, I shall digress a little, believing that the reader will be interested by some particulars concerning the Eskimos. Having in former expeditions spent nearly two years among these people, I had abundant opportunity for studying their habits and customs of life. Some of the observations thus made I shall record in the next two chapters.

ICELANDIC SETTLER.

AN ESKIMO.

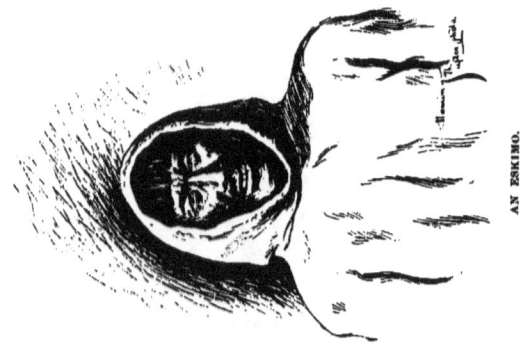

ESKIMO WOMAN.

CHAPTER X.

THE ESKIMOS.

THE Eskimos, the most northerly inhabitants of the globe, are in many respects a strange and interesting people. In appearance they are short and well-built, with fat, round faces, usually almost entirely devoid of hair; the eyebrows and eyelashes are so scanty as to be scarcely discernible, giving to their brown, oily faces a singularly bare and homely appearance. Their hair, like that of the Indians, is black and straight. By the women it is worn plaited, and twisted up into three knots, one at either side of the head and one at the back. The men wear theirs short, and well down over their forehead, for protection from the cold in winter and from the sun in summer.

While the Eskimos as a rule are short and homely in appearance, still I have met with some very handsome, stalwart men, quite up to the standard height of Canadians, and a few pretty, charming women. Most of them have bright soft brown eyes, which of themselves are features of beauty; but they serve these savages a better and more useful purpose, furnishing marvellous powers of vision and enabling their owners to see objects clearly at great distances. The eyes of the Anglo-Saxon, even when aided by the telescope, are not a match for the bright brown orbs of these "children of the cold."

The clothing of the Eskimo is made entirely of the skins of animals, chiefly of the seal and reindeer, the former being used for summer and the latter for the winter. They are nicely softened and dressed, and are neatly made up by the women, whose chief duty it is to provide clothing for their husbands and children.

The cut of the native garb, both for the men and the women, is somewhat peculiar. A man's suit may briefly be described as follows: Commencing at the foundation, it consists of a pair of fur stockings or duffles, covered by long waterproof moccasins which reach to the knees and are just met by short seal or deerskin trousers. The suit is completed by a jacket or jumper, made of the same material as the trousers, which is pulled on over the head, there being no opening in front to admit of its being put on like a coat. This jacket is provided with a hood, which takes the place of a cap, and may either be worn over the head or pushed back when not required.

In the summer season, a single suit of seal-skin, made as above, constitutes a man's entire clothing, but in the winter time he wears two such suits, the inner one having the hair on the inside, and the outer one reversed.

The female costume is rather more complex in make-up than the above. The foot-wear is the same with both sexes, but in place of the trousers worn by the men, the women wear leggings and trunks, and in place of the jacket a peculiarly constructed over-skirt, having a short flap in front, and a long train, in shape some-

THE ESKIMOS.

thing like a beaver's tail, just reaching to the ground behind. The back of the over-skirt is made very full, so as to form a sort of bag, in which the mothers carry their children. Like a man's jacket, it is provided with a hood, but of much larger size, so as to afford shelter for both mother and child. The women are very fond of decorating their dresses with beads or other ornaments, and all their garments are made with great neatness.

Like many other savage people, the Eskimos, and especially the women, tattoo extensively. They do not all thus adorn themselves, but many of them have their faces, necks, arms or hands all figured over in such a way as to give them a wild and savage appearance.

Many of the ladies, when in full dress, wear headbands, usually made of polished brass or iron, over their foreheads. These are held in position by being tied with a cord behind the head.

A stranger custom still is that of wearing stones in the cheeks, upon each side of the mouth. This practice is not universal with the Eskimos, but, as far as my knowledge extends, it is limited to those inhabiting the Mackenzie River district. The natives of this region have the reputation of being a bad lot, and it is said that when they are heard to rattle their cheek-stones against their teeth it is time to be on the look-out. The stones are cut in the shape of large shirt-studs, and are let through the cheeks by cutting holes for them.

As to the origin of the Eskimo people, very little is known, but the most probable theory accounting for their existence on this continent is that they were originally Mongolians, and at some very early date crossed over the

Behring Straits and landed in Alaska. This theory is based upon the fact that a similarity is traced between the Eskimo language and the dialects of some of the Mongolian tribes of northern Asia. A certain Eskimo tradition would rather tend to bear out this theory. It is something like this: A very long time ago there were two brothers made by the beaver and placed on an island in the Western Sea. There they lived and fed upon birds which they caught with their hands, but at length food grew scarce, and the brothers, being hungry, fought for the birds they had taken. This quarrel led to a separation, and one brother went to live in the western portion of our "Great North Land," and became the father of the Eskimos in that region; while the other went still farther east, and became the father of the natives of Hudson Bay and Straits.

The range of the Eskimos is very large, extending completely across the northern part of North America —toward the south, to about the sixtieth parallel of latitude, west of Hudson Bay, but east of the bay, to about the fifty-fifth parallel; while toward the north their range is almost unlimited. They are a very thinly scattered race, roving in small bands over great treeless wildernesses.

My first meeting with the Eskimos led me to think them a wild people. There were thirty-six of them, all women and children, piled into one of their "oomiacks," or skin boats, and all were whooping and yelling at the top of their voices, while those not paddling were swinging their arms (and legs, too) in the wildest manner. They were natives of Prince of Wales Sound, Hudson

Straits, coming out from shore to meet the steamship *Alert*, which to them was a fiery monster of mystery.

Accompanying them was a party of men in kyacks, and all were preparing to board the ship without invitation; but the first officer, by brandishing a cordwood stick, and threatening to hurl it at them if they came too near—backing up the menace with the liberal use of some strong English which they did not understand—induced them to await his convenience to receive them.

When the ship was past the shoals near which she was steaming, and safely into harbor, the natives were allowed to come on board. They were an odd-looking crowd, some of them curiously dressed. One old grey-haired chief had apparently reached a stage of civilization in his attire not common among the Eskimos, for outside of his seal-skin clothing he wore a long white cotton nightshirt, of which he was evidently very proud. The Eskimos are always pleased with the acquisition of white men's garments, but their ideas as to how and when they should be worn do not always agree with ours.

Early navigators have described the Eskimos as being savage tribes, greatly to be feared, and it is true that unfortunate crews have fallen into their hands and been murdered by them; but often in such cases the fault has been as much with the whites as with the poor savages. They really possess very simple, childish natures, but at the same time are characterized by a quiet determination and deep jealousy, which, when aroused, is likely to lead to acts of violence. From my own observation, I do not think that the Eskimos would, without considerable provocation or great temptation, harm any one falling into their hands.

Though not usually quarrelsome or vicious, they do fight with each other, but only at appointed times, when all old grudges and differences of opinion are cleared up at once. On the appointed day, all the disagreeing parties of the camp pair off, and standing at arm's length from each other, strike turn about, and in this deliberate, systematic way take satisfaction out of each other, until one of the combatants cries, "Ta-luh" (enough).

The food of the Eskimo, as his name implies, is chiefly raw flesh; so the preparation of his meals is an extremely simple operation. The culinary department of civilization has no place in his life. Reindeer, seals, white whales and walruses are to the Eskimo the staple articles of food; but polar bears, Arctic hares and other animals, besides most of the Arctic birds, are considered equally good.

It is rather a novel, if not a repulsive sight, to witness an Eskimo feast. The occasion of the feast is the capture of a seal, or perhaps a reindeer, which, according to custom during the winter season, becomes common property, so that all are invited to the lodge of the fortunate hunter to share in the festivities.

The animal's carcase is trailed into the middle of the lodge, and when all the guests are assembled, they seat themselves on the floor about it. The carcase is then skinned by the host, and the pelt laid down to form a dish or receptacle for the blood.

All things being ready, the party, armed with knives, are invited to help themselves, and this they do with great dexterity, and continue to do—not until they have had sufficient, but until the supply is exhausted and absolutely nothing remains but the skin and skeleton. The blood, being considered very fine, is dipped up with skin cups or horn spoons, and consumed with the flesh.

The blubber, or outer layer of fat, which is found on most Arctic animals, is separated from the skin and cut into long strips about an inch square. Thus prepared it is swallowed, though not eaten. It is simply lowered down the throat as one might lower a rope into a well. During the summer season the blubber is not used as food, but is saved for oil, to be used for lighting purposes during the long dark nights of the succeeding winter.

An Eskimo appears to have no idea of a limited capacity for food, but usually eats until the supply fails. I knew of one exception, however, where an old woman, after doing heroically, was forced to yield.

A party of Eskimos were having a big feast on the carcase of a whale, which they consider very good food, when this woman, in her ambition, overestimated her capabilities and ate until she became quite torpid. Her friends, supposing her to be dead, trailed her out and buried her in the snow, but a day or two afterwards she kicked off the snow that covered her and rejoined her astonished companions.

Next to stowing capacity, an Eskimo's stomach is noted for its powers of digestion. For instance, both the flesh and hide of the walrus are common articles of food with them, and yet these are so hard and gritty that when skinning or cutting up the animal one has to be continually sharpening his knife.

The skin of a walrus is a good deal like that of an elephant, and is from half an inch to an inch and a half in thickness; but, notwithstanding this, and the hardness of its structure, the little Eskimo children may often be seen running about gnawing pieces of walrus hide as if they were apples. Sometimes, however, they have no walrus hide or meat of any kind to gnaw, for occasionally in the spring season the condition of the snow and ice is such as to render hunting impossible, and though they store up meat in the fall for winter use, it is often exhausted before spring.

When this state of things occurs the condition of the Eskimos is deplorable in the extreme. They are forced to kill and eat their wretched dogs, which are even more nearly starved than themselves, and next they resort to their skin clothing and moccasins, which they soak in water until they become soft, though perhaps not altogether palatable.

HALF-BREED HUNTER WITH WOODEN SNOW-GOGGLES.

Next to starvation, perhaps the most severe affliction the Eskimo has to endure is that of snow blindness. This trouble is very prevalent in the spring season, and is caused by the exposure to the strong glare of the sun upon the glistening fields of snow and ice. Snow blindness is thus in reality acute inflammaiton of the eyes, and the pain caused by it is excruciating, being like what one would expect to suffer if his eyes were filled with hot salt. I speak from experience.

In order to guard against the occurrence of snow-blindness, the Eskimos wear a very ingenious contrivance, in the form of wooden goggles. These are neatly carved so as to fit over the nose, and close in to the sockets of the eyes. Instead of colored glasses, which the Eskimos have no means of getting, these goggles are made with narrow horizontal slits, just wide enough to allow the wearer to see through. Thus the excess of light is excluded, while the sight is not entirely obstructed.

Like many people in southern Canada, the native of the frozen zone possesses a summer and winter residence, and occupies each in turn as regularly as the seasons change. His winter dwelling is built of snow; his summer lodge is made of oil-tanned seal or deer-skins, neatly sewn together, and supported by poles, if such can be procured, or pieces of drift-wood spliced together. A flap is left for the door, but there is no opening at the top, as in the Indian wigwam or tepee, for, having no fire, they have no need of a chimney.

The atmosphere of these tents or "topicks," as they are called, is usually very sickening to one not accustomed to them, for the skins of which they are made are dressed in their natural oil in order to make them water-proof, which has the effect of making them rank and odorous to a degree.

Topicks vary in size, according to the wealth or requirements of the occupants. Sometimes they are scarcely large enough to allow two or three little people to huddle into them, while others are quite commodious, capable of seating twenty persons. The commonest form of topick is that of a cone, very similar to an Indian tepee, but it is sometimes rectangular and built with vertical walls about four feet high.

The furniture of these summer dwellings is simple, consisting usually of a few skins lying about the rocky floor, to serve as seats in the daytime and bedding at night; two or three seal-skin sacks of oil, two shallow stone vessels used as lamps, a few hunting implements, some little deer-skin bags, used as ladies' work-baskets; several coils of seal-skin line, a few pairs of moccasins scattered about, and at one side of the door the some-

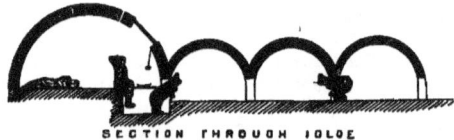

SECTION THROUGH IGLOE

what repulsive remains of a carcass consumed at the last meal. Such is the Eskimo summer house.

His winter dwelling in the snow is more interesting and curious. It is called an "igloe," and is built in the form of a dome with large blocks of snow. The common size of the dwelling apartment of an igloe is twelve feet in diameter, and eight feet in height. This is approached by a succession of three or four smaller domes, connected by low archways, through which one has to crouch in order to pass.

The innermost archway opening into the dwelling apartment is about three feet high, and as one enters he steps down a foot or more to the level of the floor of the front portion of the dwelling. The back part, about two-thirds of the apartment, is three feet higher than the entrance.

The front or lower section of the igloe corresponds to a front hall, and it is in it that the occupants, as they enter, beat the snow off their clothing, or remove their outer garments, when they wish to step up into the higher living apartment.

The floor of the entire igloe consists simply of snow, but in this upper apartment it is well covered with deer-skin robes, so that it is not melted by the warmth of those who sit or lie upon it.

Above the doorway of the igloe is placed a window to admit light into the dwelling. This is formed of a large square slab of ice, neatly inserted into the wall of the dome, and it serves well the purpose for which it is intended, admitting a pleasant soft light. Above the window a much-needed ventilating hole is usually made. This, because of the passing current of warm air, becomes rapidly enlarged, and requires to be frequently plastered up with snow.

Sometimes one of the long approaches or corridors is made to serve for two or three dwellings, each of which is connected by low archways with the innermost of the smaller domes. Usually, opening out of the inner dome, each family has one or two small pantries, where they keep a supply of meat sufficient for a week or two.

The furniture of the snow-house is much the same as that of the skin topick already described, but the stone lamps come more into prominence, contributing light to the dwelling during the long dark winter nights. These lamps are simply stone vessels, usually half moon shaped, and formed neatly of some description of soft rock. The rounding side of the vessel is made much deeper than the other, which shoals up gradually to the edge. The wick of the lamp consists of dried decomposed moss, pressed and formed by the fingers into a narrow ridge across the shallow or straight edge of the dish. In this position it absorbs the seal oil which is placed in the vessel, and when lit, burns with a clear bright flame, free from smoke. The lamp is then made self-feeding by suspending a lump of seal blubber above it, at a height varying according to the amount of light and consequent supply of oil required. This melts with the heat of the flame and drips into the vessel of the lamp. One lump keeps up the supply for a considerable length of time, the intensity of light being increased or diminished at will by lowering or raising the lump of blubber suspended above the flame.

A lamp is usually placed at either side of the entrance in the upper apartment. Both are kept burning brightly the greater part of the long cold, dark days of winter, but during the hours of sleep they are "turned down," that is, the lumps of blubber are raised; or sometimes one lamp is extinguished and the other made to burn dimly. These lamps, though chiefly designed to furnish light, also contribute a considerable amount of heat to the igloes. It is often necessary to turn them down, to provent the snow walls from being melted by the heat, though the temperature outside may be 40 or 50 degrees below zero.

Towards spring the snow-houses become very damp, and to prevent the roofs from being melted away fresh snow has to be added to the outside. Before they are abandoned for the skin tents they sometimes become so soft that they cave in upon the occupants, causing much sickness in the form of colds and pneumonia.

In their workmanship the Eskimos are always neat. Wood is used for manufacturing purposes when it is available, but all they are able to procure is of a f gn ry nature, such as has drifted from some distant sho. or from the wreck of an unfortunate vessel. It is from this rough and scanty material they frame their kyacks, make their sleds, tent-poles, and the handles of their spears and harpoons; from it they fashion their bows and many other useful or ornamental things, and by exercise of untiring perseverance and skill they manage to produce marvellous results. For example, a paddle is often made of two or three pieces of wood, but these are joined together so neatly that if it were not for the seal thong lashings the joints would not be noticeable.

The lashings are put on green, or after having been softened in water, and are drawn tightly, so that when they become dry and shrink they produce strong and rigid joints.

The process by which these lashing-thongs and heavy lines for hunting purposes, as well as the small thread for sewing, are manufactured is very interesting. A heavy harpoon line, used in the hunt for securing walruses, is made from the skin of the "square flipper" seal, a large species about eight feet long. For such use the skin is not removed from the carcase in the usual way, but is pulled off without cutting it, as one might pull off a wet stocking. The whole hide is thus preserved in the form of a sack. It is then placed in water, and allowed to remain there for several days, until the thin outer black skin becomes decomposed. This, together with the hair, is readily peeled off, and a clean white pelt remains.

Two men then take the pelt in hand, and with a sharp knife cut it into one long even white line, by commencing at one end and cutting around and around until at length the other end is reached. One skin in this way will make three hundred feet of line. In this condition it is allowed to partially dry, after which it is tightly stretched and dried thoroughly in the sun. The result obtained is a hard even white line three-eighths of an inch in diameter, but equal in strength to a three-inch manilla rope.

I have seen such a line, when imbedded in the flesh of a walrus at one end, and spiked to the hard ice at the other by a stout iron pin, as well as being held by six men, plough a furrow six inches deep through the ice, bend the spike and drag the six men to the edge of the ice, where the tug of war ended, the walrus, victorious, taking the unbreakable line with him into the deep.

Smaller seal thongs, such as are extensively used as lashings for komiticks, kyacks, handles, etc., are made in much the same way as I have described, except that the hide of smaller seals is used, and often the process of removing the outer black skin is omitted, the hair being simply scraped off with a sharp knife or scraper.

Finer lines, such as those used for fishing or for winding whip-stocks, and thread for sewing purposes, are manufactured from reindeer sinew. The best is that obtained from along the spine, which is always saved from the carcase. It is prepared for use by first drying and then rubbing till it becomes quite soft, when it is readily frayed out into fine fibres, in which condition it is used for fine needle-work; but when coarser thread or stout cord is required, these individual fibres are plaited together, with wonderful neatness and rapidity. One woman can make fifty or sixty yards of this cord or thread in a day.

With the Eskimos all joints, of whatever kind, are secured by these thongs, they having no nails or screws to supply their place. In making a komitick, the cross slats are all secured to the runners by seal thongs. In framing a kyack the numerous pieces are lashed together,

ESKIMO KYACK.

usually with seal or deer-skin, though sometimes, and preferably, with whalebone.

The Eskimo kyack or canoe consists of a light frame neatly made from all sorts of scrap-wood, and strongly jointed together in the way just described. The frame having been completed, it is then covered with green skins, either of seal or deer, dressed, with the hair removed. The skins are joined to each other as they are put on by double water-tight seams, and are drawn tightly over the frame, so that when they dry they become very hard and as tight as a drum-head.

A full-sized kyack thus made is about twenty-two feet long, a foot and a half wide, and a foot deep. It is completely covered over on the top, excepting the small hole where the paddler sits, so that though an extremely cranky craft in the hands of a novice, it is used in perfect safety, even in very rough water, by an expert. Indeed the Eskimos have an arrangement by which they can travel while almost submerged in the water. They have a thin waterproof parchment coat which they pull on over their heads in rough weather. This they place on the outside of the rim at the opening of the kyack, and tie securely, so that if the boat were to turn upside down the water could not rush in.

An Eskimo in his kyack can travel much faster than two men can paddle an ordinary canoe. I have known them to make six miles an hour in dead water, whereas four miles would be good going for a canoe.

ESKIMO OOMIACK.

The "oomiack," or woman's boat, is a flat-bottomed affair of large carrying capacity. Like the kyack it is a skin-covered frame, the many pieces of which are lashed together with thongs of skin or whalebone; but instead of being covered on top it is open, and is of a much broader model, and not so sharp at the ends. It is chiefly used by the women for moving camp from place to place, but is never used in the hunt. It is essentially a freighting craft, whereas the kyack is used only for hunting or speedy travel. Oomiacks are often made large enough to carry thirty or forty people. They are propelled by ordinary paddles, not by the long double-bladed ones used with the kyacks.

The komitick is a sled of rather peculiar design, consisting simply of two parallel runners, twelve or fourteen feet long, built of wood and placed about eighteen inches apart, upon the top of which are lashed a number of cross bars or slats. The runners are shod either with ivory or with mud, the latter answering the purpose exceedingly well. The mud covering is, of course, put on in a soft state, when it can be easily worked and formed into proper shape. When the mud is on, and the surface nicely smoothed off, it is allowed to freeze, and speedily becomes as hard as stone. In order to complete the vehicle, and put it in good running order, there is one thing to be done. The shoeing, whether of mud or ivory, must be covered with a thin coating of ice, in order to do which the Eskimo overturns the komitick, fills his spacious mouth with water from some convenient source, and then from his lips deposits a fine stream along the runner, where, quietly freezing, it forms a smooth glassy surface.

During the winter season the komitick forms an important factor in the Eskimo's life. It is drawn by a team, not of horses, nor even reindeer, but of dogs. The number of animals forming a team varies greatly, sometimes consisting of not more than three good dogs, but at other times fifteen or more are attached to a single sled. Each dog is attached by a single line, the length of which varies according to the merits of its owner. Thus the best dog in the team acts as leader, and has a line twenty or twenty-five feet in length.

In order to control the team the driver carries a whip of somewhat startling dimensions. This instrument of torture has a short wooden handle only about eighteen inches long, but what is lacking in stock is more than made up in lash, for this latter, made of the hide of the square flipper seal, is nearly thirty feet in length. An Eskimo can handle his whip with great dexterity, being able not only to reach any particular dog in the pack, but to strike any part of its body, and with as much force as the occasion may require.

Another curious Eskimo practice, observed by the women, is that of daily chewing the boots of the household. As already intimated, these boots or moccasins are made of oil-tanned seal or deer skins. The hair is always removed from the skin of which the foot of the moccasin is made, but not always from that part forming the leg. However, the point is this, that these moccasins, after having been wet and dried again, become very hard, and the most convenient or effective—or possibly the most agreeable—way of softening them seems to be by mastication. Whatever may be the reason for adopting this method, the fact is that nearly every morning the native women soften the shoes of the family most beautifully by chewing them. What to us would seem the disagreeable part of this operation cannot be thoroughly understood by one who has not some idea of the flavor of a genuine old Eskimo shoe.

In one of my trips in the land of the Eskimo I had an escort composed not only of men and women, old and young, but also of little children, several of whom could not have been more than five or six years old, and it was marvellous to see the powers of endurance of these little creatures, for they travelled along with the rest of the party, a distance of twenty-five miles, having no other object in view than that of seeing the white stranger.

The "shin-ig-bee," or Eskimo sleeping bag, is an article essential to the comfort of the traveller when making long overland journeys during the cold winter season. It consists of a long oval water-proof skin bag, lined with another of similar shape, made of soft but heavy winter deer-skins. The opening is not at the top, but near it, across one side, and is made with flap and buttons, so that it can be closed up as closely as desired.

When the traveller is provided with this kind of a bed he does not trouble himself to make a snow lodge for the night, as without it he would have to do, but he simply crawls into his "shin-ig-bee," buttons up the opening on the windward side, and goes to sleep, no matter what the weather or temperature may be. With the mercury at 40 below zero a man may in this way sleep warm and comfortable, without any fire, out upon the bleak frozen plains.

DOG-WHIP, WALRUS TUSKS AND BOWS AND ARROWS.

CHAPTER XI.

CUSTOMS OF THE ESKIMOS.

Deer-hunting is perhaps the most favored and remunerative occupation of the Eskimos. In some districts seal and other animals are extensively sought, but the reindeer is the universal stand-by. It is hunted with the bow and arrow or spear, and with guns as well, when these can be obtained.

Having already stated that the only wood obtainable by the Eskimos is broken fragments of driftwood, the inquiry may arise, Where do they get material from which to make bows? The answer is, that lacking material for making such bows as are ordinarily used, their ingenuity comes to the rescue and designs a composite bow, which answers the purpose equally well. This implement of the chase is, in the first place, made either of pieces of wood or of horn, neatly joined together. In order to give it strength and elasticity, a stout plaited sinew cord is stretched from end to end, around the convexity of the bow, and then twisted until it is brought to the required tension. By this mode of construction, when the bow is drawn the wood or horn is only subjected to a compressive strain, while the sinew thong takes up the tension.

Thus very powerful bows are made, though of rough

materials; but in order to use them with effect in killing deer, the sagacity of the hunter is often severely tested, for with the Eskimo there is no cover behind which to hide or creep upon his prey. The hunter's first precaution is, of course, to keep the deer to windward, for the moment they catch the scent of an enemy they are off, and to get within range of the wary animals upon the open plains or rocky barrens is often a difficult matter. A common way of working, when several hunters are together, is for some to take up positions in concealment, while the others drive the deer their way, causing them to pass within range of the deadly shafts. At a moderate distance an Eskimo with his ingeniously constructed bow can drive an arrow its full length into a deer.

Occasionally vast herds of deer, numbering many thousands, are met with, and at such times their numbers appear to give them confidence. The hunter then has no trouble in approaching them, but may go up and kill as many as he desires, either with bow and arrow or with spear.

The spear, however, is chiefly used for killing deer in the water. At certain seasons of the year, when travelling north or south, the deer cross streams, rivers, or lakes in great numbers, and these crossings are commonly effected year after year in the same place. The hunter, knowing their habits, lies in wait at the crossings, and often from his kyack spears large numbers as they are swimming past.

When more deer are killed than are required for immediate use, the carcases are "cached," that is, they are covered over by piles of stones to preserve them from the wolves and foxes, and the place of their burial is marked, so that during the next winter and spring, if food becomes scarce, these meat stores may be resorted to. When required, the meat thus stored is often quite blue or decomposed, but it has to be pretty bad when a hungry Eskimo will not eat it.

Seal hunting is a most curious and interesting form of sport. The seals are hunted in entirely different ways at different times of the year.

During the entire winter season they keep holes open through the shore ice, but because of the depth of snow are not seen until the warm spring sun exposes their hiding places. The Eskimo hunter has, however, a way of finding them out before this. He harnesses a dog that has been trained for the work, and, armed with his seal harpoon, leads him out to the snow-covered field, where the two walk in a zig-zag course, until the sagacious animal catches the scent of the seal and takes his master straight to its secret abode.

Here, under the hard crusted snow, it has formed for itself quite a commodious dwelling, but, unlike the Eskimo snow-house, its doorway opens into the water instead of into the air. This doorway, which is in the form of a round hole, just large enough to admit the seal, is kept from freezing up by the wary animal, which ever keeps itself in readiness, upon the slightest suspicion of danger, to plunge into it.

Usually upon the arrival of the hunter, the seal, if at home, hearing the footsteps above, quickly vacates the premises. The Eskimo then, taking advantage of its absence, ascertains the exact locality of the hole in the ice, by thrusting his long slender spear down through the snow. When the exact position of the hole is found, its centre is marked by erecting a little pinnacle of snow directly above it.

This done, a long and tedious wait follows, during which time the patient hunter often suffers much from the cold, for he is obliged to remain quite still, not uncommonly from early morning until evening. In order to keep the feet from freezing, while thus remaining for hours upon the snow, a deer-skin bag is commonly used to stand in.

During the interval of the seal's absence from home the doorway becomes frozen over, and it is on account of this fact that the hunter is made aware of its return, for when the seal comes back to its hole and finds it crusted over, it at once commences to blow upon the ice to melt it. This is the hunter's long-desired signal, and the moment he hears it he places the point of his harpoon at the mark on the snow, and thrusts the weapon vertically down into the hole, almost invariably with deadly effect. The seal, thus harpooned in the head, is instantly killed, and is then hauled out by the line attached to the spear.

Some seasons, when the ice is covered by a great depth of snow, the dogs are not able to scent the seals' houses, and then the Eskimo has to depend upon other sources for food, or else go on short rations.

In the spring, as the snow disappears, the seals' winter quarters are demolished, and they themselves are exposed to view. Then the Eskimo is obliged to resort to other methods of getting at them. When one is observed, the direction of the wind is first noted, then the hunter, keeping himself to leeward of the seal, walks to within about a quarter of a mile of it; but beyond this he begins to crouch, and advances only when the seal's head is down. The seal is one of the most wide-awake of all animals, and has the habit of throwing up its head quickly every few seconds to guard against danger. When its head is down upon the ice, its eyes are shut, and it is said that in these brief intervals it takes its sleep. However this may be, the hunter, by carefully watching the seal's movements, is able, without much difficulty, to get within about two hundred yards of it, but at closer quarters he is obliged to pursue other tactics. He now lies down at full length upon the ice, and here the real sport begins.

The seal takes the Eskimo, who is able to *talk seal* perfectly, to be one of its kinsmen; and indeed there is a great deal of resemblance between the genera, for both are similarly clothed, and the Eskimo, living largely upon the flesh and oil of the seal, is similarly odorous. As the two lie there upon the ice, a most amusing sort of conversation is kept up between them. Seal makes a remark and flips his tail. Eskimo replies in a similar manner, making the gesture with his foot, and at the same time throws himself a little forward. Seal soon has something further to say, and again flips his tail. Eskimo replies as before, and closes up slightly farther the distance between them.

When the seal's head is down, the hunter, who ever keeps his eye on his prey, is able to approach still nearer by dragging himself forward upon his elbows. This manœuvring goes on for some time, until the distance between the performers has been reduced to a few yards, or sometimes to a very few feet.

When near enough to make a sure shot, the Eskimo

takes his bow and arrow from his side and sends a swift shaft through the head of his outwitted companion. Sometimes, instead of the bow and arrow, a harpoon is used with equal effect.

I knew an Eskimo who was so expert at this kind of sport that he was able to catch seals with his teeth.

In order to secure one by shooting it, as just described, it is necessary to kill it instantly, for if only shot through the body, or even through the heart, it will throw itself into its hole and thus be lost.

During the season of open water still another method of seal-hunting has to be adopted. There is now no ice to perform upon, so the kyack has to take its place, and in this light craft the Eskimo pursues his prey in the open sea, or in the channels of water among the ice.

The weapon now used is not the bow, but a specially designed style of harpoon, which may be thrown long distances from the hand. The bow and arrow are useless, because of the difficulty of instantly killing the seal by a shaft aimed from a kyack. This harpoon is a light form of spear, having an adjustable ivory head to which is attached a long plaited sinew line. This line is wound on the handle of the harpoon, and attached to the end of it is a small float.

When a seal makes its appearance within twenty or thirty yards of the hunter the harpoon, thus arranged, is thrown, and if the seal is struck, the ivory head, which becomes buried in the flesh, is detached from the shank, and as the seal plunges about, or dives, the line is quickly unwound from the floating handle.

Unless killed outright, the seal quickly disappears with line and float; but as it can remain under water only a few minutes at a time, it must soon reappear, and as it again nears the surface, the little float comes to the top and shows the hunter where to prepare for the next charge. Thus the poor wounded animal's chances of escape are small.

Perhaps the most exciting and dangerous sport of the Eskimo is that of hunting the walrus.

This animal, sometimes called the sea-horse, is large, powerful, and often vicious. It is considered valuable both as food and for the supply of ivory which its immense tusks yield. The walrus is hunted chiefly from the kyack, either in open water, in the neighborhood of sandy shores, or about the edge of floating ice, upon which it delights to lie and bask in the sunshine.

A special equipment is required for this kind of hunting. It comprises, besides the kyack and paddle, a large harpoon, a heavy line and box in which to coil it, a large inflated seal-skin float, and a long lance. This walrus harpoon is an ingeniously devised weapon, consisting of an ivory shank fitted to a block of the same material by a ball and socket joint. These are stiffly hinged together by stout seal-skin thongs, and the block is then permanently attached to a wooden handle about four feet in length. The ivory shank, which is about fifteen inches long, is slightly curved, and tapers to a rounded point at the end remote from the handle. To this point is again fitted an ivory head, about four inches long, let into which is an iron or steel blade. Through the centre of the ivory head a heavy line is passed and strongly looped. Then, the shank and head being in position, the line is drawn tightly, and fastened to the wooden handle by an ivory pin and socket catch.

1. Walrus Harpoon; 2. Walrus Lance; 3. Seal Harpoon; 4. Seal Spear; 5. Bird Spear; 6. Small Seal Harpoon.

The remaining portion of the line is neatly coiled, and is provided at the end with a small loop.

The line used is that made from the skin of the square-flipper seal, as already described, and may be two or three hundred feet in length, though sometimes not so long. The line box is simply a small round parchment-covered frame, about the size of the lid of a cheese-box, and is fastened to the top of the kyack, behind the paddler.

The seal-skin float is a peculiar-looking object, consisting of the entire skin of a seal, removed from the carcass, as before described, without cutting it. The hair is removed from the pelt, which is then dressed as black parchment. The natural opening at the mouth of the skin sack is provided with an ivory nozzle and plug. By blowing into the nozzle the skin is inflated, and may be kept in that condition by inserting the plug. At the tail-end of the float is an ivory cross-head, to which the loop at the end of the harpoon line may be readily attached.

The lance completes the walrus hunter's equipment. This instrument is formed of a long iron or ivory bar having a steel blade point. The bar is fitted to a wooden handle by a ball-and-socket joint, and stiffly hinged with thongs as in the case of the harpoon. The object of the joint is to prevent the lance from being broken when thrust into a walrus, as otherwise it would be, by the animal plunging about.

Equipped as above, the Eskimo hunters go out during the season of open water in pursuit of walruses, which, feeding upon clams, are usually found about sandy shores or islands. Single animals are sometimes found, but more commonly they are in small herds. When feeding they remain in about the same place, but can stay under water for only about three minutes at a time. They come to the surface to breathe, sport about for a short time, then go down to the bottom and dig clams from the sand for some three minutes, and then rise again to the surface. The Eskimo, taking advantage of their necessity, advances on them only when they are busily occupied at the bottom of the sea. When a walrus reappears at the surface, the hunter, who, with harpoon in hand and line attached to float, awaits its return, hurls his harpoon with great force and precision, burying it deeply in the walrus's flesh.

The wounded monster, maddened by pain, plunges into the water, dives to the bottom, and endeavors to escape. The plunging readily causes the ball-and-socket joint of the harpoon to give, and this allows the head of the harpoon, which is buried in the animal, to become detached and form a button on the end of the harpoon line.

The detached handle floats upon the water, but the line is securely fastened to the body of the walrus, which, in trying to escape, takes with him the line and attached inflated seal-skin; but though he may take this buoy under, and keep it down for a short time, he cannot do so long.

Soon it reappears at the surface, and the hunter seeing it, makes for the spot, and awaits the returning walrus. The moment his head appears, harpoon or lance are hurled at it as before, and unless with fatal results, the same manœuvres are repeated. In this way often two or three harpoon lines and floats are attached to one walrus, but when so hampered it is considered well secured, and is finally despatched by the long keen lance.

When, however, the attack is made in the neighborhood of heavy ice, as it frequently is, the hunt is much less likely to result successfully. Because of the floating crystal, the hunter often finds it difficult to follow the movements of his game, and even if successful in this and in placing a harpoon or two, he is often defeated in the end by the line being torn from the float, which has become fast in the broken ice. Thus once freed, the wounded animal usually makes good his escape.

Occasionally these walrus contests result disastrously to the hunter, for the sea-horse is by no means a passive, harmless creature, submitting without resistance to the attacks of its enemies. Frequently one—or a number of them together—will make a charge upon the assailants, attacking them viciously with their huge tusks, which, if brought in contact with an Eskimo, are likely to make a sorry-looking object of him. Of course, through long experience and practice in the chase, the Eskimo hunters become very expert in dodging and foiling a charge, but sometimes they are caught and roughly handled by these uncouth monsters of the sea.

Upon one occasion an old hunter whom I knew, named Coto, met with a bad accident while hunting walruses in his kyack. A number of them charged upon him suddenly, and being unable to get out of their way quickly enough, his frail craft was broken and torn to shreds, and his body was frightfully bruised and lacerated. The poor fellow recovered, however, but only after months of sore suffering.

For a short time during the autumn season the sea-horse is hunted without the assistance of the kyack. The new ice being thin, the walruses break up through it at any place, and sport about in the water-holes which they make. Then the hunters—for several of them usually go together—march out upon the ice and attack them from the edge of the water-holes. This method of hunting is, however, rather dangerous, as the animals have an ugly habit of noting the position of their assailants, then disappearing below the water, and in a moment presenting themselves below the ice at the spot where the men stand.

The Eskimos, who are familiar with this manœuvre, always change their position the moment one of the crafty brutes goes down, and stand, harpoons in hand, ready to receive him when he returns crashing through the ice with deadly designs upon his craftier adversaries.

It is an easier matter to harpoon a walrus thus in the ice than it is to secure him, for here the "oweta" or float cannot be used to advantage, and it is no easy matter to hold a three thousand pounder of the sea. However, this is attempted, and when one or more harpoons are made fast to the walrus the ends of the lines are spiked down to the ice by stout spikes, and in this way the brute is very powerfully anchored; but, as I have before stated, in spite of all that can be done, he often breaks away and takes the lines with him into the deep.

Polar bear hunting is an extremely dangerous and exciting sport. An Eskimo rarely ever cares to tackle a bear single-handed, but two men, armed with lances, do not hesitate to attack this monarch of the north.

The method adopted in hunting a polar is as follows: Two men, armed only with lances, approach it from opposite sides at the same time. Then, as they close upon it, and the bear charges either man, the other rushes forward with his lance. Thus they let out its life-blood. It requires cool heads and steady nerves to be able to cope successfully with a polar in this way, but both of these characteristics the Eskimos possess in a marked degree, and it is comparatively seldom that accidents happen while thus engaged.

These bears, which live almost entirely upon seals, are usually found near the sea-shore, and often out some distance, swimming in the water, where they can live for a considerable length of time. The Eskimos attack them here as well as upon the land, but in the water they are treacherous enemies to deal with, as they are expert swimmers and divers. They are very liable to surprise one by suddenly disappearing and reappearing at embarrassingly close quarters.

The Eskimo custom in bear-hunting is, that whoever first sees a bear is the owner of the carcase, no matter who kills it, but the skin is divided up among the several hunters.

A bear-skin is so heavy that the Eskimo has no special object in preserving it whole, but he finds the greatest use for it when it is cut up into small pieces. In this condition it is commonly used by hunters as mats, which they tie under them when crawling over the ice after seals, or across the wet plains after deer. The pieces of bear-skin act as skates, upon which they can easily drag themselves along.

The Eskimo method of hunting birds is chiefly with a

spear of somewhat peculiar design. It is in all about five feet long, and consists of a wooden handle terminated at one end by a slender barbed ivory or iron rod, sharply pointed. About half way up the handle, three pointed barbed ivory fingers are securely fastened. The handle is then fitted into a wooden socket, which is held in the hand, and from which the spear is thrown. It is claimed that by means of the wooden socket the spear can be thrown with greater precision than by the bare hand, to which it would adhere more or less. However that may be, an Eskimo can hurl his bird-spear a marvellously long distance, and with deadly effect.

If the point of the spear misses the bird, one of the side fingers is almost sure to pierce it, or catch it between the fingers and the spear handle.

In this way, ptarmigan, ducks, and other land and sea fowls are obtained in considerable numbers. They are usually speared while sitting in flocks upon the snow or in the water, but they are also frequently killed in this way when on the wing. Sometimes the bow and arrow is used for bringing down the feathered game, but the spear is the instrument chiefly employed.

Fish are caught both by spearing and with the hook. The latter is of the crudest design, and is used in trolling. A troll consists of a heavy iron hook, fastened to the face of a small ivory disk, to which is attached a fine, strong line, made from plaited deer-skin sinews.

Fish are not, however, caught so much with the hook as they are by the spear. Indeed, it is chiefly by means of the harpoon and spear that the Eskimo larder is supplied. The fish-spear is a kind of three-pronged barbed fork, fastened to a handle. It is used chiefly for spearing fish through the ice, and with good results if in the hands of an expert.

I tried fish spearing in the north, but lacked the patience necessary for success. Many times, however, I purchased from the Eskimos the magnificent trout and white-fish by which their efforts were rewarded.

The way in which they spear is this: First, the most favorable spot of the lake or river is selected, and then a hole cut through the ice. With some kind of a bait, which they lower into the water by means of a string, they endeavor to attract the fish to the hole; when they appear they are thrust through by the spear and hauled out upon the ice. Great numbers of beautiful fish are caught by the Eskimos in this way during the fall and winter seasons.

Trapping is not extensively followed, unless it is by the Eskimos living within reach of the Hudson's Bay Company's posts, perhaps because of the inefficiency of the native traps, but also owing to the comparatively slight value to the Eskimos of the animals which may be caught. For instance, the wolf is an animal little sought for, because his flesh is not considered good food, and his skin is no better for clothing than the skin of the deer, which is much more easily procured. So also with the fox. Both wolves and foxes are, however, caught to some extent by "dead fall" traps, built of stones, or of snow, and so arranged that when the animal enters the trap and touches the bait, a heavy stone is caused to fall and kill or imprison him.

The Eskimo, or "Ennit," as he calls himself, being of a jovial, merry disposition, has various forms of amusement. A common one among the men is that of competing with each other in throwing the harpoon at a mark on the snow. With such practice they become powerful and expert throwers.

A rather amusing incident happened in this connection at one time during my Eskimo experiences. I, too, had been diligently exercising myself in the art of harpoon throwing, and one day, having become somewhat expert, was thus amusing myself when a party of natives came along. One of their number, doubtless supposing me to be a novice, stood up at what he thought a safe distance, and cried, "*Attay me-loo-e-uk took*" (Go ahead, throw). Promptly accepting the challenge, I hurled my harpoon, which made so straight for the astonished man's breast that he did not know which way to jump, and barely got out of the way in time to save himself. As the shaft passed him and went crashing through a flour barrel behind where he had stood, his companions had a great laugh at his expense.

Another source of much amusement is the game of foot-ball, which they play with the bladder of a walrus. Their game is played neither according to Rugby nor Association rules, but wholly without rule or system. Men and women, old and young, join in the chase after the ball, with equal delight. "Here a woman, carrying her child on her back, may be seen running at full speed after the ball, and the next moment lying at full length with her naked child floundering in the snow, a few feet beyond her. A minute later, the child is in its place, and the mother, nearly choking with laughter, is seen elbowing her way after the ball again."

A popular kind of indoor sport, played much during

the long days of winter, is a game something like our old game of cup and ball. It is played with a block of ivory, cut so as to somewhat resemble the form of a bear, which it is supposed to be. The ivory is drilled full of holes in a regular and systematic way, and to the neck of the block an ivory pin four or five inches in

ESKIMO GAMES AND TOYS.

length is attached by means of a sinew cord about a foot long. To prevent twisting of this cord, a little ivory swivel is inserted in the middle of it, and the game is played by swinging up the ivory block and catching it upon the pin. The various holes in the block count differently, so that there is really a good deal of skill in the game.

Running and wrestling are sometimes indulged in, though not often continued with interest.

The children play among themselves much as they do in the civilized south. Their favorite amusement is that of playing house, at which they may be seen busily engaged almost any pleasant summer day about an Eskimo village. The play-houses consist simply of rings of stones, and for dolls the Eskimo children are content with pretty pebbles or chips of wood or ivory. The actors, with their families, go visiting from one house to another, and have their imaginary feasts and all the rest just as our children have.

At Cape Prince of Wales, Hudson Straits, the Eskimos have been observed to play at a game of tilting. For this sport a very large igloe is built, having a great pillar in the centre of it. Ivory rings are hung from the roof, and the players, armed with spears, walk rapidly round the pillar, and vie with each other in catching the rings on their spears.

The people are not noted for being musical, though they have some songs.

The home or family circle is, as a rule, a happy one. It is not broken up by the brawling sot, nor is it often the scene of poverty and want—never is this the case while the rest of the community have plenty. All families share alike in times of famine, and in seasons of plenty all rejoice together. Thus there is no such thing as class distinction among them, but all are upon an equal footing; every man provides for the wants of his own family by hunting. They have therefore no need for workmen's unions, nor for protective associations, but all live together in peace and unity.

Of course, I am here speaking in a general way, for I have already spoken of the occasional fights which take place.

The Eskimo marriage is an exceedingly simple institution, and is not performed in any ceremonious way. It is purely a love union, requiring only the sanction of the parents of the bride. When a young man and young woman come to the conclusion that they were made for each other, and desire to become one, having the consent of the girl's parents they simply take each other and start up an igloe of their own. Eskimo brides are usually very young, and often very bonnie creatures. They lose much of their beauty, however, in early life, and at about forty mature into ugly old dames.

An Eskimo family rarely consists of more than three children, and these, in turn, for about two years are carried in the hood upon their mother's back. During this time they have no clothing apart from their mother's. New-born infants are licked by their mother's tongue, and are sometimes kept in a rabbit-skin or bag of feathers for a time before being carried upon the mother's back.

It is usual for a man to have only one wife, though it is not uncommon for him to have two, or even three, if he can provide for them. The first Eskimo encountered on our recent visit to the north, as I have related, had two wives, each having three children. As a rule the men are faithful to their wives, although sometimes they trade with each other for a few weeks or months, and afterwards receive again their first loves.

If any member of the family is seriously ill, a peculiar kind of prayer is repeated over the afflicted one by the

father or mother of the family. The prayer—for it can
hardly be called anything else—is loaded with super-
stition. The parent prepares for the ceremony by
placing a "poalo," or mit, upon the left hand. Then,
bending over the afflicted one, he or she mutters, wails
and gesticulates in the strangest manner, also blowing
with the mouth and motioning the departure of the evil
spirit. This kind of audible supplication is often carried
on for a considerable length of time.

The Eskimo, like almost every other people under the
sun, possesses some form of worship, and believes in a
spirit world. He believes in the existence somewhere of
good and evil spirits, which govern and control this
world. The Great Good Spirit (*Cood-la-pom-e-o*), they
believe, dwells in an upper world, of which the sky is
the floor; but the evil spirits, governed by their chief,
"Tornarsuk," dwell in a world beneath ours, which forms
a kind of great roof over the world below. The earth
and this under-world are connected with each other by
certain mountain clefts, and by various entrances from
the sea. The spirits of those who meet with violent
deaths go to dwell with *Cood-la-pom-e-o*, in the upper
world; but for those who die from other causes there
is a place prepared below in the land of plenty, with the
evil spirits.

These latter deities are supposed to have the greater
power of the two upon earth, and consequently their
favor is sought, and to them supplication is usually made,
though over certain forces, events and circumstances
the Great Good Spirit is supposed to have control. For
example, he is believed to be the deity governing the
frosts, so that in the fall of the year, when the ice is

insufficiently strong for hunting purposes, his favor is invoked.

Communication with the spirits is usually held through wizards or "angokokes," who are looked upon as wise men by the people, and are appointed to fulfil this function. They are ordained for their sacred calling when youths, and as a distinguishing mark of their profession wear upon their backs a string of ornaments, mostly made of seal or deer-skin. These are given them at the various places visited by them in recognition of their office. The angokokes are appointed because of their qualifications. There may be a number of them in the same community, but some rise to much greater distinction than others.

These wizards are said to be taught from youth by one of the deputy chief friends, named "Tornat," and some of them are supposed to have great power with the spirits.

At times, when the people are threatened with famine, or are in distress of any kind, the angokoke is requested to intercede for them. Supposing it is food that is wanted, he arranges for an interview with Tornarsuk, the chief of the devils. In order to do this, the angokoke, accompanied by one other man, goes down to the water's edge in the early morning at the hour of low tide. Here his companion binds him in a doubled-up position, so that his knees meet his face, and lashes him up with stout thongs so tightly that he is unable to move hand or foot. In this helpless condition his companion leaves him, with his walrus harpoon lying by his side and the rising waters lapping at his feet. What immediately follows only the angokoke knows, but I have been informed by the wizards themselves— and it is fully believed by the Eskimo people—that the devil comes to his rescue and releases him from his bonds, but at the same time seizes the harpoon found on the ground and thrusts it through the angokoke's breast. The point projecting through his coat behind, and blood trickling down in front, the excited wizard rushes up from the shore to the village, trailing behind him the harpoon line. He bursts into the first igloe in a frenzied condition, snorting and blowing like a walrus. As he enters all sharp tools are quickly put out of sight, so that the angokoke may not harm himself with them, and at the same time water is sprinkled on his feet. This done he bounds out of the igloe, and as he does so the occupants seize the harpoon line trailing behind, but are not able to hold him, for he is as strong as a walrus.

The magician then enters the next igloe, where a like performance is repeated, and in the same manner the round of the village is made, but none is able to hold the excited man. Having completed the round of the dwellings in the village, he returns to the sea-shore, where it is said he is again met by Tornarsuk, who extracts the harpoon from his breast and assures him that the prayers of the people shall be heard, and that plenty of walruses shall be sent to satisfy their hunger.

Whether or not Tornarsuk is as good as his word I can only conjecture, but the poor Eskimo pagans have great faith in the intercessory powers of their angokoke.

Intercession is sometimes made to the Good Spirit, and as before, the angokoke acts as intercessor; but instead of going to the shore, he is bound in an igloe and left there by his people. While still in this bound condition he is said to ascend through the roof of the igloe, and to meet and hold communication with *Cood-la-pom-e-o*, and having arranged matters with him he returns to earth, re-enters the igloe through the door, and reports the result of this interview.

The following are some of the laws of the Eskimos:

"1. No man shall after sunset do any work requiring the use of tools. The women may sew, make garments, or chew boots." (Thus the hours of ach day after sunset form the Eskimo's Sabbath.)

"2. No person shall eat walrus and deer meat on the same day.

"3. The carcases of all large animals slain during the winter season shall be equally divided among all members of the community.

"4. All kinds of rare game are common property during all seasons.

"5. Any person finding drift-wood secures ownership by placing stones upon it.

"6. Any other kind of goods found remains the property of the original owner.

"7. When a seal is harpooned and gets off with the harpoon, the first harpooner loses all claim to it when the float becomes detached.

"8. If two hunters strike a bird at the same time, it shall be equally divided between them.

"9. Whoever is first to see a bear has first ownership, no matter who slays it.

"10. After slaying a bear, the man who kills it shall hang up his hunting implements, together with the bladder of the beast, in some high conspicuous place, for at least three days, and for four days shall be separated from his wife.

"11. When a walrus is slain, the successful hunter shall be separated from his wife for at least one day.

"12. The borrower of tools shall not be bound to give compensation for damages.

"13. No person shall '*muckchucto*' (sew) while any member of the family is ill.

"14. If any man from any cause whatsoever slays his neighbor, the wife and family of the deceased shall become the family of the slayer, and shall be taken care of by him as if they were his own."

One Eskimo legend regarding the origin of the people has already been related. Another of special interest, regarding the occurrence of a flood, runs something like this: A very long time ago there was a great rain, which was so terrible that it flooded the earth and destroyed all people, with the exception of a few Eskimos who constructed a raft by lashing together a number of kyacks and took refuge upon it. Upon this raft they drifted for a long time, until they were much reduced by cold and starvation. Then at length in their distress their angokoke stood up and cast his harpoon and all their ornaments into the flood of waters. This act sufficed to appease the angry spirits, and the flood subsided.

This legend is particularly interesting since it adds one to the large number of similar legends belonging to other savage tribes and nations.

Another romantic Eskimo legend explains the origin of the sun and moon.

As a rule the aged and feeble members of the Eskimo community are treated with respect and kindness, but during times of distress and famine they are often forgotten in the general struggle for existence. For

CUSTOMS OF THE ESKIMOS. 171

instance, when the supply of food at any particular place becomes exhausted, and through starvation the people are forced to go elsewhere in search of the necessaries of life, the aged or feeble, or those who have become too weak to travel, are left behind to perish. If, however, food is soon found, a portion is at once taken back, and after all, what more could be done, even by white people?

When an Eskimo at home in the igloe, his body is never taken away burial by carrying it out through the doorway, but an opening must be made in the rear for its removal. The place chosen for the burial of the dead is some almost isolated point of land, a hilltop difficult of access, or some remote island where there is the least danger of the bodies being disturbed by wild beasts.

The deceased are first wrapped in their skin robes, then laid to rest and covered over with piles of stones.

At times these graves are made very large, while in other cases the bodies are barely covered over. Usually some kind of a memorial is raised over the grave: frequently a long stone, but more often a topick pole or paddle, to the top of which a flag or streamer is fixed to mark the last lonely resting-place of the departed.

Beside the lonely grave are placed the hunting implements of its occupant, and there, upon the dreary waste, imprisoned in his rocky tomb beneath the snows of many a winter storm, the poor Eskimo lies awaiting the sound of the last trumpet.

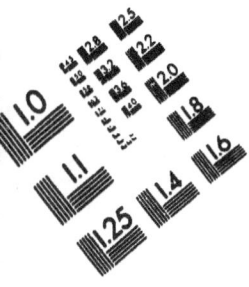
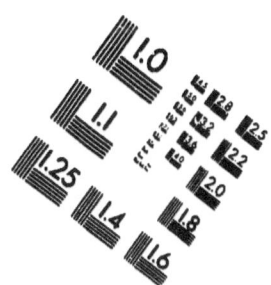

**IMAGE EVALUATION
TEST TARGET (MT-3)**

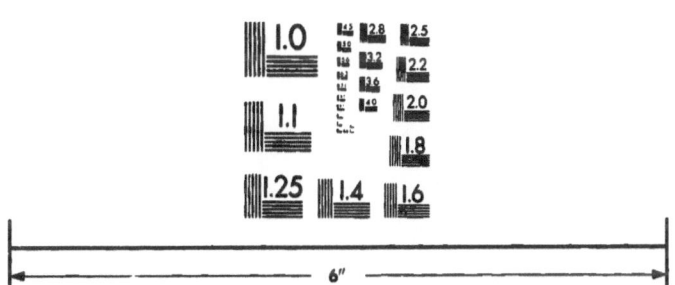

← 6" →

Photographic
Sciences
Corporation

23 WEST MAIN STREET
WEBSTER, N.Y. 14580
(716) 872-4503

CHAPTER XII.

DOWN TO THE SEA.

BAKER LAKE, about seventy miles in length and perhaps half that in breadth, was originally discovered and rudely mapped by one Captain Christopher, about the year 1770. In searching for the North-West Passage he sailed into it with two small vessels from Hudson Bay, passing *en route* through Chesterfield Inlet and the two rivers flowing into it from Baker Lake. Having with us a copy of Captain Christopher's map, though of a very sketchy character, it afforded us some information as to our future course.

Since leaving the shores of Black Lake we had traversed to this point a distance of just eight hundred and ten miles, through an entirely unknown country. We had occupied more time in doing so than we had expected, on account of the extraordinary character of the weather, but, however, on this evening of the 2nd of September we found ourselves at the mouth of "the great river flowing to the northward," as described by the Black Lake Indians.

From our astronomical observations and survey it was found that the extremity of the lake as determined by Christopher, and as located on the existing maps of Canada, was nine miles too far south and about fifty miles too far west. At the mouth of the river the water was found to be shallow—in some places not more than three or four feet in depth—and for some distance out into the lake shoals were observed. Small sailing vessels or York boats would, however, have no difficulty in getting in, but it would be difficult to take the former any great distance up the river on account of the rapids. Large properly constructed river boats might be taken up stream without difficulty for a distance of 150 miles to the confluence of the west branch, and how far they might be able to ascend that large stream it is impossible for me to say. With the exception of perhaps one spot—the canyon rapid north of Tobaunt Lake—I believe the whole river from the Height of Land to Baker Lake might be navigated by river or York boats with comparative ease. At the rapid a portage could be made or possibly a navigable channel might be discovered.

I think it important to mention the above possibilities of access to this country, on account of the fact that from Tobaunt Lake to Baker Lake there stretches an extended area of promising mineral-bearing Huronian schists and trappean rocks, a series precisely similar to the silver, copper and gold bearing rocks of the north shore of Lake Superior and Lake of the Woods districts. The time must come—it may not be far distant—when the prospector and the miner will occupy all this vast field of mineral wealth.*

From the head of Baker Lake we were now to com-

---

* For full geological and mineralogical details regarding this district, see J. B. Tyrrell's report for 1893, published by the Geological Survey Department of Canada.

mence a new stage of the journey. The rough maps we
had enabled us to form a fair idea of what lay ahead.
From our camp to the mouth of Chesterfield Inlet on the
coast of Hudson Bay measured about 250 miles, and
thence down the coast of the Bay to Fort Churchill, a
Hudson's Bay Company's post and the nearest habitation
of white men, measured 500 more; so that 750 miles
was the least distance we had to figure on travelling
in canoes before the close of navigation.

It was now the month of September, and as winter is
known to set in in the vicinity of Hudson Bay during
October, my brother and I felt that our time must be
employed to the very best advantage. The weather had
been extremely adverse all summer, but it was now
liable to be more so. Within the course of two or three
weeks the equinoctial gales might be expected. The
tides also would be a new feature of difficulty.

In consideration of these prospects, and in order to
stimulate the men to greater exertions, it was thought
best to explain our position to them, for up to this time
they had little idea as to where they were, whether in
the vicinity of the North Pole or within a few days'
travel of civilization. The effect produced by thus informing the canoemen was as desired. They resolved
as one man to make longer days and put forth greater
exertion.

Before daylight on the morning of the 3rd, camp was
aroused by the sound of many voices, and a few minutes
later, before we had turned out from our blankets, the
door of the tent was pulled half open and two or three
black burly heads with grinning faces were poked in.
They were those of some of our friends from the Eskimo

village who had come over to pay us an early morning call, before we should finally leave their shores. They all held in their hands nicknacks of one kind or another which they were anxious to trade, chiefly for needles, and some would have come in and made themselves at home had I not dismissed them until we were dressed and ready to do business at a little greater distance from our blankets, which we were desirous should be inhabited only by ourselves. Later, a few fishing-lines, spoons and such trifles were purchased.

As soon as possible, the wind happily being fair, our canoes were loaded, and with many "tabowetings" to the natives and a hurrah for Baker Lake, we started out to the eastward along the north shore. But soon the wind grew strong and caused such a high sea to run that we were forced to seek shelter, which we found in the mouth of a small river. We had then made fourteen miles. Here we waited, hoping that toward evening the wind might moderate, but on the contrary it grew worse, so on the lee-side of a bluff point camp was pitched to afford us shelter from the cold piercing blast. A high wind continued all night and during the following day, when it was accompanied by snow and sleet. The temperature was so low that the fresh-water ponds were frozen over. Such a condition of climate, together with a small and rapidly diminishing stock of provisions, made us chafe at the delay; but on the morning of the 5th we were enabled to launch, and during the day made a good run of about forty miles. The shore of the lake consisted chiefly of Laurentian rock, from 150 to 300 feet in height, but at some places broad low flats a id long points of sand and boulders separated the hills from the water.

During the afternoon of the 6th, the northerly of the two rivers discharging the waters of Baker Lake was discovered. The approach to it is well marked on the north bank by a round bluff some two hundred feet in height. At first no current could be observed in the river, which, in reality, was a deep narrow fiord, but when we had advanced a distance of about two miles a stiff current, almost approaching a rapid, was met; but instead of moving with us, as would naturally be expected, it was flowing to the westward. At first sight it caused some doubts as to whether we were on the right road. The canoemen were all persuaded that we were ascending some big river and would have at once turned back, but concluding that we had already reached tide water, though sooner than we had expected, we pulled on, and before long witnessed the seemingly strange phenomenon of a river changing its direction of flow.

So smooth and bare were its glaciated shores that we had some difficulty in effecting a landing. One night was spent on this rocky bank, and the day following being fair and bright, saw us on the waters of Chesterfield Inlet. The magnetic compasses were now found to work very unsatisfactorily, but for one day the sunlight enabled me to make liberal use of my solar instrument. During the next and several succeeding days the weather was dark and gloomy, and we encountered such tide rips in the Inlet that my survey was much interfered with.

On the 10th of September, as we were pulling down

the Inlet under a strong side wind, through extremely rough water, we were glad to find about noon a sheltered cove on the north side of a large island near the south shore. Here we landed to await an improvement in the weather. While the cooks were preparing our mid-day meal, my brother and I set out for the summit of the island, a mile or more to the south, for the purpose of taking observations. In due time the breezy elevation was reached. While sighting to a prominent point to the southward, there suddenly appeared from behind it what seemed a phantom ship. For a moment I gazed upon it in amazement, but then realizing that the appearance was a real, not an imaginary one, I called my brother's attention to it.

The object, which was several miles distant, was clearly made out to be a two-masted sail-boat, and it was heading to the westward. By whom could it be manned? We could not imagine, but there it was, with two square sails set to the wind and tearing up the inlet. By the aid of our field-glasses we could make out many moving figures on the boat, but as to whether they were whalers, Hudson's Bay Company's traders from Churchill, or who else, we could not conceive. If, however, they were to be more to us than a vision it was necessary to bestir ourselves, for they were rapidly passing. From my pocket I drew an immense red handkerchief and waved it most energetically, while my brother discharged several shots from his revolver. We soon saw from the boat's movements that we were observed, but instead of coming in towards us they only bore away more to the southward. Still I vigorously waved the red handkerchief, and finally, much to our delight, the sails flapped loosely in the wind, then in a moment were refilled by the strong breeze and the boat swept in toward us.

The appearance of a sail-boat in Chesterfield Inlet, and especially at this late season of the year, puzzled us much, and as it drew nearer we watched it intently. It had the appearance of being a large whale-boat, and was evidently well manned, but by whom we could not tell. Whoever they might be, perhaps they could be hired to take us down the coast of the Bay to Churchill, and if so we might be saved weeks of hard travel on a very exposed and dangerous coast. We sincerely hoped that the strange mariners, or at least their boat, might be available for the voyage. When they had approached sufficiently near we could see that there were Eskimos on board, and a moment later their anchor was cast out, and several of them, making a sort of raft out of three kyacks they had in tow, paddled in to the rocky shore where we stood. In vain did we look for the face of a white man. They were all natives, and as we gazed at each other in mutual amazement, I broke the silence with the question, "*Kudlsonah petehungetoo?*" (Is there no white man?) "*Petehungetoo*" (There is none), was the reply, so the whole party, which consisted of several families, men, women and children, were Eskimos, and with them in their boat they had their dogs and other necessary hunting and camping equipments. They informed us they were moving up into the interior from the coast to spend the winter, and so it was not surprising that nothing we could offer would induce them to consider the question of taking us down to Churchill or of selling their boat to us. We offered what to them would have been fabulous wealth, but to no purpose. There they were with all their belongings on their way to the westward, and westward they were determined to go.

The Eskimos in turn expressed surprise at finding two solitary white men upon such a lonely, barren island, and not unnaturally asked, "*Nowtimee ibbee kyette?*" (Where do you come from?) I replied, "*Uvagut kyette tellipea washigtooeloo townonee koog-du-ak*" (We come from the west very far, down a great river). We were then asked if we had seen any more of their people, and replied, "*Uvagut tacko-namee hipunga Enuit coonetookeloo manee tacko Enuit amasuit washigloo tellipea iglooanne attowsha sissell ungayo.*" (We have seen no other Eskimos near here, but saw plenty far to the westward beyond the first big lake). They informed us that another large boat-load of their people had gone up from the coast on the previous day, and were surprised that we had not seen them. Though we were not able to purchase or charter the boat from the natives, we obtained much valuable information and a sketch-map of the coast of the Bay from the mouth of the Inlet down to Fort Churchill. After a brief stay they returned to their boat and we to the rocky hills, upon the other side of which our party awaited our return. The wind still continued to blow too strongly to admit of travelling by canoe, so we went back again and spent the rest of the day on the hills.

Next morning we were up early. The wind had fallen somewhat and the canoes were soon launched. We managed to travel until after eleven o'clock, when, because of the high wind and rough water, we were again obliged to make for the shore, and in order to do so had to pull through a heavy surf breaking over the low sandy beach. During the afternoon at this point observations for longitude were obtained, and close by upon a prominent hill a large cairn of rocks was erected to mark the spot for the benefit of future explorers.

The two following days were marked by rough weather and little progress, but finally we reached the mouth of the great Inlet through which for several days we had been paddling.

For having completed another stage of the journey we were exceedingly glad, but coupled with this fact there was another, viz., that before us was a five-hundred-mile voyage to be made in open canoes down an exposed sea-coast. Here we would be surrounded by entirely new conditions and confronted with new difficulties.

HALF-BREED BOY.

CHAPTER XIII.

ADVENTURES BY LAND AND SEA.

STARTING southward down the coast of Hudson Bay on the 13th of September, with the weather beautifully calm, we made a capital run past a rocky coast, skirted by a succession of shoals and reefs, and at night camped upon the shore about twelve miles north of Marble Island, whose snow-white hills of quartzite could be distinctly seen on the horizon.

Marble Island—so called because of the resemblance its rounded glaciated rocky hills bear to white marble—is well-known as a wintering station for New England whalers. Its geographical position was determined in 1885 and 1886 by Commander Gordon, of the Dominion Government Hudson Bay Expedition, of which the writer was a member, so we were glad to avail ourselves of the opportunity of connecting our survey with so well-fixed a landmark.

We had been informed by the Eskimos that there were no whalers now at the island, and we satisfied ourselves of the truth of their report by the use of our long-range binoculars. Had there been we would have endeavored to arrange with one of them to take us down to Churchill, but in their absence we could only stick to the canoes. Near camp, on the shore, we found part of the skeleton of an immense whale, but unfortunately not the part that is of commercial value. This doubtless had been carried away by the Eskimos or by some whaling crew.

During the following day the weather continued fair, and feeling that nature was favoring us we made good use of our time. As we followed the coast in a southwesterly direction the outline of Marble Island could be seen against the southern sky; while to the north extended the bold, dark coast-line of rock, unbroken in appearance excepting where here and there lay great banks of snow.

About noon we discovered, on landing, what must very recently have been a large Eskimo encampment. Several kometics (sleds) and other articles were found. The wreck of a large whale-boat lay on the shore, and several dogs were seen lurking about. This camping-place was the summer home of the Eskimos we had met sailing up Chesterfield Inlet, and from a sanitary point of view was no credit to them, for filth and putrefaction everywhere abounded.

The rocks of this locality were of an interesting character, being dark green hornblendic schists of the Huronian formation.

Following these two days of exceptionally fair weather we enjoyed still another, and were permitted to traverse the mouth of Rankin Inlet, which would have required two or three days to coast had the weather been anything but calm. During these three days we had made a distance of just one hundred miles, which, upon such an exposed coast, we considered good progress.

Though we saw little game we still had some dried

meat left, and at this rate of travel two weeks would take us to Churchill. By carefully rationing ourselves we had meat enough to last for five or six days, and the balance of the time could, if necessary, be spent without provisions.

On the night of the 15th, however, being camped upon a little sand island in the mouth of Corbet's Inlet, our hopes were blighted by the approach of a gale, and all the next day we lay imprisoned upon the sand-bar without any fresh water to drink. Toward evening the wind was accompanied by a chilling rain, which continued all night and the greater part of the next morning. On the following afternoon the wind suddenly fell, and though a heavy sea continued to roll in from the east, the waves ceased to break.

Fearing to lose one hour when it was possible to travel, we launched our canoes upon the heaving bosom of the deep and started across the mouth of the inlet on an eight-mile traverse. As we passed out beyond the shelter of the island we found the seas running fearfully high, but so long as they did not break upon us we had little to fear, and this would not likely occur unless the wind should spring up again; but when we were well out in the middle of the inlet that is just what did occur. The wind began to rise from exactly the opposite quarter, and speedily increased in force, whipping the crests off the waves in such a way as to make things appear anything but reassuring. Our situation was indeed perilous. Every effort was made to guide the canoes so as to brook least danger, but in spite of all we could do the seas dashed in upon us, and it looked as if we would never reach the shore.

My brother and I laid down our paddles, and with tin kettles applied ourselves vigorously to bailing out the water. Many times the great tumbling billows seemed as if they would surely roll over us, but our light cedars, though sometimes half-filled with water, were borne up on the crest of the waves. At length we neared the rocky shore toward which for several hours we had been struggling, but, to our dismay, only to find it skirted by a long line of rocks and shoals, upon which the full fury of the wild sea was breaking. What were we to do? Without a harbor we would be dashed to pieces upon the rocks—and it was impossible to retreat against the storm. On we were borne by the force of the gale, but, thanks to a kind Providence, just as the crisis appeared to have come, a way of escape was discerned. One rock could be seen standing out in advance of the others, and behind this we managed with a supreme effort to guide the canoes. Then in shallow water, with the force of the seas broken, we all sprang out, and with great exertion succeeded in landing the boats in safety.

The country here was entirely barren and rocky, comparatively level, and of a most dreary aspect, without a sign of vegetation. The storm continued for two days longer, during which time we were obliged to remain on shore. As our provisions were now about exhausted, attention was chiefly devoted to hunting, but all that could be found was a small duck and two gulls. The broken remains of an Eskimo kyack were found upon the shore, and these were carefully gathered up so that a kettle of water might be boiled and our gulls cooked for supper.

On the morning of the 20th, the wind having fallen, camp was called at four o'clock and without breakfast our journey resumed. Later in the day each man had a small piece of dried meat, quite insufficient to satisfy his appetite; but, hungry though we were, the motto plainly written on every man's face was, "Speed the paddle." Thus we pressed on for two days, making good progress, but having scarcely anything to eat the work began to tell on us.

On the 22nd we were again storm-bound by a heavy gale with snow, which lasted four days. During this time we suffered considerably from the violence of the storm as well as from want of food. As soon as it had abated sufficiently, which was not until the morning of the 25th, two of the men, Pierre and Louis, were sent out with the shot-guns to hunt for food, and with our rifles my brother and I set out for an all-day tramp into the interior. We found our camp was situated near the end of a long narrow point at the back of which was Neville Bay. The point consisted in places of extended fields of water-washed boulders, and in order to reach the mainland we had to cross these. The necessity of doing this, together with the fact that we were walking with weakened limbs into the teeth of a gale, made travelling extremely difficult.

Shortly after leaving camp a hare jumped out from among the rocks, and coming to a fatal stand, was perforated by a slug from my "Marlin." Not wishing to carry it all day, it was left with Pierre and Louis to be taken to camp. By three o'clock, after a long and laborious march and securing nothing but a solitary ptarmigan, my brother and I reached the bottom of the bay and there discovered the mouth of a large river which flowed into it. We would gladly have stayed some time in this vicinity, but as the day was already far spent, and we were pretty well used up, we dare not. Finding a little dry moss we made a fire, roasted and ate the ptarmigan, and then started back to camp. In some localities the fresh snow was deep and soft, and this added greatly to the fatigue of the trip. But before we had proceeded far we met with encouragement in the discovery of deer-tracks. They were a day or so old, for they were frozen, but they led away nearly in the direction of camp, so we eagerly followed them, and from every hill-top keenly scanned the country.

The shades of evening were gathering and we were tired and hungry. Nothing could we see of the deer, and fearing to lie out all night without blankets in the rough, cold weather, we pushed on towards camp as fast as our weary limbs would carry us. We were frequently obliged to sit down to rest, and consequently when still several miles from camp we found ourselves enveloped in darkness and groping our way laboriously through a field of boulders. For a considerable distance we had to feel the way with hands and feet, between and over the rocks. After about two hours of this sort of experience we gained the more level country, and shortly afterwards, guided by the light of a candle in one of the tents, we reached camp thoroughly used up. We were not, however, obliged to go to bed hungry, for Pierre and Louis, having been more successful than ourselves, had secured several ptarmigan and rabbits. From these a *bouillon* had been prepared, and part of it saved for our supper. It was a most thoroughly appreciated meal, and after partaking of it we were soon rolled up in our blankets, all unconscious of the storm that howled without or of the fact that we had not another meal in camp. On the morning of the 26th we were glad to find that the wind had fallen sufficiently to allow us to launch. Without delay the canoes were loaded and a fair run made. Several sea-ducks were shot during the day, and thus supper was secured.

The next day, again storm-bound by a gale from the south-west, the whole party started out to hunt for food. We were not altogether unsuccessful, assembling in the evening with five marmots (little animals about the size of squirrels).

The following morning, though a strong breeze was blowing, we determined to make a start, for to remain where we were meant that we must soon starve to death. We were already much reduced and weakened from the effects of cold and hunger, and the condition of the weather had of late been most disheartening. Churchill, the nearest habitation of man, was still fully three hundred miles distant. We had not one bite of food. The country was covered with snow, the climate piercingly cold. No fuel was to be had, and worst of all, the weather was such, the greater part of the time, that we were unable to travel. It was difficult to be cheerful under such circumstances, but we kept up courage and pushed on.

While we were bending to our paddles, after making perhaps seven or eight miles south-westerly along the coast, a band of deer was seen upon the shore. Our course was quickly altered and a landing effected, though with some difficulty, as the tide was falling and the water rapidly receding. The men were left to keep the canoes afloat while my brother and I, with our rifles, went in pursuit of the deer, which were at this time much more difficult to hunt than earlier in the season, when they run in great herds. The country here was a vast and dreary plain, affording no cover for the hunter save that of a few scattered boulders. Concealed by some of these we crept for long distances, but finding it impossible to get within any kind of medium range, we opened fire at a distance of four or five hundred yards. At first the deer trotted about in confusion, but soon locating their enemies they fled straight away across the plains. For several hours we followed, vainly seeking for opportunity of nearer approach, but being unsuccessful, retraced our weary steps to the shore, where we arrived faint and exhausted. We found the men had been unable to keep the canoes afloat because of the ebbing tide. They were now high and dry, and the water of the Bay barely visible in the distance—such was the extremely low and flat character of the coast.

BLACKFOOT BOY.

CHAPTER XIV.

POLAR BEARS.

As it was impossible to launch until the return of the tide, Pierre and Louis were given our rifles and sent off to try their fortunes. As they departed and left us lying in the shelter of a rock we sincerely wished them success. We had done our utmost and had failed; if they also should fail it was too apparent what must soon be the result. Two of the other men were sent off with shot-guns; then anxious hours of waiting followed. No shots were heard, but towards evening Pierre and Louis, and afterwards the other men, could be seen returning in the distance. None of them appeared to be bringing any game, as we had hoped they might, and at the sight I confess my heart grew sick. As they came nearer, however, Louis, holding up something in his hand, exclaimed, "I got him." It was the claw of a polar bear, and we soon learned with joy that, sure enough, he had killed a bear, which he had unexpectedly come upon at the edge of a lake while following the deer.

The encounter had taken place about six miles inland, and Louis was alone at the time, his brother having gone off on a diverging track. The meeting was a mutual surprise, for the bear, which was lying on the snow near the ice, being very white himself, was unobserved until the hunter's approaching footsteps aroused him. There was then a distance of not more than fifty yards between them, and no time for consideration.

The bear, springing to his feet, made straight for Louis, who met his charge with a slug and brought him to his knees. He was up in an instant, though, and followed the Indian, who had taken to the ice, thinking that in a conflict he would there have the advantage. But in this he found he was mistaken. The bear was quickly overtaking him, being at home on the ice, so he turned and with a second shot again, knocked the animal down.

As Louis made for the shore the bear regained his feet, and with blood streaming from his wounds, and a roar of fury, made one more desperate charge. He was now within a few feet of Louis. The intrepid hunter, realizing his situation as critical, turned quickly and by a well-aimed shot laid his savage pursuer dead at his feet.

It was a most fortunate shot for our whole party, as well as for the Indian, who, being unable to handle the carcase himself, had returned for assistance, meeting his brother by the way. We all gladly followed him to the scene of the combat, where, judging from the tracks and blood, there was abundant proof of the veracity of his story.

On a hill near the carcase some dry moss was discovered, and with this, even before the skinning had been completed, some of the flesh was toasted and greedily devoured. The reviving effect produced upon the spirits of our party was marked. Though the flesh

of the polar bear is famed for its rankness, we would
not have exchanged it at that time for its weight in
silver.

The carcase was found to be extremely poor, the only
food found in the stomach being the droppings of reindeer. At the first meeting, therefore, Louis must have
been considered a very desirable prize. It was merely a
question of which should eat up the other in order to
prolong existence. Fortunately for our party the Indian
proved to be the fittest survivor. No part of the carcase
was wasted, but every scrap, amounting to between
three and four hundred pounds, including the hide, was
placed in bags and carried to the canoes, which we
reached with much difficulty long after dark.

Next morning a strong east wind, driving a wild surf
in upon the shore, made it impossible to launch, but we
were thankful during the delay to have a supply of
meat on hand with which to satisfy the cravings of
hunger. Advantage was also taken of the opportunity
afforded for obtaining moss. Though five or six miles
distant, a quantity of this fuel was gathered, and several
large kettles of meat boiled—almost sufficient, it was
hoped, to take us to Churchill. But alas for our hopes!
The gale which had arisen increased in fury until it
became a terrific storm, accompanied by sleet and snow.
This continued for five long days.

One night the tent occupied by my brother and I was
ripped up the back by the force of the gale, and with
difficulty kept from being carried away. So piercingly
cold was the wind that without shelter we must soon
have perished. We were already numb with cold, but
in the midst of snow and darkness I managed to find in

my bag a sail needle and some twine, and then having lowered the tent to the ground while my brother held it, I stitched up the rent. When the tent was again raised our bedding was buried in snow, but the blankets being our only comfort, the drifts were shaken off, and in a half-perished condition we again crept beneath them.

Besides the discomforts occasioned by the storm at this camp, I suffered a serious experience of poisoning. Our cook, thinking to give my brother and me a treat, provided for our dinner a dish of fried liver. Perhaps because of its rank flavor, my brother partook sparingly and so partially escaped, but I ate of it freely and at once became fearfully ill. For a whole day I lay in the tent, retching and straining, though throwing off nothing but froth, until I thought I should have died. My brother urged me to take some brandy, a little of which still remained in a flask we had brought with us, but for some time I declined. Towards evening, however, finding that I would have to take something or give up the ghost, I yielded to his advice, and soon began to recover. I have since learned that polar bear's liver is considered to be poisonous, both by the Eskimos and by the north-sea whalers.

While on the subject of bears, it may be of interest to relate here a rather exciting personal experience I once had, which took place several years before on the barren ice-bound shores of Hudson Straits.

We were a small detachment of explorers, travelling at the time in the little steam launch of a scientific expedition, and occupied in the geographical determination of a group of hitherto unknown islands. The *personnel* of our party, without giving full names, was as follows: The Doctor, who occupied a position in the stern of the boat and acted as steersman; Mac., who, contrary to orders, had smuggled a small rifle on board and come with us for sport; Con., an able seaman from Newfoundland, and myself.

The reason for orders having been given by our commander to take no rifles with us was doubtless that we might not allow sport to interfere with the object of our commission. Besides Mac.'s single-shot rifle, I had in my belt a 38-calibre S. & W. revolver, and these two arms, a knife and an axe constituted our defences; but no special thought was given to these things as at six o'clock on that summer morning, in the shadow of the Arctics, our little expedition steamed away on its mission, following and mapping the various points and bays of the rocky shore, and giving all attention to our work as we ploughed through the cold blue waters.

Before we had proceeded many miles it became necessary to go ashore in order to obtain fresh water for the boiler of the launch. Accordingly, observing what appeared to be a little cascade falling over broken cliffs into the sea, our course was shaped towards it; but before we could gain the shore our purpose was for the time forgotten, because of the sudden appearance, only a few yards ahead, of two polar bears—a large one and her cub—swimming in the water.

Mac. and I quickly took our position in the bow and opened hostilities, but on account of the roughness of the sea and the tossing of the boat the shots were ineffective, and so far as the old bear was concerned an opportunity was not afforded for repeating them. Quick as a flash she disappeared, leaving her fleecy cub paddling about on the surface.

Though the engine of our boat had been stopped, the momentum carried us on rapidly past the little swimmer, which was about the size of a half-grown sheep. As we passed, Con. seized master bruin and endeavored to land him on board, but in this he, perhaps fortunately, failed, and was prevented from pursuing his ambition by the sudden appearance from the deep of the enraged mother, who, with a roar, made a plunge for the stern of the boat, where the doctor was seated, and seized the gunwale in what were afterwards described as her "devilish-looking jaws."

To say that this sudden turn of events was a surprise to us all but feebly describes the expressions depicted upon the faces of our party. With the other occupants and the engines between us and the bear, Mac. and I were unable to fire a shot. Con. came to the rescue, and with several desperate thrusts of the iron-pointed gaff he persuaded the bear to release her hold, when with the engine again running, a separation was effected, but not before we had learned an interesting lesson regarding the habits of the polar bear.

As a matter of discretion, the lesson of experience, the boat was now kept at a safe distance from the bears. Several shots were fired, one or two slight wounds being inflicted on the mother, but as fast as the little one could travel, though no faster, they maintained a steady course for the nearest point of land. Apparently nothing would induce the mother bear to forsake her little one, and though wounded herself, her whole anxiety seemed to be for her offspring. Sometimes she

would swim a short distance in advance, but only to
return in a moment, as if to urge on the little creature
to greater exertion.

The shore was soon gained by the swimmers, who then
beat a rapid retreat up the rocky cliffs and disappeared
among the distant hills. As they fled, the exhibition of
motherly affection shown by the old bear was very
remarkable and pleasing. She would never allow the
cub to be separated more than a few feet from her,
and would govern her own pace to suit that of her
"bairn."

As the bears made good their escape, self-reproach and
disappointment filled our souls, and more than one emphasized denunciation was heaped upon our commander's
head because we had been prevented from having our
rifles with us.

After a few moments of bitter reflection as to what
"might have been," our thoughts reverted to surveying
and the obtaining of fresh water, but before thought
could be followed by action, strange to say, two other
large bears were sighted ahead. They were near the
shore, and not very far from the foot of the falls for
which we had been steering.

A brief consultation was held, and it was decided to
advance cautiously upon the game. Mac. with his rifle
and but a half-dozen remaining cartridges, again took
his position in the bow of the boat, but prompted by
recent experience I remained at the stern with my revolver, while Con. stood amidships armed with the gaff.
The bears, observing us, landed upon a high point of
broken cliffs close by, and as they did so, Mac. gave them
a couple of slugs, which evidently took effect, but caused

them no particular inconvenience. A moment later they were lost to sight among the rocks. Resolved upon preventing their escape if we possibly could, Mac. and Con.—the latter armed with the axe—were allowed to go ashore and head off the retreat, while we in the boat skirted along the shore where the bears might be most likely to take to the water. Our land party had no sooner reached the summit of the first ridge of rock than "bang" went Mac.'s rifle, and a moment later, as he crammed in another cartridge, there appeared over the ridge, not more than five yards from his feet, the blood-bespattered heads of the two furies.

It was a critical moment for our two sportsmen, and one of breathless suspense for those of us who looked on. Con. stood with uplifted axe ready to strike as Mac., again levelling, fired into the face of the foremost bear, now almost at his feet, and sent a slug boring through his head. To ordinary bears this would have been received as sufficient intimation to drop dead, but it seemed only to "rattle" this polar, so that instead of proceeding to demolish Mac. and Con., he plunged over the steep cliff into the sea and there terminated his career.

The other bear, seeing the fate of his comrade, retreated and took to the water, and as he did so, leaving a trail of blood upon the rocks, Mac. sent his last slug after him. He and Con. then, descending to the shore, came on board, and with us gave chase to the wounded animal, who was swimming off at a rapid pace. Our launch, however, soon overtook him, and as we passed I gave him a volley from my revolver, which appeared to have little more effect than to increase his rage.

"Con. stood with uplifted axe . . . as Mac. . . . fired into the face of the foremost bear." —p. 196.

As I was about to fire again he disappeared, and a moment later reappeared at the side of the boat, threw one paw over the gunwale, and with open blood-thirsty jaws, made a lunge for my leg. Fortunately for me his reach was a little too short, and the result was he got the worst of the scuffle. Putting my revolver up to the side of his head, I gave him the contents of the five chambers before he could retire. These shots, however, did not penetrate the skull, and beyond causing a withdrawal, only had t⁣ fect of further enraging him.

Hostilities having been commenced at close quarters, we continued the fight until I had fired my last cartridge and bruin's scalp was riddled with lead. But the wounded fury still swam powerfully, and with ammunition now exhausted it appeared as if we would not be able to complete the task we had undertaken. For a short time we watched his movements, and observing that he seemed inclined to go ashore, we decided upon a new plan of action. Steaming away around the point we beached the boat, and armed with axe, ice-gaff and knife, we climbed the farther side of the cliff, and there concealed ourselves in such a position that we were able to watch the enemy's movements.

We had not long to wait, for, thinking himself unobserved, he swam ashore at the foot of the bluff and hid among the broken rocks. Feeling that our opportunity had now arrived, we descended stealthily from ledge to ledge and from rock to rock, taking care that we should not be scented or observed. Step by step we drew nearer, until close to the foot of the cliff, and almost at our feet, we came upon the wounded bear. He was much out of humor, and feeling sore enough from his many wounds, but before he had time to demonstrate his displeasure, Mac. had thrust the gaff through his skull, Con. had cleft his head with the axe, and my knife had spilled his heart's blood upon the rocks.

In the animal world the polar bear is admittedly the monarch of the north. He is the bear of bears, being described by all Arctic travellers as possessing enormous strength and great voracity. Of the score of polars whose more or less intimate acquaintance I have had occasion to make, I have seen at least two whose tracks in the snow measured fifteen by eighteen inches, whose length measured over nine feet, and whose slain carcases tipped the steelyard at from fifteen to sixteen hundred pounds.

Consequently I have always had great respect for the sentiments expressed in the following lines by an author whose name I regret being unable to recall:—

> "Of the black bear you need not be afraid,
> But killing white ones is a dangerous trade.
> In this be cool, and well direct your lead,
> And take your aim at either heart or head;
> For struck elsewhere, your piece not level'd true,
> Not long you'll live your erring hand to rue."

CHAPTER XV.

LIFE OR DEATH?

AFTER the great five days' storm, which lasted until the 4th of October, the whole country was buried in snow, and every possibility of finding even a little moss for fuel was excluded. Winter indeed had overtaken us. Ice was forming all along the shore of the Bay, and it was evident that within a very few days travel by canoe must be at an end.

On the above date, though light snow continued to fall, the wind had gone down sufficiently to admit of launching the canoes after a long portage out to meet the tide. In spite of the most vigorous exertion, all we were able to make during the day was ten miles, and that through a chilling spray which froze upon us and encased canoes and men in an armor of ice. We had great difficulty in getting ashore at night, having again to portage a long distance over the low-tide boulder flats.

On the following morning the water of the Bay was out of sight, and it was not until about noon, when the tide flowed in, that we were able to float the canoes. We were so obstructed by the new ice and a strong head-wind, that we were not able to make more than a mile or two before being again forced to struggle to the shore. At this rate we would be a long time in reaching Churchill. We had now been more than three weeks on the coast, and were still at least two hundred and fifty miles from our haven.

Some different mode of travel must be adopted or we should never get in. The shore ice was forming rapidly and might now block us at any time. We had not more than enough meat for another day or two, and the game had all left the country. What was to be done? My brother and I talked the matter over during the night. The plan suggested itself of abandoning everything but rifles and blankets, and starting down the shore on foot. But then, how could the numerous large rivers, which were still open, be crossed? Again, to this plan there was the objection that having been in canoes all summer, our party, though still strong enough to paddle, was in very poor condition to walk. The only other feasible plan was then suggested. It was to abandon dunnage, instruments, rock collection, etc., everything except note-books, photographs, plant collection, rifles, blankets, and two small tents, and with these to start out in only two light canoes, and with the increased force in them to travel for our lives.

This plan was decided on, and in the morning the men were set to work to cache all our stuff excepting the articles above mentioned. This occupied the whole morning, and to us it was a sad and lonely task, but as it seemed to be the only way by which we might hope to escape from this dreary ice-bound coast, it was felt to be a necessary one. As secure a cache as we could build was made, and then with heavy hearts we turned our steps toward the shore.

After launching the two canoes it was with great danger and difficulty we were able to force a way through the broken but heavy shore-ice to the open water beyond. Having once gotten clear, we were able to make good progress, and even at great risk of being smashed upon some of the many rocks, we paddled far into the night; but at a late hour, being sheathed in ice from the freezing spray, we landed, and, without supper, lay down to sleep upon the snow.

Eight more dreary days passed, six of which were spent in battling with the elements and two in lying storm-stayed in our tents. During this interval our party suffered much from cold and lack of food, and to make matters worse, dysentery attacked us, and it appeared as if one of our men would die.

The ice had been all the while forming, rendering it more and more difficult to launch or get ashore. Our frail crafts were being badly battered, and often were broken through by the ice, and the low character of the coast had not improved. Still with hollow cheeks and enfeebled strength we struggled on, sometimes making fair progress and at others very little, until on October the 14th, as we advanced, the ice became so heavy, and extended so far out to sea, that in order to clear it we had to go quite out of sight of land.

Towards evening we began to look about for some opportunity of going ashore, but nothing could be seen before us but a vast field of ice with occasional protruding boulders. We pushed on, hoping to find some bluff point or channel of water by which we might reach the shore, but the appearance of things did not change in the slightest. We stood up in the canoes or climbed upon boulders, vainly hoping to at least get a glimpse of the land. Of course, we knew the direction in which the shore lay, but it was so low, and we were so far out, that it was beyond our view.

Soon the shades of night began to fall about us, our canoes were leaking badly and the weather was bitterly cold. Failing to reach the shore, we resolved to wait for high tide, about ten o'clock, hoping we might with it do better. The tide came, but left us still in the same condition, no more able to penetrate the ice or gain the shore than before. It had become intensely dark, and we were in great danger of being smashed on the ice or rocks. We were utterly helpless and could do nothing but remain where we were, or go where the tide chose to carry us, until the return of daylight.

The hours of that night were the longest I have ever experienced, and the odds seemed to be against us surviving until morning; but at last the day returned and found us still alive. My brother was nearly frozen, having been obliged to sit or lie in icy water all night. Poor little Michel had both of his feet frozen, and the rest of us were badly used up. Still we were in the same position as on the night before. We could not hold out much longer; we must gain the shore or perish. At the time of high tide, the ice being somewhat loosened, our canoes were thrust into the pack, and by great exertion as well as much care we succeeded about one o'clock in reaching solid ice, upon which we were able to land and, for the last time, haul out our noble little crafts. We had been in them just thirty hours, battling with the ice, exposed to a chilling winter blast, our clothing saturated and frozen, and our bodies faint and numb with starvation and cold. But we were now within reach of the land, and all of us who were able gladly scrambled out upon the ice to stretch our cramped and stiffened limbs. My brother was in a perishing condition from the exposure of the night. He had been barely able to keep his canoe afloat by bailing, and had sat in the icy water for seventeen hours. I wrapped him up as warmly as I could and administered half a bottle of Jamaica ginger, the last of our stock. We then set about hauling the canoes over the ice to the shore, which we soon reached, and where we were so fortunate as to find drift-wood. A fire was quickly made, camp pitched, and better still, a meal prepared. On the previous day a seal, the only one secured on the trip, had been shot, and we were now in a position to appreciate it. The three western men were still fairly strong, but the remaining five of us were very weak and badly used up. We knew now, however, that we could be no great distance from Churchill, for we had again reached the wooded country, and two or three miles back from the shore could be seen dark clumps of spruce trees. This was a most consoling fact, for besides having meat for several days, we felt that we would have shelter and fire.

As to launching our canoes again, that was entirely out of the question. If we would reach Churchill at all it must be by land.

As most of us were unable to walk, the only course open appeared to be to send on some of the stronger men to, if possible, reach the fort and bring back a relief party. This plan was proposed, and two of the western men, "Jim" and John, volunteered to undertake the walk. We thought the distance could not be more than fifty miles, and it might be considerably less. On the morning of the 16th the two men set out on their journey, while those of us remaining proceeded to move our tents back from the shore about two miles to the nearest woods, where we might make ourselves more comfortable, to await the success or failure of the relief party.

A sheltered spot was selected for camp, in a thick grove of spruce trees, and after clearing away about two feet of snow which covered the ground, tents were pitched, then well carpeted with spruce boughs, and a big camp-fire made. This was indeed a happy change from lying in canoes in the ice-pack. Clothing and blankets were now dried, and with the seal meat, and some ptarmigan which we shot in the grove, we were soon comparatively comfortable, with the exception perhaps of poor Michel, who suffered much from his frozen feet.

The reviving effect of the camp-fire upon our numb and half-frozen bodies was soon felt, though with the exception of François, the western half-breed, all of us at the camp were still very weak. Our veteran Pierre, who had done such good service with the paddle, now staggered in his walk, and as we were moving the tents from the shore back to the woods, he fell from sheer exhaustion and had difficulty in regaining his feet. Now in camp, however, and with meat enough to last us for a day or two, we were in a position to take a rest from our labors. Poor Michel's feet were in a bad state, and having no proper means of treating them, they

caused us much anxiety. His brother Louis was also
in a wretched condition from the effects of severe
dysentery caused by exposure and starvation, and was
unable to walk.

On the morning of the 17th, feeling somewhat revived
after a long night's rest, I undertook to go hunting
ptarmigan, which we were glad to find were plentiful
in the woods about us. Had it not been for the fact
that our ammunition was almost exhausted, the occurrence of these birds in abundance would have afforded
us greater consolation, but being, as we were, reduced
to a dozen or two charges, the opportunity for living
on feathered game seemed limited to a short period.
We were hoping that Jim and John might be successful
in reaching Churchill. Before I had walked a hundred
yards from camp, I was forced to realize how weak I
had become, and after making a circuit of about half a
mile and shooting only two or three birds, I was
scarcely able to crawl back to the tent. On my return,
François, taking the shot-gun, went out and returned in
the evening with a fine bag of game.

On waking the next morning, my brother amused us
by relating an extraordinary dream, in which he imagined
he was luxuriating in good things, and particularly sweet
currant cakes, for which he was exhibiting a wonderful
capacity. But alas! with the visions of the night the
cakes had vanished, and for breakfast he was forced to
be content with unseasoned boiled ptarmigan.

At about one o'clock in the day, as we were seated
within the tent partaking of our second meal, we were
suddenly startled by hearing the exclamation, "Hullo,
Jim!" The eagerness with which we scrambled over

dinner and dishes to the tent-door can better be imagined than described, and on looking out, sure enough there was Jim returning. Was he alone? No, thank the Lord! Behind him, a moment later, emerged from the woods a number of men, followed by teams of dogs and sleds. One after the other there came scampering along no less than four teams, hauling long empty sleds capable of furnishing accommodation for our whole outfit.

After a hard two days' tramp, Jim and John had reached the Fort, where they had found kind friends ready to send us prompt assistance. Dog teams had been placed at their disposal, provisions supplied, and early on the morning of the same day on which they had found us, the train had set out for our relief. With light sleds they had travelled at a rapid pace over the thirty miles of snowy plains which separated us from Churchill. Another day of good travel in the canoes would have taken us in, had this been afforded us.

As the relief party drew up at our camp, Jim advanced and handed letters to my brother and myself expressing kind wishes and sympathy from Mr. and Mrs. Lofthouse, the Church of England missionary and his wife at the Fort, whose friendship I had the privilege of making on two former visits to Churchill. Along with the letters was handed a box, which when opened was found to contain the very good things of my brother's dream, even to the sweet currant cakes. Staple provisions were also produced, and it is scarcely necessary to say that they were joyfully welcomed. It would be impossible to describe our feelings upon this occasion, the termination of so many hardships and sufferings.

During the afternoon preparations were made for the journey to the Fort on the following day. The canoes were hauled up from the shore, where we had been obliged to leave them, and loaded upon two of the dog-sleds. Camp outfit and provisions were loaded upon the others, and as far as possible everything was put in readiness for an early start in the morning.

A change in the weather was already forecast, the wind shifting around to the south, and towards evening it became decidedly milder. During the night a rain set in, and between it and the warm wind a wonderful change was wrought before dawn. It began to look very much as if the fates were against us, and that now with the sleds and dog-teams we should have no snow to travel on. But before daylight camp was astir, and finding that enough yet remained, breakfast was partaken of by the light of the camp-fire and at the first streaks of dawn the journey on sleds to Churchill was begun.

Out of the woods there was comparatively little of the snow left. Under cover of the trees it was still deep, but too soft and heavy for the teams, so we kept along on the open plains between the woods and the shore, and made fair progress.

The arrangement of our party was as follows: As guide an Indian named James Westaseccot led the way some distance ahead of the train. Next after him came a team of six big Eskimo dogs hitched two and two abreast to a long sled carrying the big canoe, in which Michel was given a passage. Following this team was another hauling the smaller canoe, in which I was rolled

up in my blankets. The third team consisted of only
four dogs and, in a carryall, hauled my brother and some
of the baggage; and at the rear of the train trotted
another full team of six dogs with Louis, the sick
Iroquois, and the camp outfit. The rest of our men
walked behind or beside the various sleds, resting themselves by jumping on when the travelling was easy, as
it often was when crossing level plains or frozen ponds
—of which latter there were very many.

The day was beautifully bright and pleasant for one
travelling as I was, but for the drivers and dogs it was
much too warm for comfort. In many places the higher
ground was bare, and progress consequently slow.

About noon a halt was made for lunch, and during
this time the opinion was expressed by the drivers that
we would not be able to reach the Fort until the next
day; but upon being promised that if they would take
us in without having to spend another night in camp
they should have whatever remained of the supplies
they had brought us, they were induced to change their
minds, and acting upon the new inspiration we were
soon again on our way. In many places the low flat
plains we traversed were overgrown by clumps of swamp
willow, and around these many large flocks of ptarmigan were seen. About three o'clock in the afternoon we
reached Grassy Island, at the bottom of Button's Bay,
and two hours later gained the base of a long range of
rocky hills. We skirted the foot of these for some time,
until we reached a low place in the ridge, where, dis-
mounting to lighten the loads, we turned up the steep
pass, and after a short climb to the crest found ourselves within full view of Fort Churchill. It was not

LIFE OR DEATH? 209

an imposing place, but even though consisting of only four or five old frame buildings, the sight to us was one of deep satisfaction. For a moment we paused on the summit of the ridge, then at the crack of the driver's whip the teams bounded forward, galloped down the steep slope, sped across the plains below, and in a few minutes landed us at the house of the Hudson's Bay Company's traders. Here, after extricating ourselves from the various conveyances, we were presently received by a tall young Scotchman, who announced himself as Mr. Matheson, Master of the Fort.

FRENCH-SALTEAUX GIRL.

CHAPTER XVI.

FORT CHURCHILL.

WITH our arrival at Fort Churchill, with its well-filled storehouses, the successful termination of the long journey seemed pretty well assured. Here was abundance of provisions to feed our small party for an indefinite length of time, so that we could either spend the winter at the post, and go south by canoes in the spring, or else remain long enough to recruit, and then continue the journey on foot.

Adjoining the Master's house, and ranged in two irregular, detached rows on the rocky bank of the Churchill River, were four or five old frame buildings, used as storehouses and servants' lodges. Two or three hundred yards down the shore was a neat little church and mission-house.

Drawn up on the beach near the church were several large open coast-boats, used during the summer by the Hudson's Bay Company in carrying on trade with the Eskimos, and beside these was a small landing and warehouse, while down at the mouth of the river, five miles distant, could be seen the ruins of old Fort Prince of Wales, once a massive cut-stone fortification.

The buildings of the traders were very old, some of them being in a half-wrecked condition, but those of the mission were new and trim, having been only recently erected by the Rev. Jos. Lofthouse, who, with his family, occupied the dwelling. In this ideal little home, from the hour of our arrival at the Fort, we were given a most hearty and hospitable welcome.

One of the first duties requiring attention, after arranging for rations and shelter, was the treatment of poor Michel's frozen feet, which upon examination were found to be in a shocking condition. Fortunately in a pocket medicine-case the proper remedies for treating him were found, and with attention and care his condition from the first began to improve, though it was evident that at best it would be many weeks, if not months, before he would again be able to walk.

Having arranged almost immediately upon our arrival at Churchill that we should proceed southward on foot as soon as the condition of the party (and that of the Churchill River, now running full of ice) would admit, we lost no time in getting into training for the tramp, which would amount to nearly one thousand miles. Daily walks were prescribed for all but Michel, and the stronger of the men were sent out to shoot ptarmigan, so that they might not only exercise their limbs, but, at the same time, supplement their daily rations, in which endeavors they were quite successful.

As regards my brother and myself, our short constitutionals almost invariably ended at the Mission House, where many pleasant hours were spent with Mr. and Mrs. Lofthouse and their little daughter Marjorie.

From the time of the establishment of the Churchill Mission—the history of which would of itself form an interesting chapter—to the time of our visit, Mr. and Mrs. Lofthouse had been devoting their lives to the noble work of teaching and helping the natives, both Indians and Eskimos, wherever they found them, and already the fruits of their labors were apparent.

Close to their home stood a neat substantial church, capable of seating three hundred people, and every nail

REV. JOSEPH LOFTHOUSE AND FAMILY.
Fort Churchill, Hudson Bay.

in the structure—which would be a credit to many a village in Ontario—was driven by the missionary's own hand. Part of the year, during the absence of the moving population of the district, such a seating capacity is unnecessarily great, but at other seasons, when the natives come in with the produce of the hunt, the little building is usually crowded.

Mr. Lofthouse preaches in the Cree, Chippewyan and Eskimo languages, and having won the esteem and affection of his people, he has a powerful influence over them, and is teaching them with much success. He and Mrs. Lofthouse together conduct a day-school for the benefit of the children of the permanent residents. These number twenty-one, and the total population of Churchill is only fifty-one. On visiting the school I was much pleased with the advancement of the children, even the smallest of whom could read from the Bible. The girls were being taught by Mrs. Lofthouse to do various kinds of needlework, and by way of encouragement were being supplied with materials.

At the trading station, besides Mr. Matheson, Capt. Hawes and his family were staying at the time, he in an unofficial capacity. He was shortly to succeed Mr. Matheson, who was to be removed to some other post. Although not so well acquainted with the Captain as with Mr. and Mrs. Lofthouse, his face was also a familiar one to me, as we had met at Churchill in former years, when he was master of the Hudson's Bay Company's ship, *Cam Owen*, since wrecked on the coast.

For nearly two hundred years it had been the practice of the Hudson's Bay Company to send out from England every year one or two small sailing vessels with supplies to their trading stations on Hudson Bay. Almost without exception these little crafts were able to make their passages successfully, deliver their cargo, and return to England with a wealth of furs, oil, and other goods obtained in trade from the natives.

Now this practice is all changed. Instead of the small sailing vessels, one large steamship is employed for the trade, and Churchill, possessing the only safe harbor on the west coast, is made the shipping port for the Bay, all goods being distributed from this centre by schooners to the other posts, and the furs here collected for shipment. Over this work of distributing and collecting goods the Captain was to have charge.

During the stay at Churchill every day brought noticeable improvement in the condition of our party. On several occasions, the weather being favorable, snowshoeing expeditions were formed and much enjoyed, though usually accompanied by great fatigue. Knowing, however, that by means of such travel we must return home in a short time, we realized the necessity of gaining strength for the long journey.

In the course of one of our outings we reached a place called Sloops Cove, about half way to Prince of Wales Fort, and there made some interesting observations. This cove owes its name to the fact that in the year 1741 the two sloops, *Furnace* and *Discovery*, sent out from England in command of Captain Middleton to search for the long-looked-for North-West Passage, spent the winter there. How two vessels could have been forced into this cove is a question which has given rise to much speculation on the part of Canadian scientists, for the cove does not now contain more than sufficient depth of water, at high tide, to float a small boat, and it is doubtful if even such a boat could get in through the rocky entrance. The historical fact remains, however, that this cove was the winter quarters of these two sloops, and as proof of the fact a number of ring-

FORT CHURCHILL.

bolts to which the vessels were secured may still be seen leaded into the smooth glaciated granite shores. Besides the ring-bolts, many interesting carvings are to be seen cut on the surface of the smooth rocks. Amongst them are the following:—"*Furnace* and *Discovery* 1741," "J. Horner 1746," "J. Morley 1748," "James Walker May ye 25 1753," "Guillford Long May ye 27 1753," "J. Wood 1757," "Sl. Hearne July ye 1 1767." In addition to many other names are several picture carvings, and notably one of a man suspended from a gallows, over which is the inscription, "John Kelley from the Isle of Wight." According to local tradition Mr. Kelley is said to have been hanged for the theft of a salt goose.

As yet during our stay at Churchill we had not been successful in reaching the ruins of old Fort Prince of Wales, but on the 3rd of November, the weather being cold and good for snowshoeing, we started off, and after an enjoyable five-mile tramp reached the memorable spot, now a scene of utter desolation. Not a tree or other sign of life could be seen on the long, low snow-driven point of rock, but there in all its solitary, massive grandeur stood the remains of what had more than one hundred years ago been a noble fortress.

The construction of this fortification—which appears to have been planned by the English engineer, Joseph Robson—was commenced in the year 1743 by the Hudson's Bay Company, which was then, as now, carrying on fur-trading business in northern Canada. So large and expensive a fortification was built probably not so much for the protection of the Company's interests as for the purpose of complying with a provision of its

Royal Charter, which required that the country should be fortified.

The building of the fort appears to have been carried on for many years under the direction of the famous Samuel Hearne, already referred to as having traversed the Barren Lands to the mouth of the Copper Mine River. In a stone barrack within the Fort, Hearne

RUINS OF FORT PRINCE OF WALES.

lived and carried on business for the Company for many years.

The fortress was in the form of a square, with sides three hundred feet long; at the corners were bastions, and on top of the massive stone walls, twenty feet in height by thirty feet in thickness at the base, were mounted forty-two guns. With such a defence one would suppose that Churchill should have been safe from attacking foes, but this does not seem to have been the case, for history informs us that on the 8th of August, 1782, the gallant La Perouse and his three vessels of war, with, it is said, naught but scurvy-smitten crews, made their appearance before the much-amazed garrison of thirty-nine men, and demanded an unconditional surrender, which was granted without resistance, and the gates of the great stone fort thrown open to the invaders. Taking possession, they spiked and dismounted the guns, in places broke down the walls, burned the barracks, and sailed away to France with Hearne, his men, and all their valuable furs.

As La Perouse left the Fort so did we find it. For the most part the walls were still solid, though from between their great blocks of granite the mortar was crumbling. The guns, spiked and dismounted, were still to be seen lying about on the ramparts and among the fallen masonry. In the bastions, all of which were still standing, were to be seen the remains of wells and magazines, and in the centre of the Fort stood the walls of the old building in which Hearne and his men had lived. The charred ends of roof-beams were still attached to its walls, where, undecayed, they had rested for the past one hundred and eleven years.

With a continuous low temperature, such as now existed at Churchill, the ice in the river, much to our satisfaction, began to set fast. This was necessary to enable us to continue the journey. On Saturday, November 4th, the thermometer registered $14\frac{1}{2}°$ below zero (Fahr.), and with that temperature the movement of floating ice ceased and the river was bridged from shore to shore. Being anxious to get away as early as possible, arrangements were made with the Company's agent for a start for York Factory on Monday morning. The assistance of one dog-team, with driver and guide, was with some difficulty secured, but three other teams were to accompany us a great part of the way, viz., to Stony River, where in the month of September the Company's servants had been obliged to

ICE-BLOCK GROUNDED AT LOW TIDE.

abandon a boatload of supplies because of severe weather, the month in which we had been canoeing on the coast five hundred miles farther north.

A bill of necessary supplies was prepared, and these were weighed out and put into sacks. Men and teams were sent off to obtain a supply of dogmeat—an indispensable commodity—from a shanty on the south side of the river. When they reached the place they found it in possession of five polar bears—three large ones and two cubs. Along with the dogmeat were brought back the skins of one old bear and the two cubs. During Sunday the thermometer fell to 21° below zero, making the river-ice strong and perfectly safe.

CHAPTER XVII.

ON SNOWSHOES AND DOG-SLEDS.

ON the morning of the 6th of November, after a stay of seventeen days at Fort Churchill, we were again ready to set out for the south. Our team consisted of six Eskimo dogs, attached tandem fashion to a sled twelve feet long and a foot and a half wide. This sled was of the regular Eskimo type, the runners being formed of sticks hewn down to the dimensions of about two inches by six inches, and slightly curved up in front.

Upon the sled was loaded about six hundred pounds of provisions, dog-meat, blankets and other dunnage, all securely lashed on within a canvas wrapper. The driver who had charge of the team was a tall young half-breed, named Arthur Omen. Our guide, whose name was "Jimmie" Westasecot, was a large fine-looking Cree Indian, of about middle age, who bore the distinction of being the most famous hunter and traveller in all that country.

The party consisted of ten. My brother and I were warmly dressed in deer-skin garbs of the Eskimo, while the rest of the party wore the white blanket suits of the traders, and with the exception of poor Michel, whose feet were still too sore to allow him to walk, each man was provided with a pair of snowshoes. As one dog-team was unable to draw all the freight, the men were obliged to haul their own dunnage, and for this purpose three flat sleds or toboggans were procured and loaded with sixty or seventy pounds each.

Thus provision was made for the transport of all necessary supplies, but what was to be done with Michel? Mr. Matheson kindly assisted us out of the difficulty by offering to take the crippled Indian on one of his sleds. Thus arrangements were completed, and, with nine days' provisions, we bade our kind friends farewell, and early on the morning of the date mentioned marched from the Fort in single file, forming into a long serpentine train, winding our way to the southward across the broad frozen river. As we departed farewell salutes were waved from the doorway of the little mission-house, and we felt that with them were wafted the most sincere and hearty good wishes.

At the outset, though we had greatly improved physically during the stay at Churchill, we were still far from being strong, and it was thought best not to attempt forced marches at the outset. The wisdom of this resolve was clearly proven before the first day's tramp was ended. That afternoon one of my knees gave out, and soon became so badly crippled that within an hour or so every step caused me excruciating pain, and it was with the greatest effort I managed to hobble along after the train until evening. We travelled about twenty-one miles during the day, on an easterly course, across open plains and snow-covered lakes. There was little timber on the route until we reached the Eastern

Woods, where it was decided to camp. Upon the open plains we found the snow hard and in good condition for travelling, so that the teams trotted along easily with their heavy loads.

Snowshoe travel was also comparatively easy for those whose legs were sound, but the moment we entered the woods down sank shoes and dogs into the soft, light snow. In soft snow it is necessary for the guide or track-breaker to wear very large shoes, that he may not sink too deeply, but those who follow in his trail get along with the more ordinary size.

The snowshoes used by Jimmie, the guide, were about five feet long and eighteen inches wide, whereas those used by the rest of us varied from three to three and a half feet in length and from ten to twelve inches in breadth. The guide's large shoes were made somewhat after the Montreal model, symmetrical on either side, framed of one stick and slightly bent up at the toe, but those used by the rest were of very different make, and more peculiar design. Though we purchased them from the Hudson's Bay Company at Churchill, they were made by the Chippewyan Indians. Their shoes are not made symmetrically, but are constructed with great bulges upon their outer sides, and are formed of two pieces of wood, tied together at both ends and held apart in the middle by cross-bars, while the toes are turned up with a sharp curve.

Having reached the shelter of the Eastern Woods, and concluded the first day's march, a camping-place was chosen. The drivers of the teams at once proceeded to unharness the dogs, make beds for them of spruce

boughs, and give them their daily meal of seal-blubber
or fish. The other members of the party busied themselves in clearing away the snow, cutting down brush
and firewood, and building the camp. This latter did
not consist of a tent, shanty, or indeed covering of any
kind, but simply of a wall of brush built crescent shaped,
to a height of three or four feet, and in such a position
as to best afford shelter from the cutting wind. The
two main elements of a good winter camp-ground are
shelter and dry wood, both of which are indispensable.

The snow was cleared away from the inside of the
wind-break, and in its stead spruce boughs were strewn
to a depth of several inches, and in front of this a big
fire kindled—and camp was complete.

These tasks ended, the preparation of supper was
commenced. Bacon and biscuits were hauled out, while
frying-pans and tea-kettles were brought and placed
with their contents upon the fire. Fresh water had
been found by cutting through the ice of a creek close
by, so nothing was lacking.

Tin plates and cups, knives and forks were provided,
but as we took hold of them they froze to our fingers,
and before we could use them they had to be heated.
After supper preparations were made for the night and
for the morrow's tramp. Socks, duffles and moccasins,
wet with perspiration from the day's march, were hung
up before the fire to dry; robes and blankets were
spread about the camp, and upon them our tired party
assembled to enjoy a rest and smoke beside the fire
before turning in for the night. Though cold, the night
was beautifully calm and clear, and when from time to

time the big dry sticks of wood were thrown upon the
fire, showers of sparks ascended until they found hiding-
places among the dark branches of the overhanging
spruce trees.

Camp-fire stories and gossip were indulged in for an
hour, then several logs were thrown upon the fire,
and each man, rolled up in his blanket and with feet
toward the fire, lay down to sleep. There was little
sleep for me, however, because of my knee, which gave
me great pain during the night.

The next morning camp was called at five o'clock, and
under the still star-lit sky all hands rolled out into the
keen frosty morning air. At the first streak of dawn,
after breakfast and other preliminaries, our march was
resumed.

It was yet dark in the woods, and to most of us there
was no more indication of a trail in one place than in
another, but our veteran guide, who possessed all the
sagacity of the ideal red-man, led the way, and all the
rest of us had to do was merely to follow his tracks.
Soon we merged from the Eastern Woods, and getting
into more open country, turned our course toward the
south, crossing broad plains, diversified here and there
by stunted, scattered trees, ice-covered ponds, and occasionally the thickly wooded valley of a winding stream.
As we travelled on my leg caused me intense pain, so
that it became impossible to keep up with the train. I
hobbled along as well as I could for a time, but finding
that I was seriously retarding the progress of the march,
arrangements were made to give me a lift on one of the
sleds. Pierre and Louis were also becoming lame from

the use of their snowshoes, to which they were not yet hardened, but were not seriously crippled.*

During the second day from Churchill a band of twenty or thirty deer was seen. Some of us were in no mood or condition to hunt, but Jimmie, the guide, our own man, Jim, and Mr. Matheson, went off in pursuit of the band. Several times during the afternoon we crossed the tracks of both deer and hunters, but when we came upon the big tracks of our guide we saw the first signs of success. He had evidently wounded a deer and was giving him a hot chase, for the Indian's strides were right upon those of a caribou, and to one side of the trail spatters of blood could be seen on the snow. Toward evening our train came up with Mr. Matheson and Jim, who had a long but fruitless run after the deer, but nothing could be seen of the guide. Some time after camp had been made for the night Jimmie walked in with a haunch of venison on his shoulder. He had wounded his deer early in the afternoon, but had been obliged to run him many miles before he could again come up with him. Lest the carcase, which was lying some distance from camp, should be devoured by wolves in the night, a team was harnessed and Jimmie himself, with another man, started off for the meat, which, a few hours later, they brought into camp. As we had had very little fresh meat for

---

* For the benefit of anyone who may be not aware of the fact, I will explain that there are various kinds of lameness commonly produced by the prolonged use of snowshoes. In thus travelling, certain leg muscles which are only accustomed to perform light service are brought into vigorous use, and are very liable to become strained and cause much discomfort and suffering.

some time past, supper of venison steak was gratefully appreciated.

During the day's march numerous wolf and polar bear tracks had been crossed, but the caribou were the only animals seen.

The next day's tramp was a short one, not in actual miles travelled by some of us, but in distance made upon the course. We had, however, a good day's sport, for at different times during the day no less than eight deer were shot. My brother and I were not able to take part in the chase, for by this time, though I was beginning to recover, my brother was as badly crippled as I had been, and for a time had to be drawn on a sled. I should not, perhaps, say we took no part in the chase, for my brother made one remarkable shot.

At about the close of day, a small deer which Mr. Matheson had been following, and at which he had been practising for some time with my brother's rifle, stood still and looked at him with innocent amazement, at a distance of about three hundred yards from our train. Probably the cause of Mr. Matheson's bad shooting was the cross wind which was blowing strongly at the time, but, however, he gave up in disgust and returned the rifle to my brother, asking him to try a shot. My brother said it was useless for him to try, as the deer had now run still farther away, and he himself had only one leg to stand on. But, dropping on his knee, he fired a shot, and down dropped the deer.

Several of the best haunches of venison secured were loaded upon the sleds, but it was not thought wise to overload the teams by trying to carry too much. The bulk of the meat was "cached" where it was killed, to be picked up by the Company's teams on their return trip and taken to Churchill to replenish the larder. Our third camp was made in a strip of wood upon the bank of Salmon Creek, and to our Indians it will be memorable as being the place at which they had the "big feed," for it took three suppers to satisfy them that night. With my brother and myself the hours of darkness had ceased to bring repose. Our knees were so painful we did not sleep, but only turned restlessly from side to side until the return of dawn. Happily for us all the weather had continued to be fair, with no extreme cold since the commencement of the journey, which was particularly fortunate on account of poor Michel, who would doubtless have suffered had he been obliged to ride upon a sled all day during severe weather. As it was, we were able to keep him fairly comfortable, bundled up in deer-skin robes and blankets.

On the fourth day, meeting with no deer, we made about twenty-seven miles, a good march under the circumstances. This brought us to the banks of Owl River, a stream two or three hundred yards in width, situated in a straight line about midway between York and Churchill.

At dawn the next morning we were again marching southward, with the expectation of that day reaching Stony River, where William Westasccot, a brother of the guide, was encamped, and where our parties were to separate.

Three more deer were shot during the day, making a total of twelve for the trip, most of them victims of the Indian guide. About four o'clock in the afternoon we arrived at Stony River, but there was no Indian camp

to be seen, and for a time we saw no signs of any human
presence. We turned down the river, and ere long came
upon the tracks of a solitary hunter. These Jimmie
knew to be the tracks of his brother, and by following
them a mile or two into a dense evergreen wood, we
came upon the camp. It was a solitary tepee, situated
in the heart of a snow-clad thicket of spruce trees and
scrub, so dense that a bird could scarcely fly through it.

The Indian lodge or tepee was built of poles placed
closely together, and arranged in the shape of a cone.
The cracks between the poles were chinked tightly with
moss, with which the tepee was then covered, excepting a foot or so at the top, where a hole was left for the
chimney. An opening made in the wall to serve as a
doorway was closed by a heavy curtain of deerskin,
and as we lifted it we saw in the centre of the lodge,
upon a square mud-covered hearth, a smouldering wood
fire burning, from which the circling smoke ascended
to find its way through the chimney, while huddled
around it by the wall were the old Indian, his squaw
and their children. Deerskin cushions were offered us,
and as we seated ourselves more wood was piled on the
fire.

William, the Indian, was a much older man than his
brother, for his long flowing locks were already whitene
with age, though he still appeared strong and athletic.
Presents of tobacco were passed around; pipes were then
lighted, and information sought and obtained, both by
ourselves and the Indian. We found that William had
seen and killed only one deer for some weeks past, and
was now almost out of food, and entirely out of ammunition. We supplied him with the latter, and told him

228 ACROSS THE SUB-ARCTICS OF CANADA.

where, within a day's travel, he might supply himself with the former.

From him we learned that the great Nelson River, which we expected to reach within two or three days, was still quite open, and that we should find a large boat, in which we might cross, some miles up the river. It was arranged, also, that William's older son should accompany us to York, and assist by hauling a flat sled.

N.-W. M. P. "OFF DUTY."

HALF-BREED DOG-DRIVER.
(Drawn from life by Arthur Heming.)

CHAPTER XVIII.

CROSSING THE NELSON.

On the morning of the 11th of November our parties arranged to separate. The route of Mr. Matheson's party henceforth lay away to the eastward, while our path still led to the south, toward the banks of the Nelson River. A place was prepared on our own dog-sled for crippled Michel; the team of six dogs was harnessed, and the flat sleds, including one for Eli, the son of old William the Indian, were loaded with all that the dogs were unable to haul. Our supplies by this time were diminished to the extent of about two hundred and fifty pounds, so that, even with the additional weight of a man, the loads were lighter than at the outset of the journey.

Loads being thus readjusted, and our feet harnessed to snowshoes, we bade farewell to our friends from the Fort, as well as to those of the forest, and made a new start.

The weather was now unusually mild for the month of November, making the snow soft, and even wet in some places. This made travelling hard for the team, as it caused the ice glazing to melt from the sled, and the mud shoeing to wear and drag heavily upon the track. My brother and I still suffered much from our crippled

limbs, but with considerable difficulty managed to keep
up with the rest. After making a small day's march we
camped for the night on the bank of a stream called by
the Indians White Bear Creek. The weather having
turned colder during the night, making the prospects for
travel more favorable, we started down stream the next
morning upon the ice of the creek, and then across
country to Duck Creek, where we found a second Indian
camp, occupied by two Crees and their families.

From one of these Indians, named Morrison, we purchased an additional dog with which to supplement our
team. The price asked was a new dress for one of the
squaws, but as we had no dress-goods with us, the best
we could offer was that the dress should be ordered at
the Hudson's Bay Company's store at York, and
delivered when the first opportunity afforded. After
some consideration, and several pipes of tobacco, the
offer was accepted and with seven dogs in our team the
journey resumed. We followed the creek till it led us
out to the low, dreary coast at the mouth of the Nelson,
where, having left the woods several miles inland, we
were exposed to the full sweep of a piercingly cold, raw,
south-west wind.

We are accustomed to thinking of a coast as a definite,
narrow shore-line; but to the inhabitants of the Hudson Bay region the word conveys a very different meaning. There the coast is a broad mud and boulder flat,
several miles in width, always wet, and twice during the
day flooded by the tide. At this time of the year the
mud flats were covered by rough broken ice and drifted
snow, but above high-tide mark the surface of the
country was level and the walking good. For several

hours we tramped southward down the coast, with the cutting wind in our faces. During the afternoon we sought shelter, but finding none our course was altered and shaped for the nearest wood, several miles inland.

The great advantage of travelling on the open plain is that there the snow is driven hard, and hence the walking is much better than in the woods, where the snow is soft and deep. Nevertheless, when the weather is rough, as it was on this occasion, the heavy walking is preferable to travelling in the open country in the teeth of the storm.

For the remainder of the day we bore southward, and about sunset made camp on the south bank of a stream known as Sam's Creek, in a lovely snow-laden, evergreen forest—an ideal Canadian winter woodland picture. From this beautiful but chilling scene our tramp was continued next morning at daylight. The low shore of the Nelson was again reached and followed, until about noon a decided change in the character of the land was observed. A boulder clay bank commenced to make its appearance, and this as we advanced rapidly reached an elevation of twenty-five or thirty feet, and as we proceeded up the river became higher and more thickly wooded. The change was a great relief from the level, treeless coast.

We were now well within the mouth of the great Nelson River, and could already, through the rising vapor, dimly see the outline of the opposite shore.

Considerable ice was coming down the river, and on this account we felt some anxiety as to crossing, but we were now within a few miles of the boat of which we had been informed, and it seemed possible that we might yet cross the stream before nightfall. In the middle of the afternoon we found the boat drawn up at the mouth of Heart Creek, where the old Indian hunter had left it. It was a large heavily built sail-boat, capable of carrying our whole outfit in one load, but unfortunately the keel was deeply imbedded in the sand and there securely frozen. The only way to free it was to chop it out, and at this task as many hands were set as could find room to work. Long pries were cut and vigorously applied, but even with our united efforts we only managed to get the boat loosened by nightfall. We were obliged, therefore, to leave it until morning, and seek a place to camp.

During the night the wind, which had been blowing pretty strongly for two days past, increased to a gale from the north-west. This unwelcome guest did not come by himself, but brought with him his friend the snow-storm, and they two held high carnival all night, vying with each other as to which should cause the strange intruders in the grove the more discomfort. The gale shrieked through the trees and threatened to level our shelter, nor was he contented with this, but also entered the camp and played pranks with our fire and blankets. The more stealthy snow-storm, making less noise than his blustering friend, before daylight had filled the ravine with white drifts and almost buried us.

Such was our condition on the morning of the 14th. As this was the ninth day from Churchill, our supply of provisions was about exhausted, but we were now only one day's march from York. After breakfast, despite the condition of the weather, all hands proceeded to the boat, and by a united effort managed to drag it out to the edge of the shore-ice, but the tide being low there was no water to float it. We therefore had to await the flood-tide, which would not be up till about noon. Meanwhile the boat was loaded where it rested upon the sand, and at twelve o'clock, being lifted by the water, a canvas was hoisted, and through a dense fog which rose from the river we sailed up the shore to find a narrow part of the stream and avoid the broad shoals which extended out from the opposite shore.

Having proceeded some three miles up, to the vicinity of Flamboro' Head, a bold headland, our course was altered and we steered into the fog for the south shore —about two miles distant. The wind was piercingly cold, instantly freezing every splash as it fell, and still blowing fresh, so that our ice-laden craft sped swiftly away on her course. Some floating ice was met, but successfully passed, and for a time it seemed as if the crossing would soon be effected; but suddenly there loomed out of the mist right ahead a dense field of ice, broken and rafted and hurrying down with the current. By putting the helm hard to starboard, and quickly dropping our canvas, we managed to keep clear of the mass; but what was now to be done?

The south shore was still hidden by dense volumes of vapor, and nothing could be seen in that direction but the adjacent fields of ice. On the north shore the dark outline of Flamboro' Head could still be discerned, and it was resolved thence to beat our retreat. We were, however, unable to sail against the wind, but taking to the oars we managed, after a prolonged and difficult struggle, to regain the place whence we had started.

Once more on land, a camp was made, and a fire kindled to thaw out our stiffened limbs, while we awaited an opportunity to cross. The mist continued the rest of the day, preventing us from making a second attempt, and so we lay up for the night.

Next morning the fog had cleared away, revealing a dismal sight. On the south side the river was frozen over, and the ice firmly set for a mile or more from shore, while the channel of open water to the north was running full of heavy ice, making it quite impossible to use the boat, and equally impossible to effect a crossing on foot.

We had no alternative but to remain where we were, and hope for a change in the condition of the river. Not the least unpleasant feature of this waiting was that our provisions were now gone.

The men were at once sent out to hunt, and returned in the evening with nine ptarmigan, with which a good *bouillon* was made for supper. Besides this, Eli, the Indian boy, gave us some comforting information as to the existence of a fish cache of his father's, not far distant. With this consoling knowledge we rolled up in our blankets and were soon dreaming of better times.

The next morning, there being no change in the river, two men and the dogs were sent after William's fish cache, and four others went off hunting, while the rest remained at camp, collected wood, and kept the fire burning.

We had nothing to eat this day until evening, when the sledding party returned with a little bag and can of pounded dried fish, two or three gallons of seal oil, and some seal blubber for the dogs, all of which, though not exactly luxurious, we were heartily glad to receive.

Later two of the hunters returned with several ptarmigan and one or two rabbits, and last of all, some time after dark, the remaining two—Jim and our noble guide—walked into camp carrying the carcase of a deer.

With careful use we had meat enough now to keep us from suffering for several days, and in order to guard against greed or waste my brother and I took possession of the stock and divided it up equally among the party, each man receiving in all about ten pounds.

Without narrating in detail the incidents following it will be sufficient to state that for ten long days our weary wait on the bleak banks of the Nelson was continued. From time to time the men were sent out to hunt, but except in the above instance were obliged to return empty-handed.

On the morning of the 19th, the guide and Jim, provided with rifles, blankets, axes and snowshoes, started up the river, determined to find deer if there were any in the neighborhood, and also to investigate the possibilities of crossing the river higher up.

Four days of bitterly cold weather passed, the thermometer varying from 12 to 15 degrees below zero, and back came our discouraged hunters without having fired a shot. Food was becoming alarmingly scarce. A fox which happened in our way was trapped and eagerly devoured.

On the evening of the 22nd, though the mercury indicated 22° below zero, the channel of the river above us was noticed to be less thickly blocked with ice than where we were encamped. It was resolved, if possible, to haul the boat a mile or two farther up stream, and there to launch and measure our strength with the floe.

All hands excepting Michel, who was still unable to walk, engaged in the work. The boat was launched, and by means of a long line we managed to tow it about half a mile up shore, but there the ice became so thick that we had to haul it out to prevent its being crushed. Our objective point was about a mile farther up, so an effort was made to haul the boat along the shore. It was all the ten of us could manage, but by about night-fall we had succeeded. The night being clear and light, we moved camp to the boat, that we might be prepared to cross in the morning if it were possible.

The next morning was bitterly cold and a fog was rising from the river. We towed the boat half a mile still farther up, until the Seal Islands were reached. Here we pushed out into the stream and commenced the struggle.

Every man was armed with an oar, a pole or an axe, and all of these were vigorously applied in forcing our way through the ice and the current. For a time we made fair progress, but before long were caught in the grip of the ice-pack and hurried down with the stream toward the sea.

We pushed and we pulled, we pounded and hacked, and at length got into a channel of open water. Again we were beset, but again got free, and so after much exertion we crossed the channel and landed upon the stationary ice. We had taken this for shore-ice, but were sorely disappointed to find it was only a jam in the middle of the channel.

What was now to be done? It was impossible to tow the boat around the upper end of the jam; and to allow it to drift down past the lower end would mean that we would be carried with the current out to sea and be irrevocably lost.

After carefully considering the situation, we concluded to portage across the island of ice and launch on the other side. Accordingly the boat was unloaded and piece by piece everything was carried safely across, but when we attempted to portage the boat it and we continually broke through the surface. We were therefore obliged to cut a channel right through the island, the full width of the boat. After much labor this was accomplished, the boat hauled through, reloaded, and again pushed out into the flowing pack, which carried us, in spite of all our endeavors, far down toward the mouth of the river.

At length we had succeeded in getting within thirty feet of the solid south-shore ice, but even then, when the shore seemed almost within reach, we were nipped in the floe and again carried helplessly downward, until it seemed as if, after all, we were going to be carried out to sea.

We used every effort to free the boat, but all of no avail. At last, however, civil war among the floes caused a split and brought deliverance. A few rapid strokes and our old craft bumped against the solid ice.

The bowman, François, quick as a flash, sprang out with the end of the tow-line, while the rushing ice again caught the boat and bore it downward. François held on to the tow-line with all his might, but the tug-of-war was going against him; he yielded, fell, and for a short distance was dragged over the broken hummocks of ice, but bracing his feet against one of these, he formed himself into a veritable ice-anchor, and with Herculean strength held us fast until others sprang out to his assistance.

All hands quickly disembarked, but as there was still between us and the shore a full mile of rough ice, liable to break adrift at any moment, no time was lost in exultation. The boat was unloaded, hauled up and the tramp commenced for the shore. After much exertion

HUDSON'S BAY COMPANY'S STORE, YORK FACTORY.

we reached land, and every man felt a thrill of exultation that the Nelson was at last to the north of us.

We were all much chilled from exposure, so a fire was made in the edge of the woods. Spruce boughs were strewn about it to keep our feet from the snow, and the cheerful warmth was most gratefully enjoyed.

A little of the pounded dried-fish still remaining was fried on a pan with seal oil, the combination forming a dish that might be described as fish-flavored chips steeped in oil, but with appetites such as ours it could be eaten—though I will not say relished.

After this "refreshment" had been partaken of, and the stiffness thawed from our limbs, snowshoes were adjusted, and with a "Hurrah for York" the march was resumed.

One more camp was made, and on the following day, the 24th of November, and the nineteenth day since leaving Churchill, we reached York Factory.

RED DEER COWBOY.

CHAPTER XIX.

THROUGH THE FOREST AND HOME AGAIN.

Upon arriving at York we were kindly received by the officer of the Hudson's Bay Company, Dr. Milne. Our men were given lodgings and rations in one of the many vacant houses in the Fort, while my brother and I were shown into the Doctor's bachelor quarters and allowed to occupy the room of Mr. Mowat, the assistant trader, who was absent at the time.

The first articles essential to comfort were tubs and warm water. With travellers in the north, particularly during the winter season, the practice of performing daily ablutions is quite unheard of. This is not due to neglect, but is rather an enforced custom due to the painful effects produced by the application of ice-cold water to the skin. During the previous summer and autumn my brother and I adhered to the habit of daily washing our hands and face, until our skin became so cracked and sore that we were forced to discontinue.

Besides Dr. Milne and an old-time servant, Macpherson, Mr. Mowat, now temporarily absent, was the only other white resident in York. He had, only a few days before our arrival, been sent off with two Indians as a relief party to look for the Company's autumn mail, which was now more than six weeks overdue. The

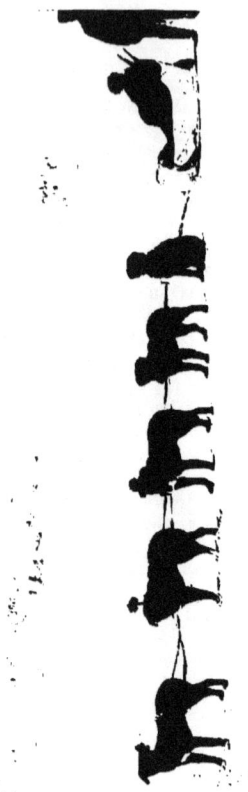

DOG-TRAIN AND CARRYALL.

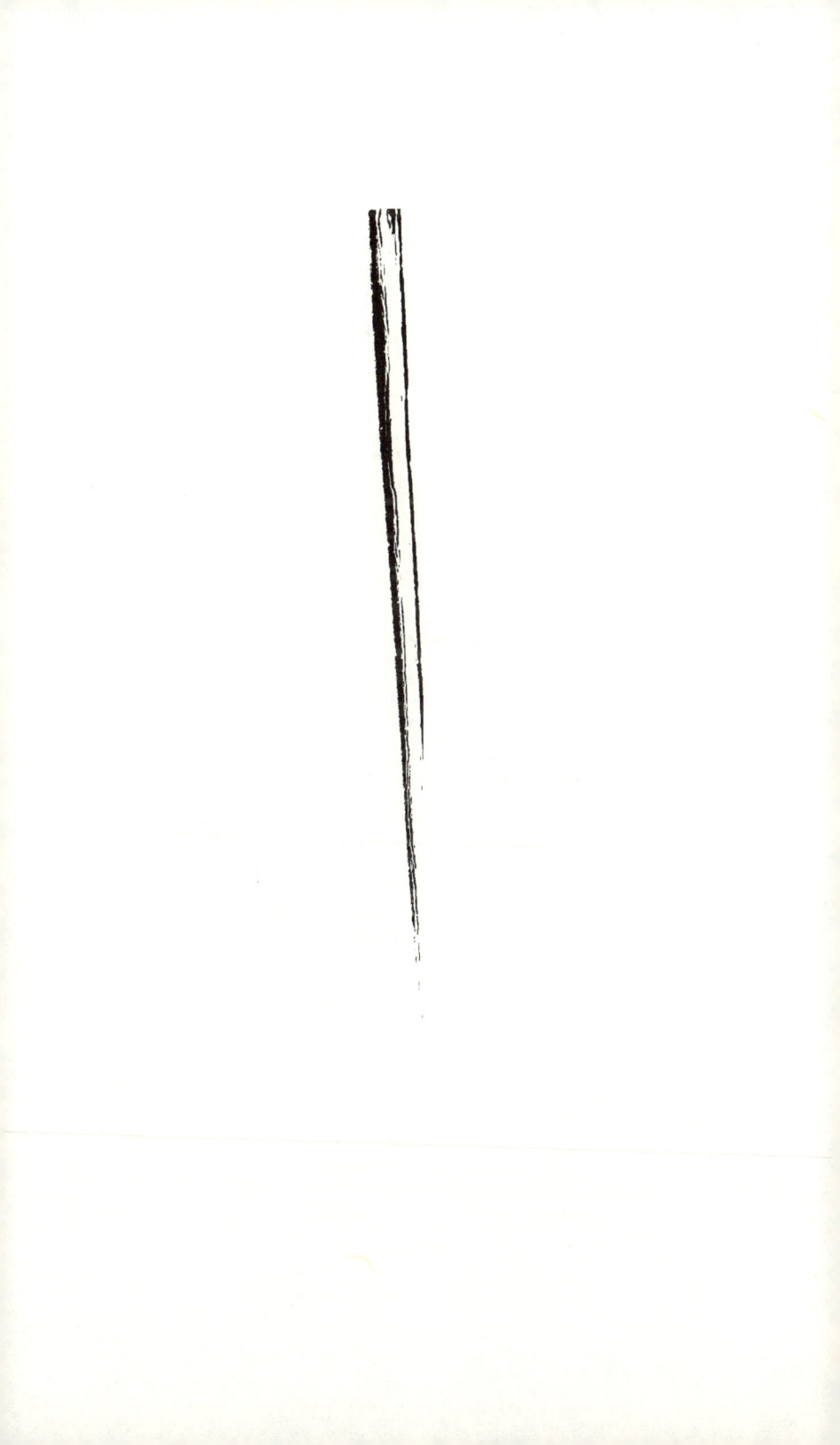

mail should have come down the Hays River from Oxford House, 250 miles distant, before the close of navigation, but as nothing had yet been heard of it or the party, fears were entertained as to their safety. It was thought they must have been lost in the river.

As to York Factory, it is one of those places of which it may be said "the light of other days has faded." In the earlier days of the Hudson's Bay Company it was an important centre of trade, the port at which all goods for the interior posts were received, and from which the enormous harvests of valuable furs were annually shipped. Such business naturally necessitated the building of large store-houses and many dwellings to shelter the goods and provide accommodation for the large staff of necessary servants. As late as the summer of 1886, when I visited York, there was a white population of about thirty, besides a number of Indians and half-breeds in the employ of the Company: but things had now changed. Less expensive ways of transporting goods into the interior than freighting them hundreds of miles up the rivers in York boats now existed, and as the local supply of furs had become scarce serious results necessarily followed. Gradually the staff of servants had been dismissed or removed, and one by one the dwellings vacated, until York was now almost a deserted village. The Indians also had nearly all gone to other parts of the country.

One of the first duties receiving our attention upon reaching York was the placing of poor crippled Michel in the doctor's hands. His frozen feet, still dreadfully sore, were carefully attended to, and it was thought that in the course of a few weeks they might be sufficiently recovered to allow him to walk. As to taking him any farther with us, that was unadvisable, for he was now in the care of a physician, and in a place where he would receive all necessary attention. Besides, we would have no means of carrying him, unless upon a sled drawn by our own men, and such an additional burden would seriously retard progress. It was therefore admitted by all that the best plan was to leave Michel in Dr. Milne's care, to be forwarded as soon as he was well enough to walk. This was promptly arranged, and with as little delay as possible preparations were made for departure.

Two dogs from our Churchill team were purchased outright from Jimmie, who happened to be the owner of them, and a third having been secured from Morrison, the Indian, we only required one more to make up a fair team, and this was procured from the Doctor. Another team was hired from the Company, and it was at first thought, with the aid of these two, we might comfortably make the twelve days' trip to Oxford House. But when supply bills were made out it was found that with the assistance of only two teams for so long a trip, each man would have to haul a heavily-loaded toboggan. The Doctor therefore, with some difficulty, raised a third team to accompany us for two days on the journey.

The next necessary preparation was the procuring of a guide and drivers for the teams. As the mail-carriers and two other Indians, Mr. Mowat's companions, had already gone to Oxford House, few men were left at the Fort who knew the route; but happily a man was found who turned out to be another brother of our guide from Churchill. He was a very dark Indian, younger than Jimmie, and of much less noble appearance, and was known by the name of Charlie. He was said to be well fitted for the purpose, and we felt that a brother of our guide could not be a very poor man. Our party, including Arthur Omen, the driver from Churchill, who had determined to accompany us out of the country, was now complete. Twelve days' rations, consisting of bacon, flour, sugar and tea, were served out to each man, with a warning to make them last through the trip or suffer the consequences. The flour was then baked up into the more convenient form of cakes. Dog-fish was also provided, and all being loaded upon the three sleds and two toboggans, the second stage of our sledding journey was begun on Tuesday morning, the 28th of November. The dog-sleds were not the same as those we had used in traversing the hard driven snow of the plains, but were what are known as "flat sleds" or large toboggans, they being better suited to woodland travel.

The condition of our party on leaving York was vastly different from what it had been on leaving Churchill. The two hundred mile tramp, although crippling some of us and causing all plenty of exertion, had hardened our muscles so much that, with the ten days' "lie up" on the bank of the Nelson River, and a four days' rest at York, we were now in first-class walking trim, and started up the Hays River at a brisk pace.

The first day's march was upon the river ice, and our first camp was made on the bank, in two feet of snow, beneath the shelter of the evergreens. Beyond this our course led through the woods to the north of the river, and by many winding ways we journeyed on.

On the morning of the third day the assisting team from York, leaving its load with us, returned to the Factory. A readjustment of loads was then made, and with the two remaining teams we pushed on, though now more slowly, for Oxford House.

At about noon on the 1st of December we were pleased to meet Mr. Mowat, returning with the long-looked for mail and party, all safe. The delay in the arrival of the mail had been caused by one of the Indians becoming ill soon after leaving Norway House, and having to return to that post. After a brief halt, each party now having the advantage of the other's track, we started on, pursuing opposite ways, they to their solitary home on the ice-bound coast of Hudson Bay, and we towards ours in the more genial south.

At this time the temperature remained pretty steady at about 25 degrees below zero, but with the exertion of the march during the day, and the shelter of blankets and the warmth of the camp-fire at night, we managed to keep fairly comfortable.

About sixteen miles beyond a large stream known as Fox River we came upon an ancient track. This in earlier days had been travelled by oxen and Red River carts, and over it hundreds of tons of freight had annually been hauled; but now it was so grown up with trees that it often required the skill of the guide to keep it. The track led directly to Oxford, so that from this forward it was to be our road.

Since leaving the banks of the Hays River no timber of any value had been seen. The wood had all been black spruce of a very scrubby character, but now poplar, birch and jack-pine were occasionally met with.

On December the 4th the temperature ran down to 34 degrees below zero, but on the following day this record was beaten, and 40 degrees below was registered. In this low temperature we naturally found some difficulty in keeping warm. When the day's tramp was over, and our position taken for the night beside the camp-fire, it was found necessary either to slowly revolve or frequently reverse our position. It was a question of roasting or freezing, or rather doing both at the same time. While one's face was turned to the fire and enduring a roasting heat, his back was freezing, and as the position was reversed the roasting and freezing process was also reversed. Our meals, after being prepared, were served up on the hot pan to keep them warm while eating, but even so they were sometimes frozen to the frying pan before they could be disposed of.

During the afternoon of the 4th and the morning of the 5th of December we crossed Deer Lake, twenty-seven miles in length, and at either end of the lake found camps of Indians. From one of them we purchased some fine whitefish, which they were catching through the ice.

By this time our guide Charlie had become pretty badly used up by the march. He was no longer able to hold the lead, but our own men managed to keep the track and Charlie hobbled along behind

During the evening of the 6th and the morning of the 7th of December we crossed a succession of thirteen small lakes and some flat open plains, but the afternoon of the latter day saw a marked change in the character of the country. With the exception of two or three isolated patches, we had seen nothing in the shape of timber of any value since leaving York —indeed, I might say since leaving Churchill, or even a thousand miles or so farther back on the road. But now we had reached a heavy forest of white spruce, jack-pine, poplar and birch trees, and the change was a pleasing one.

For a distance of six or eight miles we trudged through this heavy forest, and then, just at night-fall, reached the shore of Back Lake, really an extension of Oxford Lake. One of my brother's feet had become so sore during the day that he had been obliged to walk with only one snowshoe. On this account we had fallen several miles behind the leaders of the party, and when we arrived at the shore of the lake above described, nothing could we see of the outfit, and both because of darkness and the hard surface of the snow, it was with great difficulty we were able to follow the track. It led away across the lake, and for a time we managed to follow it. While doing so we carefully noted its bearing, but soon the faint tracks could no longer be followed, for the night was becoming dark. We feared to lose them, as there might be a change in their course and then our bearing would not lead us aright. For a time, upon hands and knees, we tried to follow the trail, but could not keep upon it continuously.

Keeping as straight a course as we could, we pressed on through the darkness toward the distant shore, the dark outline of which could just be discerned against the lighter sky. At length we reached the shore, when, after passing through a narrow strip of woods, to our joy there suddenly flashed out before us, a few yards ahead, the lights of Oxford House. A few minutes later we were the guests of Mr. and Mrs. Isbister, one of the most hospitable old couples it has ever been my good fortune to meet. Mr. Isbister was the local agent of the Hudson's Bay Company, and was a thorough old-time Canadian, one of those men filled with reminiscences of early Canadian life in the north and whose many stories were a delight to hear.

Having reached Oxford in safety, preparations were at once commenced for our journey to the next post—Norway House—150 miles farther west. Some delay was occasioned in getting dogs, but at length three miserable half-starved teams were secured, and with a new guide and drivers we set out on the third stage of our winter journey. Without narrating the many incidents by the way, I need only say that after a six days' tramp, with the thermometer in the neighborhood of 40 degrees below zero, we arrived safely at Norway House, an important Hudson's Bay Company's post, situated at the northern extremity of Lake Winnipeg. Two of the dog-teams procured at Oxford had been intended to haul my brother and myself, and for a time they did so, but the poor animals were in such a wretched condition from the effects of former hard work that we preferred to walk most of the time, and before we reached our destination considered ourselves fortunate that we escaped without having to haul the dogs.

At Norway House the difficulties of the journey, so far as my brother and I were concerned, were practically ended. Enough strong, capable dogs were here secured to admit of our travelling in carry-alls for the remaining four hundred miles still separating us from West Selkirk, the northern terminus of the railway; but of course the Indians had to stick to their snow-shoes. It was here decided to divide our party, and send the three western men home, assisted by the team of Eskimo dogs which had accompanied us the whole six hundred miles from Churchill. The valley of the Saskatchewan River would be their most direct course, in taking which route they would reach their several homes by travelling about the same distance as ourselves. Arthur Omen, the driver from Churchill, chose to go up the Saskatchewan with the western men, so that of the original party there only remained the two Iroquois, Pierre and Louis, to accompany my brother and myself. With the least possible delay four good dog-teams, as many drivers, and a guide were procured from Mr. J. K. Macdonald, the Hudson's Bay Company's Factor, who showed us much kindness, and two days before Christmas the last and longest division of our journey was begun.

My brother and I were now warmly rolled up in robes and blankets and lying in our carry-alls. Supplies and baggage were all loaded upon the two remaining sleds, and with a driver trotting along beside or behind each team, the guide running before, and the two Iroquois sometimes before and sometimes behind, we travelled on an almost due south course over the ice along the shore of Lake Winnipeg. About the same time that we started for the south, the other section set out across the lake to the westward for the mouth of the Saskatchewan River.

Our teams, of four dogs each, were for the most part fine powerful animals, and we soon found there was no necessity for my brother or myself exerting ourselves more than we desired. The teams travelled all day, and, indeed, day after day, at a rapid trot, sometimes breaking into a run, so that it gave the Indians all they could do to keep up with them.

Taking smooth and rough together we made an average of about forty miles per day, and some days as much as forty-six or forty-seven miles. When we had made about half the distance to Selkirk, and were in the neighborhood of a fishing station at the mouth of Berens River, poor Pierre played out; but, most opportunely, we met a man teaming fish to Selkirk and secured a passage for him, while we ourselves pushed on. When we had made another hundred miles Louis, the remaining Iroquois, also became crippled. Arrangements were made to have him, too, driven in with a horse and sleigh, and without delay we pursued our journey.

At length, after a long and rapid trip, which occupied ten days, on the evening of the 1st of January, 1894, under the light of the street lamps of the little town, our teams trotted up the streets of West Selkirk, and thus was completed a canoe and snowshoe journey of three thousand two hundred miles.

I need hardly say that the telegraph office was soon found, and messages despatched to anxious friends, who, having heard nothing from us for some months, had begun to entertain grave fears for our safety. Thirteen hundred miles more of travel by rail and we were home again, after an absence of just eight months.

CREE HUNTER'S PRIZE.

APPENDIX I.

CLASSIFIED LIST OF PLANTS.

Collected by J. W. TYRRELL, C.E., D.L.S.,

in 1893, along the line of route between Lake Athabasca and the west coast of Hudson Bay; with which is incorporated a small collection made in 1885 at Ashe Inlet, on the north shore of Hudson Strait, and a collection made by Miss Marjorie Lofthouse at Fort Churchill.

The species collected from the Barren Lands are marked *B*; those from the forest country south of the Barren Lands, or in isolated groves of timber on the banks of the river, north of the general limit of the forest, are marked *W*. Any species collected both from the woods and from the Barren Lands are marked *W.B.*, or *B.W.*, according to whether they are woodland species extending into the Barren Lands, or Arctic species extending south into the forest.

Determined by Professor John Macoun, M.A.

I. RANUNCULACEÆ.

1. *Anemone patens*, L., var. *Nuttalliana*, Gray.—*W*.
    Fort Chippewyan, Lake Athabasca, June 19.
2. *Anemone parviflora*, Michx.—*W.B.*
    North shore of Lake Athabasca. Limestone Island in Nicholson Lake, and the west shore of Hudson Bay at Fort Churchill.
3. *Anemone Richardsonii*, Hook.—*W*.
    Telzoa River, just below Daly Lake.
4. *Anemone multifida*, Poir.—*W*.
    Woodcock Portage, on Stone River.

5. *Ranunculus affinis*, R. Br.—B.
   Barlow Lake, Telzoa River. Telzoa River, between Schultz and Baker Lakes. South shore of Chesterfield Inlet, near its mouth. Fort Churchill.
6. *Ranunculus Lapponicus*, L.—B.
   West shore of Tobanut Lake, near the mouth of Telzoa River.
7. *Ranunculus hyperboreus*, Rottb.—W.
   Telzoa River, just below Daly Lake.

II. PAPAVERACEÆ.

8. *Papaver nudicaule*, L.—B.
   Telzoa River, between Schultz and Baker Lakes. This species was also collected at Ashe Inlet, on the north shore of Hudson Straits, in 1885.

III. FUMARIACEÆ.

9. *Corydalis glauca*, Pursh.—W.
   North-west and north shores of Lake Athabasca. Esker, near the Narrows of Daly Lake.
10. *Corydalis aurea*, Willd.—W.
    Rocky Island, on the north side of Lake Athabasca, west of Fond du Lac.

IV. CRUCIFERÆ.

11. *Cardamine pratensis*, L., var. *angustifolia*.—B.
    Island near the centre of Boyd Lake. Limestone Island, in Nicholson Lake. Fort Churchill.
12. *Arabis lyrata*, L.—W.
    North shore of Lake Athabasca.
13. *Arabis humifusa*, var. *pubescens*, Wat.—W.
    North-west angle of Lake Athabasca. Esker, near the Narrows of Daly Lake. This species had not previously been found west of Hudson Bay.
14. *Barbarea vulgaris*, R. Br.—W.
    Cracking Stone Point, north shore of Lake Athabasca. Red Hill, on the west shore of Hinde Lake.
15. *Sisymbrium humile*, C. A. Meyer.—W.
    Fort Chippewyan, Lake Athabasca.

16. *Cardamine digitata*, Rich.—*B*.
    London Rapid, above Forks of Telzoa River. Mouth of Chesterfield Inlet. Not found elsewhere since it was collected by Sir John Richardson near the mouth of the Coppermine River.
17. *Draba hirta*, L.—*B*.
    Limestone Island, Nicholson Lake, London Rapids, above the Forks of Telzoa River. Also at Ashe Inlet, on the north shore of Hudson Strait.
18. *Draba incana*, L.—*B*.
    London Rapids, above the Forks of Tulzoa River. Fort Churchill, on the west coast of Hudson Bay.
19. *Draba nemorosa*, L., var. *leiocarpa*, Lindb.—*W*.
    Fond du Lac, Lake Athabasca.
20. *Draba stellata*, Jacq.—*B*.
    North-west shore of Tobaunt Lake.
21. *Cochlearia officinalis*, L.—*B*.
    Mouth of Chesterfield Inlet.
22. *Eutrema Edwardsii*, R. Br.—*B*.
    North-west shore of Tobaunt Lake.
23. *Nasturtium palustre*, D. C.—*W*.
    Fond du Lac, Lake Athabasca.

V. VIOLACEÆ.

24. *Viola palustris*, L.—*W*.
    East and north shores of Carey Lake. These are the most northern localities in Canada where this species has been found.
25. *Viola canina*, L., var. *Sylvestris*, Regel.—*W*.
    Fond du Lac, Lake Athabasca. South end of Daly Lake.

VI. CARYOPHYLLACEÆ.

26. *Silene acaulis*, L.—*B*.
    Tobaunt Lake, west shore. North end of Wharton Lake. Also at Ashe Inlet, on Hudson Strait.
27. *Lychnis apetala*, L.—*B*.
    Mouth of Chesterfield Inlet.
28. *Lychnis affinis*, Vahl.—*B*.
    Tobaunt Lake, north-west shore.

29. *Arenaria lateriflora*, L. — W.
   Near the south end of Daly Lake.
30. *Arenaria peploides*, L. — B.
   Ashe Inlet, on the north side of Hudson Strait.
31. *Stellaria longipes*, Goldie. — B. W.
   Barlow Lake. Carey Lake. Wharton Lake. Tobaunt Lake, west shore. London Rapids, above the Forks of Telzoa River. Fort Churchill.
32. *Stellaria longipes*, Goldie, var *lœta*, Wats. — B.
   Barlow Lake and Limestone Island, in Nicholson Lake.
33. *Stellaria borealis*, Bigel. — W.
   Red Hill, on the west shore of Hinde Lake.
34. *Cerastium alpinum*, L. — B.
   Limestone Island, in Nicholson Lake. Wharton Lake. London Rapids, above the Forks of Telzoa River. Telzoa River, between Schultz and Baker lakes. Mouth of Chesterfield Inlet. Fort Churchill. Ashe Inlet, on the north side of Hudson Strait.

VII. GERANIACEÆ.

35. *Geranium Carolinianum*, L. — W.
   North shore of Lake Athabasca, a short distance west of Fond du Lac.

VIII. SAPINDACEÆ.

36. *Acer spicatum*, Lam. — W.
   Fort Chippewyan, Lake Athabasca. This is the most northerly locality in Canada from which this species has been recorded.

IX. LEGUMINOSÆ.

37. *Astragalus alpinus*, L. — W.
   North shore of Lake Athabasca at Fond du Lac, and near Big Fowl Island. Esker, near the Narrows of Daly Lake.
38. *Spiesia* (*Oxytropis*) *Belli*, Britt. — B.
   London Rapids, above the Forks of Telzoa River. Mouth of Chesterfield Inlet.
   The only other locality from which this species has been collected is Digges Island, Hudson Bay, where it was found by Dr. Bell in 1884. It was described by Mr. Britton in 1894 from the specimens collected at the second and third of the above localities.

39. *Oxytropis campestris*, L., var. *cærulea*, Koch.—*R.*
   Ashe Inlet, on the north shore of Hudson Strait.

40. *Oxytropis leucantha*, Pers.—*R.*
   Telzoa River, between Shultz and Baker lakes. Mouth of Chesterfield Inlet. Fort Churchill.

41. *Hedysarum boreale*, Nutt.—*B.*
   London Rapids, above the Forks of Telzoa River.

42. *Hedysarum Mackenzii*, Richard, L.—*R. W.*
   Fort Churchill. Ashe Inlet, on the north side of Hudson Strait.

X. ROSACEÆ.

43. *Prunus Pennsylvanica*, L.—*W.*
   North-west angle of Lake Athabasca. Esker, near Narrows of Daly Lake.

44. *Rubus chamæmorus*, L.—*W. R.*
   Fort Churchill. Common in swampy places from Lake Athabasca northward to the edge of the woods. Grove on the north shore of Carey Lake, and at London Rapids, near the Forks of Telzoa River. It was also found at Ashe Inlet, on the north side of Hudson Strait.

45. *Rubus arcticus*, L., var. *grandiflorus*, Ledeb.—*W.*
   North shore of Lake Athabasca. Barlow Lake. North shore of Carey Lake. Fort Churchill.

46. *Rubus strigosus*, Michx.—*W.*
   Banks of Stone River. In an isolated grove of white spruce on the north shore of Carey Lake. This would seem to have been an isolated locality, at some considerable distance north of its general northern limit.

47. *Dryas integrifolia*, Vahl.—*R.*
   Carey Lake. Limestone Island, in Nicholson Lake. West shore of Tobaunt Lake. London Rapids, above the Forks of Telzoa River. Fort Churchill. Ashe Inlet, on the north shore of Hudson Strait.

48. *Fragaria Canadensis*, Michx.—*W.*
   North shore of Lake Athabasca and Woodcock Portage, on Stone River.
   This species, which has usually been confounded with *F. Virginiana*, was also collected in the same year by Miss Taylor at Fort Smith, on Slave River.

49. *Potentilla Norvegica*, L.—*W.*
   Woodcock Portage, on Stone River. Red Hill, on the west shore of Hinde Lake.

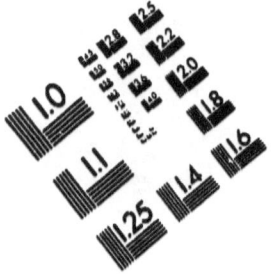

**IMAGE EVALUATION
TEST TARGET (MT-3)**

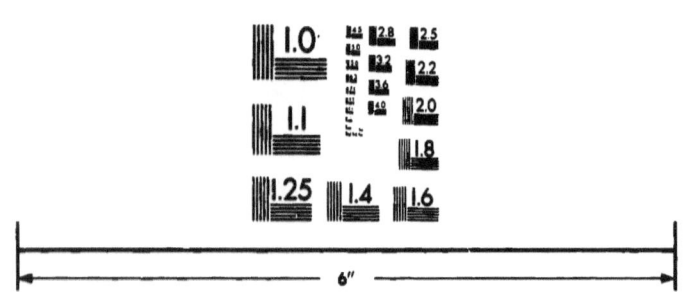

← 6" →

Photographic
Sciences
Corporation

23 WEST MAIN STREET
WEBSTER, N.Y. 14580
(716) 872-4503

50. *Potentilla nivea*, L.—*B.*
    Telzoa River, between Schultz and Baker lakes. Mouth of Chesterfield Inlet. Fort Churchill.
51. *Potentilla palustris*, Scop.—*W.*
    Stony flats on the banks of Telzoa River, just below Daly Lake.
52. *Potentilla fruticosa*, L.—*W.*
    North shore of Lake Athabasca, a little distance west of Fond du Lac.
53. *Potentilla nana*, Willd.—*B.*
    Shore of Hudson Bay, north of Marble Island. Ashe Inlet, on the north shore of Hudson Strait.
54. *Potentilla tridentata*, Solander.—*W.*
    Woodcock Portage, Stone River.
55. *Amelanchier alnifolia*, Nutt.—*W.*
    North-west angle, Lake Athabasca.

XI. SAXIFRAGACEÆ.

56. *Saxifraga oppositifolia*, L.—*B.*
    Telzoa River, between Schultz and Baker lakes. Mouth of Chesterfield Inlet. Ashe Inlet, on the north shore of Hudson Strait.
57. *Saxifraga cæspitosa*, L.—*B.*
    Telzoa River, between Schultz and Baker lakes. Mouth of Chesterfield Inlet. Ashe Inlet.
58. *Saxifraga rivularis*, L.—*B.*
    Loudon Rapids, above the Forks of Telzoa River. Ashe Inlet.
59. *Saxifraga cernua*, L.—*B.*
    North-west shore of Tobaunt Lake. Loudon Rapids, above the Forks of Telzoa River. Telzoa River, between Schultz and Baker lakes. Mouth of Chesterfield Inlet. Fort Churchill.
60. *Saxifraga nivalis*, L.—*B.*
    Mouth of Chesterfield Inlet.
61. *Saxifraga hieracifolia*, Waldst and Kit.—*B.*
    North shore of Tobaunt Lake.
62. *Saxifraga punctata*, L.—*B.*
    North-west shore of Tobaunt Lake.
    This species had not previously been recorded east of the Rocky Mountains.

63. *Saxifraga Hirculus*, L.—*B.*
    North-west shore of Tobaunt Lake.
64. *Saxifraga tricuspidata*, Retz.—*B. W.*
    Fort Chippewyan, Lake Athabasca. North shore of Carey Lake. Wharton Lake. Loudon Rapids, above the Forks of Telzoa River. Mouth of Chesterfield Inlet. Ashe Inlet.
65. *Chrysosplenium alternifolium*, L.—*B.*
    Limestone Island, Nicholson Lake.
66. *Parnassia Kotzebuei*, Cham. and Schl.—*W.*
    South end of Daly Lake.
67. *Parnassia palustris*, L.—*W.*
    Fort Churchill.
68. *Ribes oxydcanthoides*, L.—*W.*
    North shore of Lake Athabasca, near Fond du Lac.
69. *Ribes rubrum*, L.—*W.*
    Fort Chippewyan, Lake Athabasca.
70. *Ribes Hudsonianum*, Richards.—*W.*
    Fort Chippewyan, Lake Athabasca.
71. *Ribes prostratum*, L'Her.—*W.*
    North shore of Lake Athabasca. Esker, near the Narrows of Daly Lake. East and north shores of Carey Lake.

XII. HALORAGEÆ.

72. *Hippuris vulgaris*, L.—*B.*
    Mouth of Chesterfield Inlet.
73. *Hippuris maritima*, L.—*B. W.*
    Red Hill, on the shore of Hinde Lake. Mouth of Chesterfield Inlet.

XIII. ONAGRACEÆ.

74. *Epilobium angustifolium*, L.—*W. B.*
    Esker, near the Narrows of Daly Lake. Ashe Inlet, Hudson Strait.
    These localities probably mark the northern range of this species.
75. *Epilobium latifolium*, L.—*B.*
    West shore of Tobaunt Lake. Loudon Rapids, above the Forks of Telzoa River, where the flowers were just appearing on August 25. Fort Churchill. Ashe Inlet.

17

76. *Epilobium lineare*, Gray.—*B.*
    Red Hill, on the shore of Hinde Lake. Mouth of Chesterfield Inlet.

XIV. CORNACEÆ.

77. *Cornus Canadensis*, L.—*W.*
    North shore of Lake Athabasca. South end of Daly Lake.

XV. CAPRIFOLIACEÆ.

78. *Viburnum pauciflorum*, Pylaie.—*W.*
    North shore of Lake Athabasca. Esker, near the Narrows of Daly Lake.
79. *Linnæa borealis*, Gronov.—*W.*
    Elizabeth Rapids, Stone River. Esker, near the Narrows of Daly Lake. North shore of Carey Lake. Fort Churchill.

XVI. RUBIACEÆ.

80. *Galium trifidum*, L.—*W.*
    Red Hill, on the shore of Hinde Lake.

XVII. COMPOSITÆ.

81. *Erigeron uniflorus*, L.—*B.*
    London Rapids, above the Forks of Telzoa River.
82. *Erigeron eriocephalus*, J. Vahl.—*B.*
    North end of Wharton Lake.
83. *Antennaria alpina*, Gærtn.—*B.*
    West shore of Tobaunt Lake.
84. *Achillæa millefolium*, L., var. *nigrescens*, L.—*W.B.*
    Woodcock portage, Stone River, Fort Churchill. Ashe Inlet.
85. *Matricaria inodora*, L., var. *nana*, Hook.—*W.*
    Fort Churchill.
86. *Artemisia borealis*, Pall., var. *Wormskioldii*, Bess.—*B. W.*
    Telzoa River, just below Daly Lake, and east end of Aberdeen Lake.
87. *Petasites palmata*, Gray.—*W.*
    Fond du Lac, Lake Athabasca.

88. *Petasites sagittata*, Gray.—*B.*
    Limestone Island, Nicholson Lake. Ashe Inlet, Hudson Strait.
89. *Arnica alpina*, Olin.—*B. W.*
    North shore of Lake Athabasca. Esker, near Narrows of Daly Lake. West shore of Tobaunt Lake. Loudon Rapids, above the Forks of Telzoa River. Fort Churchill. Ashe Inlet.
90. *Senecio palustris*, Hook., var. *congesta*, Hook.—*B.*
    West shore of Tobaunt Lake. Fort Churchill. Ashe Inlet.
91. *Senecio aureus*, L., var. *borealis*, Tor. and Gr.—*B.*
    Limestone Island in Nicholson Lake.
92. *Senecio aureus*, L., var. *balsamitæ*, Tor. and Gr.—*W.*
    Fort Churchill.
93. *Saussurea alpina*, Hook.—*B.*
    North end of Wharton Lake.
94. *Taraxacum officinale*, Weber, var. *alpinum*, Koch.—*B.*
    Loudon Rapids, above the Forks of Telzoa River. Mouth of Chesterfield Inlet. Fort Churchill.

XVIII. CAMPANULACEÆ.

95. *Campanula uniflora*, L.—*B.*
    Loudon Rapids, above the Forks of Telzoa River.

XIX. VACCINIACEÆ.

96. *Vaccinium Canadense*, Kalm.—*W.*
    South end of Daly Lake.
97. *Vaccinium uliginosum*, L.—*W. B.*
    North shore of Lake Athabasca. Telzoa River, just below Daly Lake. Carey Lake. Tobaunt Lake. Loudon Rapids, above Forks of Telzoa River. Fort Churchill.
98. *Vaccinium Vitis-Idæa*, L.—*W. B.*
    North shore of Lake Athabasca. Daly Lake. Tobaunt Lake. Loudon Rapids, above the Forks of Telzoa River. Fort Churchill.
    While both this and the preceding species extend for a considerable distance into the Barren Lands, the bushes are small and bear very little fruit.

99. *Oxycoccus vulgaris*, Pursh.—*W*.
   Esker, near the middle of Daly Lake, and stony banks of Telzoa River, just below the lake.

XX. ERICACEÆ.

100. *Arctostaphylos alpina*, Spreng.—*B. W*.
   Island near the middle of Boyd Lake. Telzoa River, between Schultz and Baker Lakes. Mouth of Chesterfield Inlet. Fort Churchill Ashe Inlet, Hudson Strait.
   (In 1894 the most southern locality at which this species was observed was on the hill south of Kasba Lake. In 1896 it was seen in the swamp at Cross Portage, north of Seepiwisk Lake. In 1896, Nelson River.—J. B. T.)

101. *Arctostaphylos Uva-ursi*, Spreng.—*W*.
   North to the edge of Barren Lands.

102. *Cassandra calyculata*, Don.—*W*.
   North-west shore, Lake Athabasca. South end of Selwyn Lake.

103. *Cassiope tetragona*, Don.—*B*.
   Shores of Tobaunt Lake. Telzoa River, between Schultz and Baker Lakes. Mouth of Chesterfield Inlet. This is one of the plants most commonly used for fuel by those travelling in the Barren Lands.

104. *Andromeda polifolia*, L.—*W. B*.
   North shore of Athabasca Lake. South end of Selwyn Lake. Esker, near the middle of Daly Lake. West shore of Tobaunt Lake. Fort Churchill.

105. *Loiseleuria procumbens*, Desv.—*B*.
   Boyd Lake.

106. *Bryanthus taxifolius*, Gray.—*B*.
   London Rapids, above forks of Telzoa River.

107. *Kalmia glauca*, Ait.— *B*.
   Fond du Lac, Lake Athabasca. Esker, near middle of Daly Lake.

108. *Ledum latifolium*, Ait.—*W*.
   North shore of Lake Athabasca. Daly Lake. Farther north it is replaced by the next following species.

109. *Ledum palustre*, L.—*B. W*.
   South end of Daly Lake. Carey Lake. Shores of Tobaunt Lake. Wharton Lake. London Rapids, above Forks of Telzoa River. Mouth of Chesterfield Inlet. Fort Churchill.

110. *Rhododendron Lapponicum*, Wahl.—*R.*
    Limestone Island, Nicholson Lake. Shores of Tohannt Lake. Fort Churchill.
111. *Pyrola minor*, L.—*W.*
    Red Hill, on the shore of Hinde Lake.
112. *Pyrola secunda*, L., var. *pumila*, Gray.—*W. R.*
    North shore of Carey Lake. London Rapids, above the Forks of Telzoa River. This is the most northerly point at which this species was observed.
113. *Pyrola rotundifolia*, L., var. *pumila*, Hook.—*B. W.*
    North shore of Lake Athabasca. Carey Lake. Wharton Lake. London Rapids, on Telzoa River. Fort Churchill. Ashe Inlet.

XXI. PLUMBAGINACEÆ.

114. *Armeria vulgaris*, Willd.—*R.*
    West shore of Tohannt Lake. London Rapids, above the Forks of Telzoa River. Mouth of Chesterfield Inlet.

XXII. PRIMULACEÆ.

115. *Primula Mistassinica*, Michx.—*W.*
    North shore of Lake Athabasca. Fort Churchill.
116. *Trientalis Americana*, Pursh.—*W.*
    Elizabeth Falls, Stone River.
117. *Androsace septentrionalis*, L.—*W.*
    Fort Churchill.

XXIII. GENTIANACEÆ.

118. *Menyanthes trifoliata*, L.—*W.*
    Woodcock Portage, Stone River.

XXIV. HYDROPHYLLACEÆ.

119. *Phacelia Franklinii*, Gray.—*W.*
    North shore of Lake Athabasca. Woodcock Portage on Stone River.

XXV. SCROPHULARIACEÆ.

120. *Castilla pallida*, Kunth.—*B.*
   Limestone Island, in Nicholson Lake. Shore of Tobaunt Lake. Loudon Rapids, above the Forks of Telzoa River.

121. *Pedicularis Lapponica*, L.—*B.*
   Mouth of Chesterfield Inlet. Ashe Inlet, on Hudson Strait.

122. *Pedicularis euphrasioides*, Stephan,—*B. W.*
   Esher, near the middle of Daly Lake. North shore of Carey Lake. Loudon Rapids, above the Forks of Telzoa River. Fort Churchill.

123. *Pedicularis hirsuta*, L.—*B.*
   Limestone Island, in Nicholson Lake. West shore of Tobaunt Lake. Loudon Rapids.

124. *Pedicularis flammea*.—*B.*
   Limestone Island, in Nicholson Lake.

125. *Pedicularis capitata*, Adams.—*B.*
   East shore of Carey Lake.

126. *Bartsia alpina*, L.—*W.*
   Fort Churchill.

XXVI. LENTIBULARIACEÆ.

127. *Pinguicula villosa*, L.—*W.*
   Daly Lake. Boyd Lake.

128. *Pinguicula vulgaris*, L.—*W.*
   Carey Lake. Fort Churchill.

XXVII. POLYGONACEÆ.

129. *Polygonum viviparum*, L.—*B.*
   Limestone Island, in Nicholson Lake. West shore of Tobaunt Lake. Loudon Rapids, above the Forks of Telzoa River. These are among the most northerly localities at which these species have been found in Canada.

130. *Oxyria digyna*, Campdera.—*B.*
   Mouth of Chesterfield Inlet.
   Ashe Inlet, on the north shore of Hudson Strait.

XXVIII. MYRICACEÆ.

131. *Myrica Gale*, L.—*W.*
North-west angle of Lake Athabasca.

XXIX. CUPULIFERÆ.

132. *Betula papyrifera*, Michx.—*W.*
North shore of Lake Athabasca.
Daly Lake.
The Indians make their canoes from the bark of this tree. Trees sufficiently large for canoes were seen as far north as the north end of Selwyn Lake and the northern bend of Cochrane River. From these places northward it gradually decreases in size, until it disappears at about the northern limit of the forest.

133. *Betula pumila*, L.
Red Hill, on the west shore of Hinde Lake.
Boyd Lake.

134. *Betula glandulosa*, Michx.
Daly Lake.
London Rapids, above the Forks of Telzoa River.
Tobaunt River, between Schultz and Baker Lakes.
Fairly common, is a small shrub on the Barren Lands as far north as Ferguson River.—J. B. T.

135. *Alnus viridis*, D.C.—*W.*
Carey Lake. Quartzite Lake, on Ferguson River.

XXX. SALICACEÆ.

136. *Salix petiolaris*, Smith.—*W.*
North-west shore, Lake Athabasca.

137. *Salix desertorum*.—*W.*
North shore of Lake Athabasca.

138. *Salix Brownii*, Bebb.—*W.B.*
North Shore of Lake Athabasca.
North-West shore of Tobaunt Lake.
Ashe Inlet, Hudson Straits.

139. *Salix Richardsonii*, Hook.—*B.*
    Mouth of Chesterfield Inlet.
    Not previously recorded from the vicinity of Hudson Bay.

140. *Salix reticulata*, L.—*B.*
    Limestone Island, in Nicholson Lake.
    London Rapids, above the Forks of Telzoa River.

141. *Salix herbacea*, L.—*W. B.*
    Esker, near the middle of Daly Lake.
    Mouth of Chesterfield Inlet.
    Ashe Inlet, on the north side of Hudson Strait.

142. *Salix rostrata*, Rich.—*W.*
    North shore of Lake Athabasca.
    Elizabeth Rapids, Stone River.

143. *Salix speciosa*, Hook and Arn.—*B.*
    Mouth of Chesterfield Inlet.

144. *Salix glauca*, L., var. *villosa*, And.—*B.*
    Tobaunt River, between Schultz and Baker lakes.

145. *Salix phyllicifolia*, L.—*B.*
    Shore of Tobaunt Lake.
    Tobaunt River, between Schultz and Baker lakes.
    Mouth of Chesterfield Inlet.

146. *Salix balsamifera*, Barratt.—*W.*
    West shore of Daly Lake.
    This species was not before known to occur north of the Saskatchewan River.

147. *Populus balsamifera*, L.—*W.*
    North shore of Lake Athabasca.
    Limbs, believed to be of this species, were found lying on the sand at the Forks of the Telzoa River, having drifted down the West Branch to that place.

148. *Populus tremuloides*, Michx.—*W.*
    North shore of Lake Athabasca.
    Esher, near the narrows of Daly Lake.
    The latter locality is the northern limit of the tree in this longitude. On the head-waters of the Thlewiaza River it was found to range as far north as latitude 60°. A few small trees were also observed on the raised beaches near Fort Churchill.—J. B. T.

XXXI. EMPETRACEÆ.

149. *Empetrum nigrum*, L.—*W. B.*

> Daly Lake.
> Hinde Lake.
> Carey Lake.
> London Rapids, on Tobaunt River.
> Mouth of Chesterfield Inlet.
> Ashe Inlet, on Hudson Strait.
> Very little fruit was found on the bushes north of the edge of the Barren Lands.

XXXII. CONIFERÆ.

150. *Juniperus communis*, L.—*W.*

> Fort Chippewyan, Lake Athabasca.
> Esker, near the middle of Daly Lake.
> North shore of Carey Lake.

151. *Juniperus Sabina*, L., var. *procumbens*, Pursh.—*W.*

> Fort Chippewyan, Lake Athabasca.

152. *Pinus Banksiana*, Lambert.—*W.*

> On dry sandy or rocky slopes as far north as the north end of Selwyn Lake.

153. *Picea nigra*, Link.—*W. B.*

> North shore of Lake Athabasca.
> Telzoa River, just below Daly Lake.
> This species occurs in scattered groves down the Telzoa River to Tolbaunt Lake. On the shore of Hudson Bay it reaches its northern limit at the mouth of Nubam River. The most northern examples are spreading shrubs, in the middle of which may be found a small upright stem four or five feet high.—J. B. T.

154. *Picea alba*, Link.—*W. B.*

> North shore of Lake Athabasca.
> The sandy eskers near Hinde and Boyd lakes were thinly covered with fine large trees of this species. Groves of large trees were also growing on the wet but well drained flats or slopes beside the Telzoa River down to within a short distance of Tobaunt Lake. Many large drifted trunks were also found at the Forks below this lake. Its northern

limit on the shore of Hudson Bay is at Little Seal River, north of Fort Churchill, where it replaces the preceding species in the wet swamps near the shore.—J. B. T.

155. *Larix Americana*, Michx.—*W. B.*

Telzoa River, as far north as Tobauntt Lake.
On the shore of Hudson Bay as far north as the mouth of Little Seal River, associated with white spruce.—J. B. T.

XXXIII. LILIACEÆ.

156. *Smilacina trifolia*, Desf.—*W.*

Esker, near middle of Daly Lake.

157. *Maianthemum Canadense*, Desf.—*W.*

North shore of Lake Athabasca.

158. *Allium Schœnoprasum*, L.—*W.*

North shore of Lake Athabasca.

159. *Tofieldia borealis*, Wahl.—*W. B.*

Barlow Lake.
London Rapids, above the Forks of Telzoa River.
Fort Churchill.

XXXIV. ORCHIDACEÆ.

160. *Orchis rotundifolia*, Pursh.—*W.*

Fort Churchill.

XXXV. JUNCACEÆ.

161. *Luzula spadicea*, D.C., var. *melanocarpa*, Meyer.—*B.*

Island near the middle of Boyd Lake.

162. *Luzula campestris*, Desv.—*B.*

Island near the middle of Boyd Lake.

163. *Luzula campestris*, Desv., var. *vulgaris*, Hook.—*B.*

West shore of Tobaunt Lake.

XXXVI. CYPERACEÆ.

164. *Scirpus cæspitosus*, L.—*B.*
   Island near the middle of Boyd Land.

165. *Eriophorum polystachyon*, L.—*W. B.*
   West shore of Hinde Lake.
   Island near the middle of Boyd Lake.
   Limestone Island, in Nicholson Lake.
   West shore of Tobaunt Lake.
   Ashe Inlet, on Hudson Strait.

166. *Eriophorum vaginatum.*—*W. B.*
   Esker near the middle of Daly Lake.

167. *Eriophorum capitatum*, Host.—*B.*
   Ashe Inlet, on Hudson Strait.

168. *Carex rariflora*, Smith.—*B.*
   Loudon Rapids, above the Forks of Telzoa River.

169. *Carex canescens*, L., var. *alpicola*, Wahl.—*W.*
   Telzoa River, just below Daly Lake.
   Boyd Lake.

170. *Carex misandra*, R. Br.—*W. B.*
   West shore of Hinde Lake.
   Mouth of Chesterfield Inlet.

171. *Carex aquatilis*, Wahl.—*W.*
   West shore of Hinde Lake.

172. *Carex vulgaris*, Fries., var. *hyperborea*, Boott.—*W.*
   Daly Lake.   Hinde Lake.
   Boyd Lake.

173. *Carex Magellanica*, Lam.—*W.*
   Esker, near the middle of Daly Lake.

174. *Carex saxatilis*, L.—*W.*
   Hinde Lake.   Barlow Lake.

175. *Carex rotundata*, Wahl.—*B.*
   Mouth of Chesterfield Inlet.

XXXVII. GRAMINEÆ.

176. *Hierochloa alpina*, R. & S.—*B*.
   West shore of Tobaunt Lake.
   London Rapids, above the Forks of Telzoa River.
   Mouth of Chesterfield Inlet.

177. *Arctagrostis latifolia*, Grisob.—*W, B*.
   West shore of Hinde Lake.
   London Rapids, above the Forks of Telzoa River.

178. *Arctophila Laestadii*, Rupr.—*W*.
   West shore of Hinde Lake.

179. *Elymus arenarius*, L.—*W*.
   Black Lake, on Stone River.

180. *Elymus mollis*, Trin.—*B*.
   Tobaunt River, between Schultz and Baker lakes.
   Mouth of Chesterfield Inlet.

181. *Calamagrostis Langsdorffii*, Kunth.—*W*.
   Black Lake on Stone River.
   Esker, near the middle of Daly Lake.
   Telzoa River, just below Daly Lake.

182. *Calamagrostis Canadensis*, Hook.—*B*.
   Limestone Island in Nicholson Lake.

183. *Poa alpina*, L.—*B*.
   London Rapids, above the Forks of Telzoa River.

184. *Poa angustata*, R. Br.—*B*.
   Boyd Lake.

185. *Poa cenisia*, All.—*B*.
   Limestone Island, in Nicholson Lake.
   London Rapids, above the forks of Telzoa River.

186. *Trisetum subspicatum*, Beauv.—*W*.
   Esker, near the middle of Daly Lake.

XXXVIII. EQUISETACEÆ.

187. *Equisetum Sylvaticum*, L.—*W*.
   Esker, near the middle of Daly Lake.

XL. FILICES.

188. *Polypodium vulgare*, L.—*W.*
    North shore of Lake Athabasca.
189. *Phegopteris Dryopteris*, Fee.—*B.*
    Island near the middle of Boyd Lake.
190. *Aspidium fragrans*, Swartz.—*W. B.*
    Daly Lake. Carey Lake.
    Tehaunt River, between Schultz and Baker lakes.
    Mouth of Chesterfield Inlet.
191. *Cystopteris fragilis*, Bernh.—*B.*
    Limestone Island, in Nicholson Lake.
    Mouth of Chesterfield Inlet.
192. *Woodsia Ilvensis*, R. B.—*W.*
    North shore of Lake Athabaska.
    Grove of white spruce on the north shore of Carey Lake.

XLI. LYCOPODIACEÆ.

193. *Lycopodium annotinum*, L.—*W.*
    Cracking-stone Point, Lake Athabasca.
    North shore of Carey Lake.
194. *Lycopodium annotinum*, L. var. *alpestre*, Hartm.—*W.*
    Telzoa River, below Daly Lake.
195. *Lycopodium complanatum*, L.—*W.*
    West shore of Hinde Lake.
196. *Lycopodium Selago*, L.—*B.*
    West shore of Tehaunt Lake.
    Ashe Inlet, on Hudson Strait.

XLII. MUSCI.

197. *Sphagnum fuscum*, var. *pallescens*, Warnst.—*W.*
    In swamp on the banks of Telzoa River, just below Daly Lake.
198. *Sphagnum tenellum*, var. *rubellum*, Warnst.—*W.*
    Telzoa River, just below Daly Lake.
199. *Sphagnum acutifolium*, Russ & Warnst.—*W.*
    Telzoa River, just below Daly Lake.

200. *Dicranum elongatum*, Schwaegr.—*W.*
   North end of Barlow Lake.
201. *Dicranum congestum*, Bird.—*B.*
   West shore of Tobaunt Lake, at the mouth of Telzoa River.
202. *Dicranum fuscescens*, Turn.—*B.*
   West shore of Tobaunt Lake, at the mouth of Telzoa River.
203. *Dicranum Bergeri*, Bland.—*W.*
   West shore of Hinde Lake.
204. *Aulacomnium palustre*, Schwaegr.—*B.*
   West shore of Tobaunt Lake, at the mouth of Telzoa River.
   Ashe Inlet, on Hudson Strait.
205. *Polytrichum strictum*, Banks.—*B.*
   West shore of Tobaunt Lake, at the mouth of Telzoa River.
206. *Webera nutans*, Hedw.—*B.*
   West shore of Tobaunt Lake, at the mouth of Telzoa River.
   Asher Inlet, on Hudson Strait.
207. *Hypnum exannulatum*, Guemb.—*B.*
   West shore of Tobaunt Lake, at the mouth of Telzoa River.
208. *Hylocomium Schreberi*, Willd.—*W.*
   Telzoa River, just below Daly Lake.
209. *Hylocomium splendens*, Schimp River.—*B.*
   West shore of Tobaunt Lake, at the mouth of Telzoa River.

XLIII. HEPATICÆ.

210. *Ptilidium ciliare*, Dum.—*B.*
   West shore of Tobaunt Lake.

XLIV. LICHENES.

211. *Cetraria aculeata*, Fr.—*B.*
   West shore of Tobaunt Lake.
212. *Cetraria arctica*, Hook.—*B.*
   River bank between Nicholson and Tobaunt Lakes.
213. *Cetraria Islandica*, Arch.—*W. B.*
   Daly Lake. Hill at the north end of Barlow Lake.

214. *Cetraria Islandica*, Ach., var. *Delisei*, Bor.—W.
    Telzoa River, just below Daly Lake.
215. *Cetraria Richardsonii*, Hook. B.
    West shore of Tolmunt Lake.
216. *Cetraria cucullata*, Ach.—B.
    North-west angle of Tolmunt Lake.
217. *Cetraria juniperina*, Ach., var. *Pinastii*, Ach.—W.
    Telzoa River, just below Daly Lake.
218. *Cetraria nivalis*, Ach.—W. B.
    Telzoa River, just below Daly Lake.
    North end of Barlow Lake.
    Ashe Inlet, on Hudson Strait.
219. *Alectoria jubata*, L., var. *implexa*, Fr.—W.
    West shore of Hinde Lake.
220. *Alectoria divergens*, Nyl.—W.
    Telzoa River, just below Daly Lake.
221. *Alectoria ochroleuca*, Nyl., var. (a) *rigida*, Fr.—B.
    North end of Barlow Lake.
    West shore of Tolmunt Lake.
222. *Parmelia physodes*, Ach.—W.
    Telzoa River, just below Daly Lake.
223. *Parmelia conspersa*, Ach.—W.
    Telzoa River, just below Daly Lake.
224. *Umbilicaria Muhlenbergii*, Tuckerm.—W.
    Telzoa River, just below Daly Lake.
225. *Nephroma arcticum*, Fr.—W.
    West shore of Hinde Lake.
226. *Lecanora tartarea*, Ach.—W.
    Telzoa River, just below Daly Lake.
227. *Stereocaulon Desprenxii*, Nyl. W.
    Telzoa River, just below Daly Lake.
228. *Cladonia decorticata*, Floerk.—W.
    North end of Barlow Lake.
229. *Cladonia gracilis*, Fr., var. *elongata*, Fr. W. B.
    Telzoa River, just below Daly Lake.
    West shore of Tolmunt Lake.

230. *Cladonia rangiferina*, Hoffm. — *W*.
    Telzoa River, just below Daly Lake.
    North shore of Barlow Lake.
231. *Cladonia rangiferina*, Hoffm., var. *sylvatica*, L. — *W*.
    Telzoa River, just below Daly Lake.
232. *Cladonia cornucopioides*, Fr. — *W*.
    Telzoa River, just below Daly Lake.
233. *Bomyces aeruginosus*, D.C. — *W*.
    Telzoa River, just below Daly Lake.

APPENDIX II.

ESKIMO VOCABULARY OF WORDS AND PHRASES.

(ORIGINAL.)

All	Ter-mok-er-mingk.
All night	Knee-en-nah.
Always	E-luk-o-she-a.
Alone	In-nu-tu-ak.
A game	Nu-glee-ta.
A herd	Ah-mik-took-too.
Another	Hi-punga.
All gone	Pet-a-hung-e-too.
Angry	Mar-ne-an-nah.
Afraid	Kay-pe-en-nah.
A while ago	Tatch-e-munny.
Ark	O-kow-te-vah-vor.
Antlers	Nug-le-yow.
Arm	Tel-oo.
Arrow	Kok-yoke.
All right	Co-id-na.
Are you sleepy	Chin-e-gin.
Autumn	Mow-yah.
Axe	Ooley-moon.
Bad	Pee-ung-e-to.
Bald	Ked-juk-yow.
Barren Lands	Nappartu-itok.
Bear	Nah-nook.
Big	Ung-a-yow-aloo.
Brother (big)	Ung-a-yowk-a-loong-a.
Brother (small)	Nung-a-yowk-a-loong-a.
Black lead	Ming-oon-nah.
Boot	Kamming.
Black	Kunnietah.
Bring	I-cluc-to.
Bullet	Uchie.
Bow	Pet-e-chee.
Blood	Owk.
Bones	Sow-ner.
Blubber	Owk-zook.
Beard	Oo-mik.
Beads	Shoong-ow-yoh.
Blankets	Kep-ig.
Bite	Kee-wah.
Big River	Koog-oark.
Black Moss	Kee-now-yak.
Cap	Nich-shaw.
Cap (for gun)	Shee-nek-tow.
Child	Noo-ta-an.
Cod-fish	On-wat.
Come here	Ki-yeet.
Cold	Ick-kee.
Coal	Kee-youk-eha.
Clouds	Ne-boo-yah.
Clothing	An-no-wak.
Canoe	Kyack.
Coat	Koo-lee-ta.
Day	Ood-loo-me.
Day before yesterday	Ick-puck sha-nee.
Dark	Ta-koo-nee.
Deer	Took-too.
Deer sinew	Took-too-Ib-a-loo.
Dead	Tuck-o-boo.
Down	Town-na-ney.
Dog	King-me.
Don't want to	Uggone.
Don't lie	Shag-lo-naw-me.

Don't under-
    stand .... Cow-you-mung-a-to.
Don't know .... Ah-chew.
Do you wish to
    go out? ..... Annic-low?
Die .... Tuck-o-boo.
Drink (give me) Emmic-ray.
Duck .... Mu-ah-tuck.

Ear .... See-yow-tee.
East .... Ka-ning-nah.
Early .... Oo-blah.
Eat .... Tun-wah-wa.
Egg .... Mun-nee.
Empty .... E-mah-ik-took.
End for end ... Ig-loo-ahnec.
Eye .... Egee.
Ermine .... Ter-re-ak.
Enough .... Ta-bah.

Far away ...... Wash-ig-too-aloo.
Fat .... Owk-shaw.
Farewell ...... Ta-bow-e-tee.
Faster .... Ook-shoot.
Father .... At-at-a.
Father (my) ... At-at-a-ga.
Female .... Ungna.
Fire .... Ick-o-ma.
Fish .... Ick-kal-luck.
Fox .... Tar-bed-ne-ah.
Fur .... Mit kote.

Game(deer, etc.) O-ko-ko.
Go .... Owd-luck-too.
Give me .... Kidj-you.
Gone .... Pete-lung-e-too.
Good .... Pee-a-uke.
Glad (I am) ... Pee-a-wee-unga.
Glove .... Po-a-low.
Glad (it will
    make me) ... Pee-a-yow-appy.
Good morning . Ah-shn-id-lee.
Good-bye ...... Ta-bow-a-ting.
Gun .... Kook-e-you.
Goose .... Ne-nck-a-luck.
Grave .... E-le-wah.

Hair of the
    head .... Noo-yah.
Hair of the face. Oo-ming.
Here (take it).. Awk.

Here(this place) Man-nee.
Hat .... Uck-che-wa-loo.
Hills .... Kak-ka.
How many ..... Katch-ening.
House .... Igloe.
How do you do
    (salute)?... Ashow-you-didlee?
Well thank you
    (reply) ..... Ta-bow-you-adlo.
Halloo .... Chimo.
Hot .... Oo-oo.
Hungry .... Ka-pa.
Hungry (they
    are) .... Kak-too.
Hard-tack .... Shee-va.

Ice (salt water). Se-ro.
Ice(fresh water) Nee-lug.
Ice (to cut with
    chisel) .... Too-y-lako.
Iceberg .... Pick-a-lnlial.
Ice chisel .... Too-woke.
I, me, mine ... Oo-wunga.
I did not see it. Tacko-naunee.
I want it ..... Oo-wung-aloo.
It is good .... Pee-a uke.
Island .... Kig-yuck-ta.
Island (large). Kuck-ee-tuck-dua.
Iron .... Sev-wick.
Ivory .... Too-wak.
Indian .... Ik-kil-lin.

Jack-knife .... Pook-ta-yon.
Jump .... Ob-look-too.
Just right .... Nah-muck-too.

Kick .... Ish-ee-ma-ac-too.
King's Cape ... Telle-pin.
Knife .... Chub-beek.
Kill .... To-ko-pah-hah.
Kiss .... Coon-e-glee.

Laugh .... Ig-luck-too.
Land .... Noo-na.
Land (main) ... Eel-a-wee-yun.
Lake .... Siscull.
Large .... Unga-yon.
Last year ..... Uck-kaw-nee.
Lead .... Uck-e-chn.
Live (reside) .. Noona-gin.
Look at it .... Tack-o-wack.

APPENDIX. 275

Line	Ud-le-ung.	Quick	Tu-quilee.
Little	Mick-a-yon.		
Little River	Koog-ah-la.	Rain	See-la-loo.
Long ago	Tap-shoo-mann-nee.	Rabbit	Ook-quil-la.
Loom	Kok-saw.	Rat	Tithen.
		Rapids	E-tem-na-zuck.
Man	Ung-oon.	Raven	Too-loo-ah.
Make	Sou-a-you.	Reindeer	Took-too.
Me	Oo-wunga.	Reindeer horns	Nug-dow.
Meat	Pak-too.	Reindeer (fawn)	No-kak.
Matches	Icko-ma.	Reindeer (young	
Medicine man	Ang-o-koke.	buck)	Nu-ka-tu-a.
Mine	Pie-ga.	Red	Owg.
Mica	Ked-luck-e-yack.	River	Koog.
Moon	Tuck-ee.	Rock	We-a-gook.
Morning	Ool-la.	Run	Ool-luk-too.
Mouse	Ah-ving-ca.	Remember	Kow-ye-mee-yow-a.
Musk-ox	Oo-ming-muuk.	Rope	Ook-so-noya.
Much	Am-o-suit.	Red-head	Ky-yow-aloo.
Mountain	King-yi.	Resolution	
		Island	Too-jung.
Narwhal	Ud-lee-ung.	Reside	Noo-naggin.
Near (very)	Koon-e-took-aloo.	River (big)	Koog-o-ak.
Near (rather)	Koon-e-took-e-maken	Resemble	Ti-ma-too.
Next year	Uek-kak-go.		
Needle	Mit cone.	Same	Ti-ma-too.
No	Au-guy, Nowk.	Seal (small)	Poo-see.
North	Wungna.	Seal	Jet-chuck.
North Star	Nicky-chew-e-too.	Seal (fresh	
Now	Man-nah.	water)	Kaus-e-gen.
Night	Oo-din-nook.	Seal (square	
		flipper)	Ug-jook.
		Seal (jumping)	Ky-aug-lee.
Oar	E-pool.	Ship	Oo-may-ne-due.
Old man	Ick-too-aloo.	Steamship	Ick-o-na-ling.
Old woman	Ning-o-wah-loo.	South	Neeg-yill.
One	Attowsha.	Stars	Ud-loo-a-ah.
One more	At-ta-loo.	Sun	Suc-e-nok.
On the other		Summer	Oak-e-youk.
side	Igloe-annie.	Spear (seal)	Oo-nah.
Out of doors	Seel-a-me.	Shut the door	Oo-may-glee.
Open the door	Mat-a-wa-goo.	Something to	
Only one	Ta-but tua.	eat	I-pa-pa.
Over there	Ti-na.	Sick	Ah-ah.
		See	Tacko.
Paper	Al-le-lay-yook.	Small	Micky-you.
Perhaps	Shug-a me.	Small (very)	Micky-nck-aloo.
Pork	Ook-e-mara.	Spots	Mee-luck.
Powder	Uck-dua.	Scars	Kidley.
Presently	Wet-chow.	Steal	Tidley-poo.
Pretty	Mah-muk-poo.	Speak	Wah-poo.

APPENDIX.

English	Eskimo
Shot	Uck-e-la.
Spear (to kill with)	Now-lick-ta.
Sew	Muck-chuck-too.
Shoot	Kook-o-ak-too.
Short time ago	Tick-e-cove.
Six	Uck-bin-e-gin.
Seven	Uck-bin-e-mok-o-nik.
Sleep	Shin-ig-poo.
Smell	Tee-pe.
Sister	Ne-yowk-a-loong-a.
Sleeping bag	Shin-ig-bee.
Spy glass	King-noot.
Swap (trade)	Ok-ke-lay-yook.
Strong	Shung-e-yook.
Spring	Oo-ping-yak.
Snow	Con-nee.
Snow-house	Igloe.
Sinew	Ih-a-loo.
Smoke	E-shik.
Smoke (verb)	Pay-u-let-ee.
Smoke (give me)	Pay-u-let-ee-de-lung-a.
Snow stick	An-owt er.
Take	Pe-e-ock-i-re.
Tent	To-pick.
Teeth	Kee you.
Thimble	Teek-kin.
Thunder	Kud-loo.
Tide rising	Ill-e-pook.
Tide falling	Tine-e-pook.
To-day	Ood-loome.
To-night	Ood-la.
To-morrow	Kow-pung.
The other day	Tatch-e-munny.
Tongue	Ook-ah.
Trade	Ok-ke-lay-loo.
Tracks	Too-n .
Trousers	Kod-ling.
Thank you	Koo-id-ne-mik.
Thread	Ih-e-loo.
Tell	Kpw-yow-ya.
That will do	Ta-ba.
Throw	Me-loo-e-ak-took.
Ugly	Pe-ne-took.
Understand	Kow-o-me-yow.
Up	Ta-pau-ney.
Warm	Oo-ko.
Water	Emmick.
Warmth (personal)	Oo-ko-ning ah.
Walrus	I-byl.
Walrus hide	Kow.
Wait	Watch-ow.
Walk	Pe-shook-too.
Wake up	Too-pook-poo.
What is that?	Kiss-yowa?
What do you want for it?	Kiss-yow-ok-a-la-loo?
What are you making?	Kiss-yow-livie?
What?	Shua?
Where	Now-te-mee.
When	Kunga.
When do you go?	Kunga-and-luck-too.
We	U-va-gnt.
Who	Kee-a.
Who owns it?	Kee-a-pinga?
Winter	Ook-e-yook.
Wind	An-a-way.
White man	Knd-loo-nah.
White	Kak-owk-tah.
Why	Kun-we-mun?
Whale	Ook-bik.
Whip	Ip-e-row-ter.
Will you?	E-ben-loo?
Wife	Nell-e-ang-nn.
Wood	Kee-yow.
Woman	Koo-nee.
Wolverine	Cow-bik.
Woman's boat	Oo-me-ack.
Wolf	Am-miow.
Work	Sen-a-yow.
White gull	Now-yah.
Yes	Ah-me-lah.
Year	Ok-ah-ney.
Yesterday	Ick-puck-shall.
Yesterday evening	Ick-puck-shall-ood-la.
You	Ib-bee (or Ich-bin).
You and I	Oo-bah-gook.

APPENDIX. 277

Young boy .... Un-nick-e-loo-ga.
Young girl .... Pen-nick-e-loo-ga.
Youngster .... Nen-ta-a.

NUMERALS.

One .... At-tow-sha.
Two .... Mok-oo.
Three .... Ping-ah-suet.
Four .... Seet-a-mut.
Five .... Ted-le-mut.
Six .... Uck-bin-e-gin.
Seven .... Uck-bin-e Mok-o-nik.
Eight .... Uck-bin-e-Mok-o-suet.
Nine.......... Uck-bin-e-seet-a-mut.
Ten .... Ko-ling.
Twenty .... Mok-ko ling.

PHRASES.

Come in ...... Ki-low-it.
Go ahead...... At-tay.
Give me a light Ik-ke-do-lung-a.
Give me a drink Im-mil-bah.
Give me a smoke Pay-u-let-e-de-lung-a.
It is good...... Pee-a-uke.
I don't know .. Shu-ga-mee.
I don't under-
  stand ...... Cow-you-mung-e-too.
What is the
  name of?.... I-ting-oṙ?
What are you
  making?.... Shu-la-vik?
Which way?.. Nel-lo-ung-nook?
Where from?.. Nuck-ke-nu-nah?
Where do you
  come from?. Nuck-ke-pe-wict?
Who is it?..... Kee-now-yah?

CLASSIFIED INDEX.

NAMES OF PERSONS.

Aberdeen, Earl and Countess of, 112.
Athabasca, Bishop of, 45, 46.
Back, Sir George, 124.
Christopher, Capt., 172.
Corrigal, James, portrait, 11; engaged, [41].
Daly, Hon. T. M., 80.
Flett, John, engaged, 9; portrait, 11.
Franklin, Sir John, 124.
French, Pierre, Louis and Michel, engaged, 9; portrait of, 11.
Gordon, Commander, 181.
Hawes, Capt., 213.
Hearne, Samuel, 213-217.
Howard, Inspector, 26, 28, 30.
Lobster, Mr. and Mrs., 247.
La Perouse, 217.
Lofthouse, Jos. (Rev.) and wife, 205, 211-213; portraits, 212.
Lofthouse, Miss Marjorie, 212, 251.
Macdonald, J. K., 248.
Mackenzie, Sir Alexander, 49.
Macoun, Prof. John, 251.
Matheson, Mr., 209.
Markham, Admiral R. N., 91. [41].
Maurice, François, portrait, 11; engaged,

Middleton, Capt., 214.
Mills, Capt. J. W., 28, 45, 53, 55.
Milne, Dr., 240, 242.
Moberly, Mr., H. B. C. officer, 9, 41.
Moberly, the guide, engaged, 53.
Mowat, Mr., 240, 242, 244.
McConnell, Mr., 28, 37.
McKay, Dr., 45, 46, 48, 52, 53, 55, 57.
Ogilvie, Wm., D.L.S., 28, 30, 48.
Omen, Arthur, 210.
Ray, Dr., 124.
Reed, Mr., 50.
Richardson, Sir John, 124.
Robson, Joseph, 215.
Russell, Mr., 48.
Schott, river pilot, 30, 32-34, 42.
Schultz, Sir John and Lady, 13, 115.
Selwyn, A. R. C., portrait, 74.
Tyrrell, J. Burr, 7, 70, 173; portrait, 210.
Westaccot, Charlie, 245.
Westaccot, James, 207.
Westaccot, William, 220.
Wolseley, Lord, 9.
Young, Bishop, 49, 52, 55.

WILD GAME, FISH, ETC.

Arctic birds, 132.
Arctic hare, 182, 185.
Bear, black, 73.
Bear, polar, 132, 158, 159, 180-198, 218, 225.
Buffalo, 80; trails of, 13.
Caribou. (See Reindeer.)
Duck, wild, 100, 184, 187.
Ermine, 98.
Fox, 161, 235.
Goose, wild, 47, 58, 102, 112.
Gull, 184.
Loon, 17.
Marmot, 187.
Moose, 23-25.

Musk ox, 107, 113.
Pike, 58.
Ptarmigan, 100, 185, 186, 204, 205, 208, 234, 235.
Rabbit, 45, 186, 235.
Reindeer (or caribou), 84-87, 95, 96, 99, 100, 132, 147-149, 180-198, 224-226.
Salmon trout, 96, 93, 101.
Seal, 127-171, 203.
Walrus, 132, 133, 140, 153-158.
Whale, 132, 133, 182.
Whitefish, 51, 60, 93, 101, 245. [225.
Wolf, 17, 23, 58, 99, 108, 120, 129, 161, 224.
Wolverine, 99, 100.

TIMBER, MINERALS, ETC.

Aspen, 81.
Balsam, 47.
Birch, 23, 40, 57, 71, 111, 245, 246.
Coal, 14, 60.
Copper, 173.
Fig, 59.
Glaciers, 81.
Gneiss, Laurentian, 57, 175.
Gold, 14, 173.
Huronian schists, 118, 173, 182.
Iron ore, 60.
Jack-pine, 16, 17, 58, 245, 246.
Lignite, 14.
Limestone, 38, 39; Cambro-Silurian, 92.

Marl, 120.
Natural gas, 30.
Poplar, 15, 21, 40, 40, 57, 245, 246.
Quartzite, 100, 181.
Sand, curious hills of, 99, 105.
Sand, "Kames," 80.
Sandstone, cretaceous, 57; soft, 111.
Silver, 173.
Spruce, 17, 21, 40, 46, 47, 57, 71, 84, 90, 93, 203, 204, 227, 245, 246.
Tamarack, 70, 84, 85.
Tar sand beds, 36, 37.
Trappean rock, 110, 173.
Willow, 111, 208.

RIVERS, LAKES AND LOCALITIES.

Aberdeen Lake, 112, 114.
Active Man Lake, 8.
Ahoska, 130.
Arctic Ocean, 8, 10, 28, 111.
Ada, 130.
Athabasca Delta, 47.
Athabasca Lake, 7, 10, 12, 15, 20, 28, 48, 56, 57, 58, 77, 80, 84.
Athabasca Landing, 15, 17, 19, 20, 29, 40.
Athabasca River, 9, 12, 15, 17, 19, 21, 29, 30, 40.
Back Lake, 246.
Baker Lake, 114, 125, 172.
Barlow Lake, 84. 124-5, 216.
Barren Lands, 7, 8, 90, 93, 101, 110, 113.
Beaver Hills, 90.
Behring Straits, 130.
Beren's River, 249.
Big Unseule, 38.
Birch Lake, 73. 172-3, 175-6.
Black Lake, 7, 8, 49, 53, 64, 68, 69, 76, 77.
Boiler Rapid, 37.
Brûlé Rapid, 36.
Button's Bay, 236.
Calgary, 13, 14.
Cary Lake, 85, 90.
Caughnawaga, 9. 179, 182.
Chesterfield Inlet, 110, 172, 174, 176, 178.
Churchill River, 210-11.
Clear Water River, 40.
Clinton Golden Lake, 112.
Copper Mine River, 94, 216.
Corbet's Inlet, 183.
Crooked Rapid, 38.
Daly Lake, 80, 81.
Deer Lake, 246.
Duck Creek, 230.
Edmonton, 10, 12, 14, 20, 91.
Fishing River, 58.
Flamboro' Head, 223.
Fort Chippewyan, 12, 45-55, 61, 63.
Fort Churchill, 107-8, 174-177, 181, 187, 191, 220, 223-224, 224, 226, 232, 236.
Fort Fond du Lac, 59, 61, 75. 242-3.
Fort McMurray, 9, 10, 20, 28, 30, 36, 40.
Fort Prince of Wales, 210-217. 142-6.
Fort Smith, 28, 46.
Fort Vermillion, 40.
Fox River, 244.
Grand Rapids, 29, 26-28, 32-36, 42.
Grassy Island, 208.
Great Fish River, 111.
Great Slave Lake, 7, 53, 112.
Great Slave River, 28, 55.
Hamilton, 7.
Hays River, 241, 243, 245.
Heart Creek, 232.

Height of Land, 8, 17, 76 81, 173.
Hudson Bay, 7, 8, 107-8, 110, 124, 130, 172, 174, 181.
Hudson Straits, 45, 53, 107, 130, 101, 192.
Isle-à-la-Crosse, 9, 41.
Lachine Rapids, 9.
Lady Marjorine Lake, 110.
Lake of the Woods, 118, 173.
Lake Superior, 173.
Lake Winnipeg, 247, 249.
Little Unseule, 38.
Long Rapids, 38.
Lower Telzoa River, 102-113.
Mackenzie River, 10, 20, 28, 48, 120.
Manitoba, 12.
Marble Island, 107, 181-2.
Markham Lake, 91, 92.
Montreal, 224.
Mountain Rapid, 37, 38.
Nelson River, 238-9, 243.
Neville Bay, 185.
North Bay, 12.
North Pole, 174.
North-West Passage, 172, 214.
Norway House, 244, 247-8.
Old Man Island, 69.
Oxford House, 241-2, 244, 247.
Peace River, 40.
Prince Albert, 9.
Prince of Wales Sound, 130; Cape, 104.
Rankin Inlet, 183.
Rapid of the Jolly Fuel, 23.
Rocky Mountains, 14.
Salmon Creek, 226.
Sam's Creek, 231.
Saskatchewan River, 14, 17, 248-9.
Schultz Lake, 115, 117.
Seal Islands, 236.
Selkirk, 249.
Selwyn Lake, 71, 78.
Sloop's Cove, 214.
Stone River, 64-5.
Stony River, 218, 226.
Telzoa River Delta, 124.
Telzoa River Rapids, 83.
Telzoa River, 77, 82, 91, 92.
Talmand Lake, 94, 99, 173.
Toronto, 7, 12.
Twin Mountains, 110.
West Selkirk, 248.
Wharton Lake, 109.
White Bear Creek, 230.
White Mountain, 110.
Winnipeg, 12.
Wolverine Lake, 8, 71, 76.
Wolverine River, 73.
York Factory, 218, 228, 230, 232, 230-246.

MISCELLANEOUS.

Adventures; in Boiler Rapid, 37; in Mountain Rapid, 39-40; with a black bear, 73; on Telzoa River, 81; on Corbet's Inlet, 183-4; at sea, 201-2; on Nelson River, 230; on Back Lake, 246.
American naturalist, meeting an, 48.

Ancient sea-beaches, 114.
Arrival at Fort Churchill, 209.
Arrival at Nelson River, 231.
Arrival at Norway House, 247.
Arrival at West Selkirk, 249.
Athabasca, steamer, 29, 35, 27.

CLASSIFIED INDEX.

MISCELLANEOUS—*Continued.*

Black flies, 66.
Bread-making, novel method of, 75.
Breeding-place of wild geese, 102.
Buffalo trails, ancient, 13.
Cacheing our supplies, 240.
Cairn of rocks built, 90, 95, 181.
Camp in the woods, 222-3.
Canadian, an old-timer, 247.   [173.
Canadian Geological Survey, 7, 37, 75, 74,
Canadian Pacific Railway, 12, 13.
Canoe race with Indians, 20.
Canoes secured, 9.
Corrigal meets with accident, 66.
Crossing Nelson River, 236-8.
Crippled, 226.
Deer vs. canoe, a race, 85.
Desperate situation, 223.
Dog-sleds, 210.
Dried fish and seal-oil, 238.
Dysentery, 201.
Encounter with polar bears, 189-90, 192-5, 218.
Encounter with wolves, 98.
Eskimo, bartering with, 107, 123, 175.
Eskimo first met with, 115.
Eskimos, photographing, 120.
Eskimo, appearance of, 127-8; clothing, 128-9; tattooing, 129; cheek-stones, 130; origin of, 130; range of, 130; temperament, 132, 163, 164; feast, 132-3; dwellings, 135-0; ingenuity, 139; implements, 139; kyack, 141; oomiack, 142; komitick, 143; dog-whip, 144; sleeping-bag, 145; customs, 147-171; weapons, 147, 153-5, 160; seal-hunting, 149-153; walrus-hunting, 155-8; polar bear-hunting, 158-9; hunting birds, 159-60; fishing, 160-1; trapping, 161; amusements, 163-4; marriages, 165; religious beliefs and ceremonies, 165-9; laws, 169-70; legends, 170; burials, 171; vocabulary, 273.
Famine at Fort McMurray, 42-3.
Feeding dogs at H. B. Co.'s posts, 51.
Finding Eskimo cache, 109.
First camp, 21.
First rapid, 23.
Flora, collecting, 70.
Forest, limit of, 83.
François' chase of wolverine, 99, 100-1.
François' tug-of-war, 237-8.
French missionaries returning, 50.
Fur trade, new conditions in, 241.
Gale on Lake Tchauni, 102.
Glaciers, 81.
Grahame, steamer, 28, 43, 46, 52, 55.
Grove of spruce, isolated, 90.
Guide procured, 53.
Guide deserts us, 62-4.
Historic ruins, 210, 216-17.
Hudson's Bay Company, 9, 12, *et seq.*
Icefields on Lake Tchauni, 105-6.
Ice, massive walls of, 22.
Ice-pack, all night in an, 202.
Indians: Chippewyan, 7, 32, 40, 48, 221;
  Cree, 23, 40, 43, 219, 230; Iroquois, 9.
Inventory of our supplies, 54.

Indian camps, 77, 227, 230; dance, 32;
  log-houses, 64; majo, 8; tepee, 227;
  tradition, 30; types of, 18.
Iroquois, craftiness of our, 71.
Kyack vs. canoe, a race, 120.
Last trees seen, 181.
Louis crippled, 246.
Louis shoots polar bear, 189-90.
Low temperature, 245, 247.
Mathematical instruments provided, 10.
Meeting an old shipmate, 45.
Michel's feet frozen, 202.
Michel left at York Factory, 242.
Missionaries, hospitable, 211.
Moose hunt, 34.
Moose-bags, 81.
Moss fuel, 101.
Mountain of iron ore, 60.
Musk-ox robes, 122, 123.
Mosquito torments, 55, 66.
Nailing up the flag of Canada, 70.
Names carved on rocks, 215.
Navigation of Athabasca River, 26-28.
Navigation of Telzoa River, 173.
North-West Mounted Police, 26; banqueted by, 28.
Our only seal shot, 203.
Our party separates, 248.
Parting with civilization, 70.   [13
Perilous situation, 236.
Picturesque scenery, 14, 19, 21-2, 40, 112-
Plants collected, list of, 261-72.
Pierre exhausted, 204.
Poisoned by polar bear liver, 192.
Portaging, an achievement in, 71.
Prairie travel, 15-17.
Provisions exhausted, 234.
Reaching tide water, 176.
Red River cart trail, ancient, 244.
Relief party from Churchill, 236.
Remarkable island, 92.
Rich mineral district, 173.
Running the Grand Rapids, 33-35.
Sand formations, curious, 89-1, 90.
Seventeen hours in ice-water, 203.
Shooting pike with revolver, 58.
Snow-blindness, 134.
Snow-goggles, 135.
Snowshoes, 221; practice with, 215.
Snow in August, 90.
Solitary grave, 60, 75.
Starving Cree camp, 44.
Stone pillars, 113.
Storm on Baker Lake, 175.
Storm on the Telzoa, 116.
Struggle with shore-ice, 199-200.
Tar wells, curious, 37.
Teepee remains, ancient, 92.
Travelling by carryall, 248-9.
Visit to Eskimo camp, 118.
Visit to Eskimo village, 122.
Water-spouts on Daly Lake, 80.
Welcome ablutions, 246.
Whale-boat on Chesterfield Inlet, 177.
Winter sets in, 199.
Without food or fuel, 187.
Wood violets, 90.
Wrigley, steamer, 28, 46.

www.ingramcontent.com/pod-product-compliance
Lightning Source LLC
Chambersburg PA
CBHW022046230426
43672CB00008B/1085